Golden Age

Writer: Brian Michael Bendis
Artist: Alex Maleev
Colorist: Dave Stewart
Letterers: Virtual Calligraphy's Chris Eliopoulos
& Cory Petit
Editor: Jennifer Lee
Executive Editor: Axel Alonso

Collection Editor: Jennifer Grünwald
Senior Editor, Special Projects: Jeff Youngquist
Director of Sales: David Gabriel
Production: Loretta Krol
Book Designer: Jeof Vita
Creative Director: Tom Marvelli

Editor in Chief: Joe Quesada
Publisher: Dan Buckley

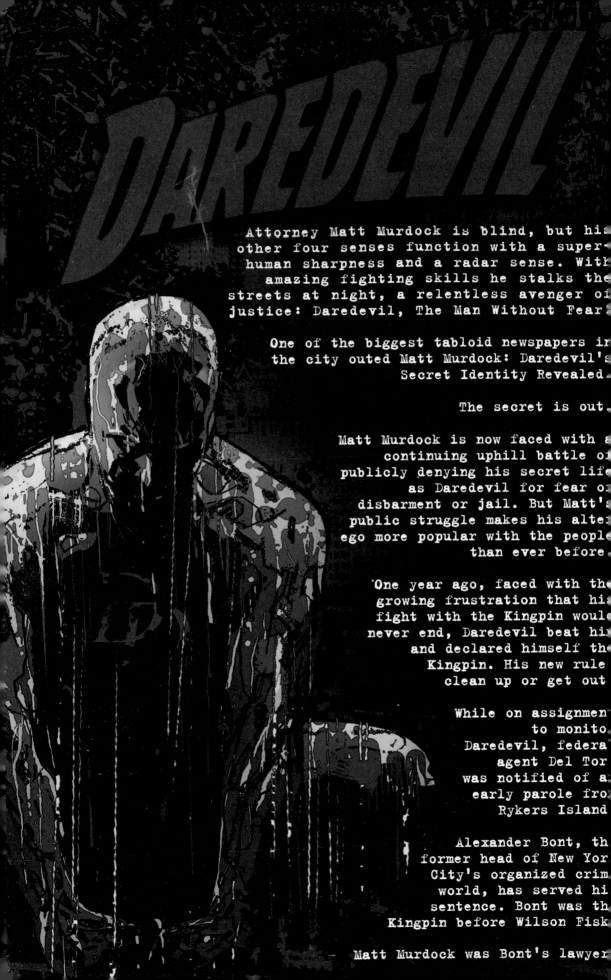

DAREDEVIL

Attorney Matt Murdock is blind, but his
other four senses function with a super-
human sharpness and a radar sense. With
amazing fighting skills he stalks the
streets at night, a relentless avenger of
justice: Daredevil, The Man Without Fear.

One of the biggest tabloid newspapers in
the city outed Matt Murdock: Daredevil's
Secret Identity Revealed.

The secret is out.

Matt Murdock is now faced with a
continuing uphill battle of
publicly denying his secret life
as Daredevil for fear of
disbarment or jail. But Matt's
public struggle makes his alter
ego more popular with the people
than ever before.

One year ago, faced with the
growing frustration that his
fight with the Kingpin would
never end, Daredevil beat him
and declared himself the
Kingpin. His new rule:
clean up or get out.

While on assignment
to monitor
Daredevil, federal
agent Del Toro
was notified of an
early parole from
Rykers Island.

Alexander Bont, the
former head of New York
City's organized crime
world, has served his
sentence. Bont was the
Kingpin before Wilson Fisk.

Matt Murdock was Bont's lawyer.

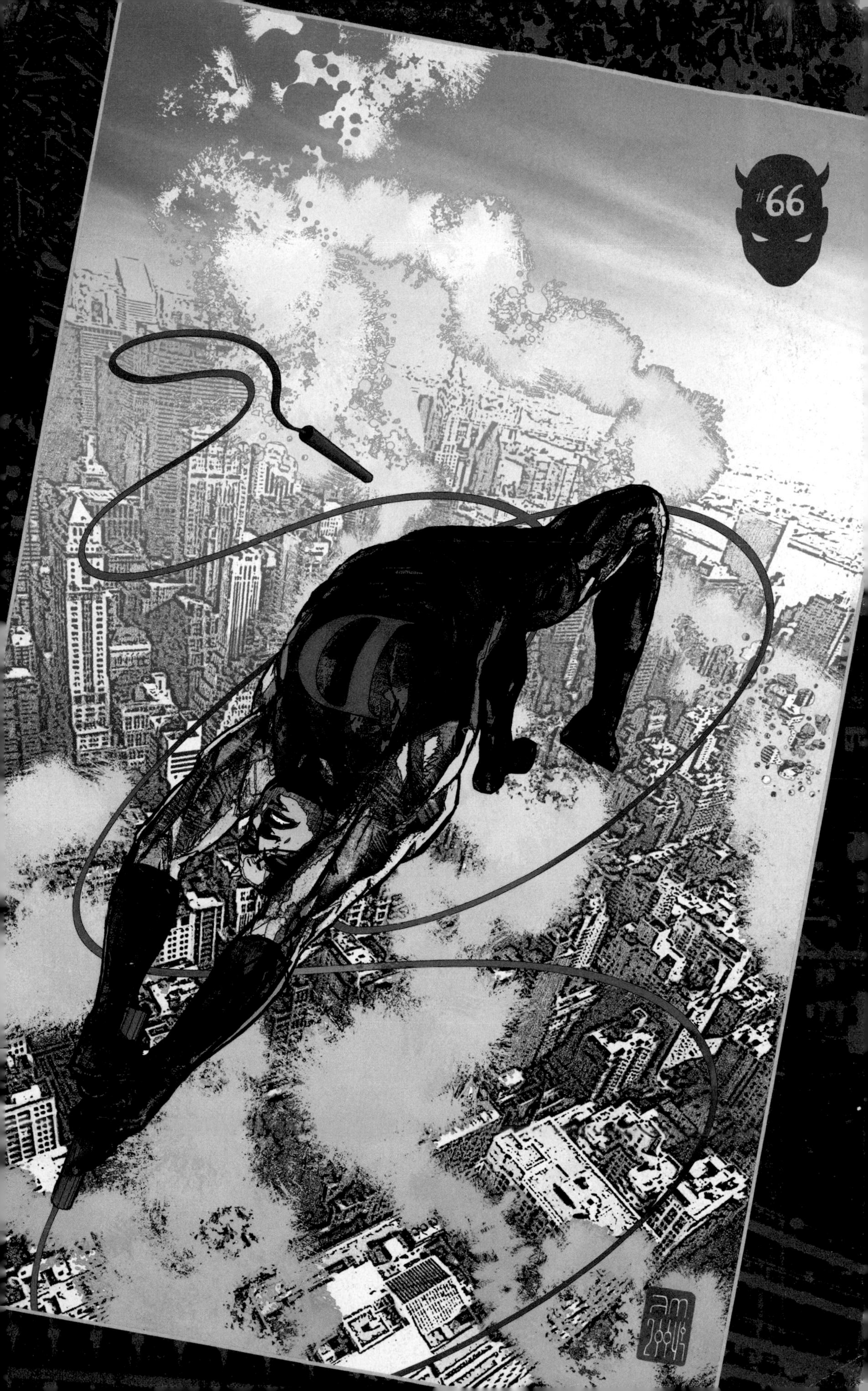
#66

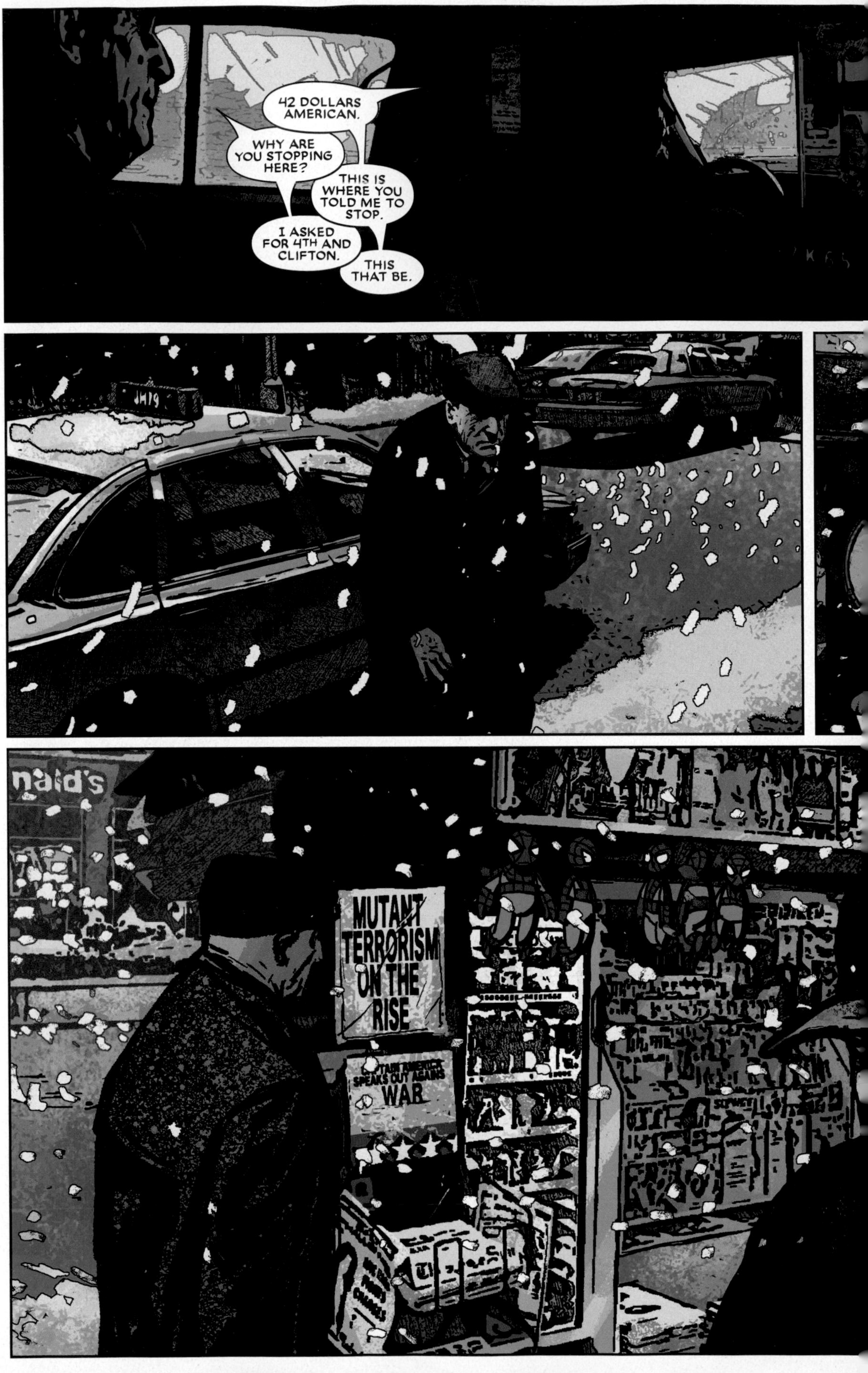
42 DOLLARS AMERICAN.
WHY ARE YOU STOPPING HERE?
THIS IS WHERE YOU TOLD ME TO STOP.
I ASKED FOR 4TH AND CLIFTON.
THIS THAT BE.
MUTANT TERRORISM ON THE RISE

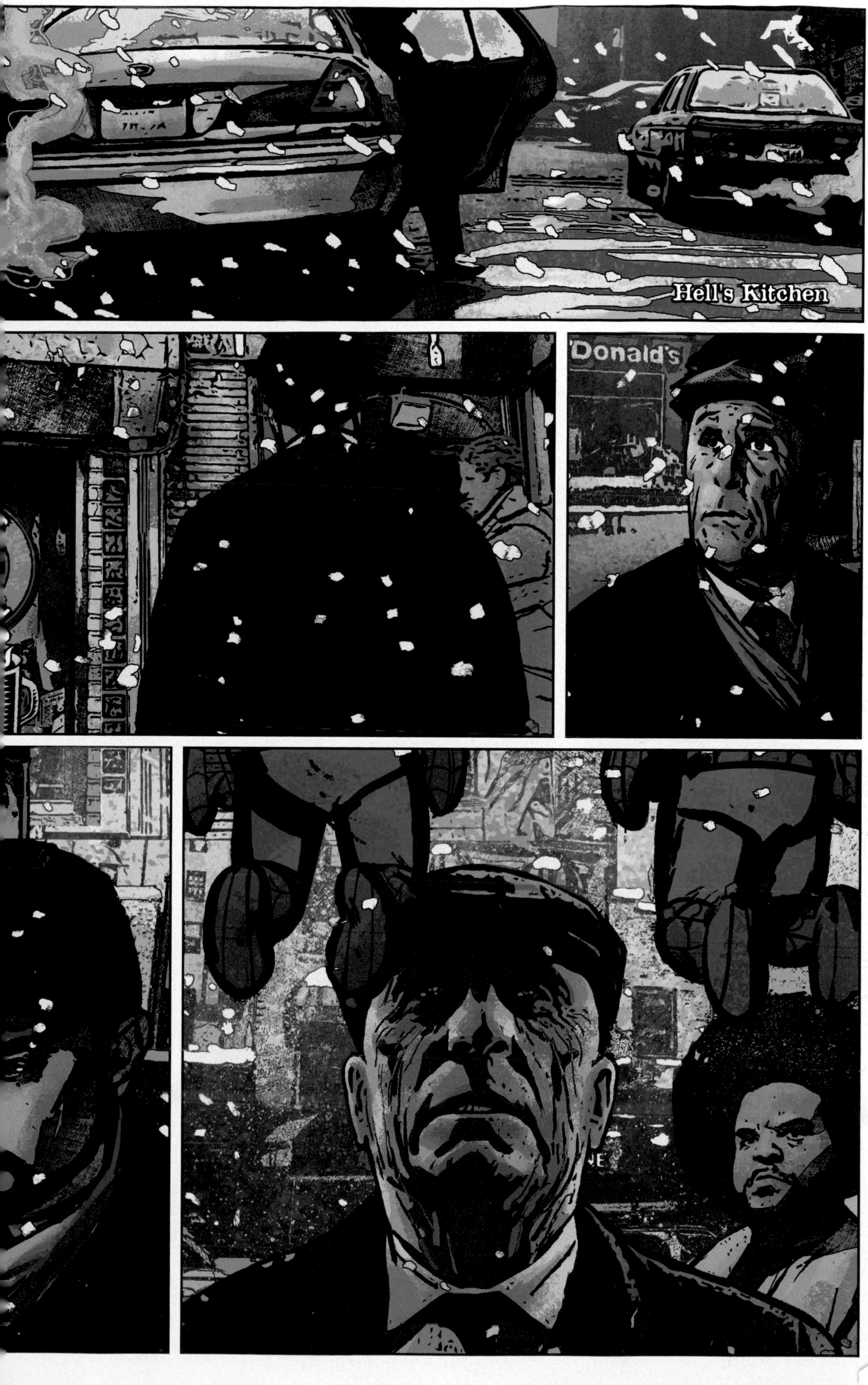
Hell's Kitchen
'Donald's

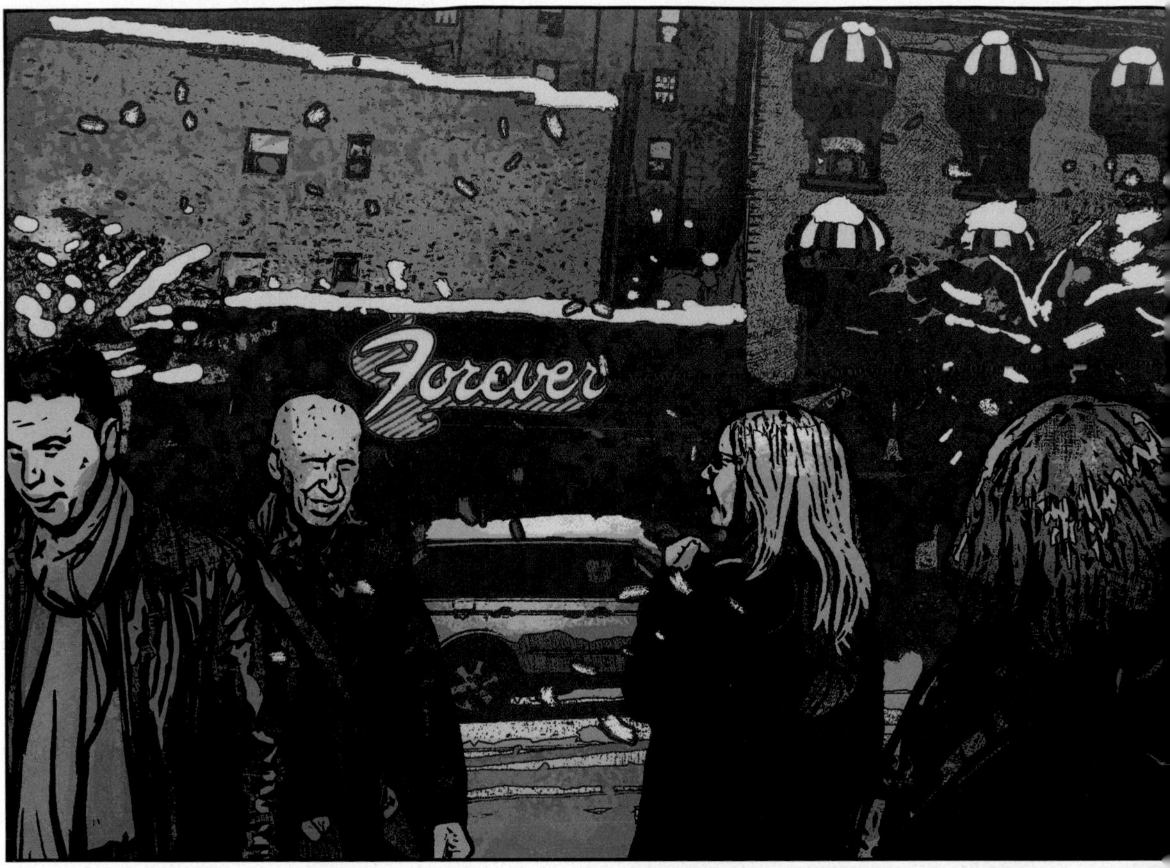
Forever

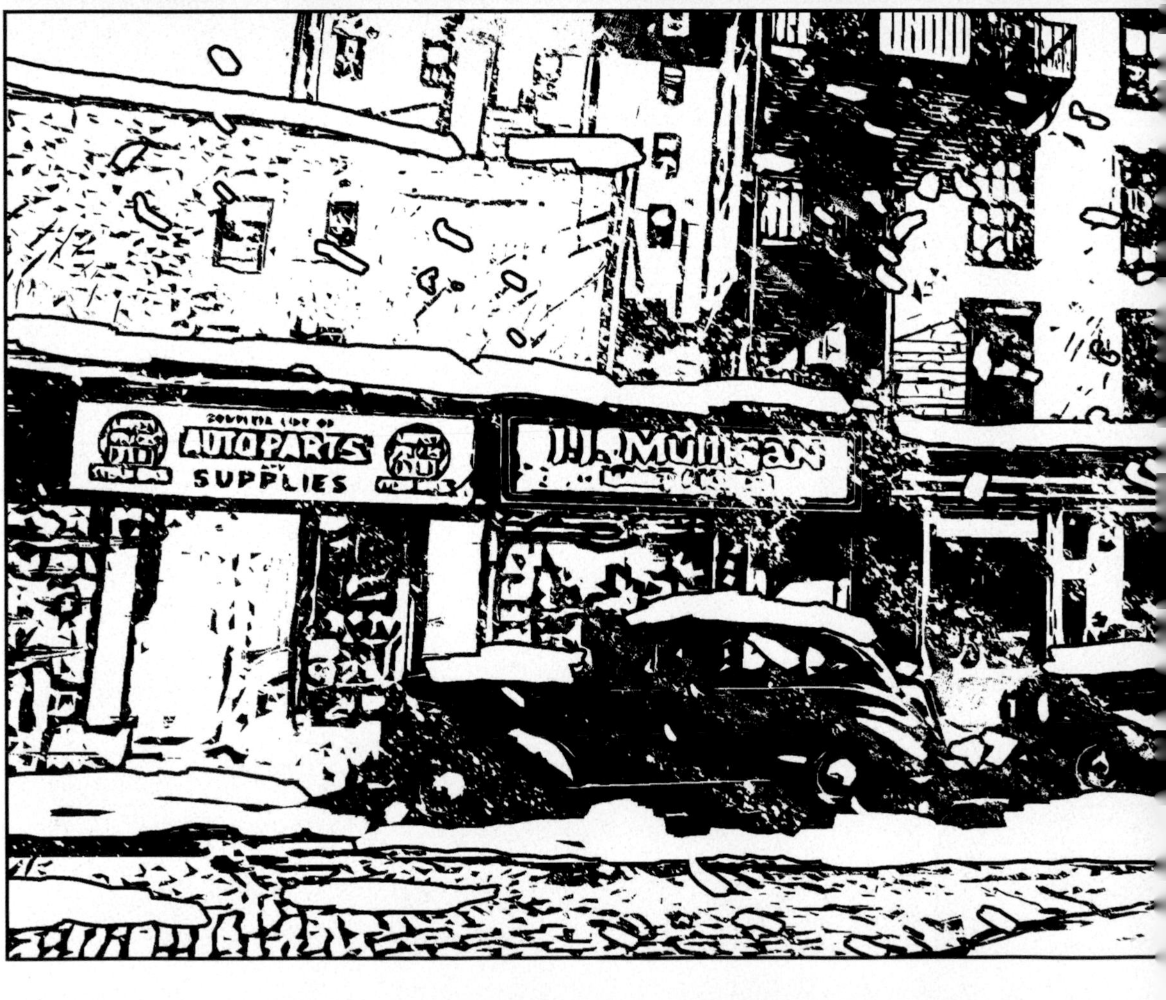
AUTO PARTS
SUPPLIES

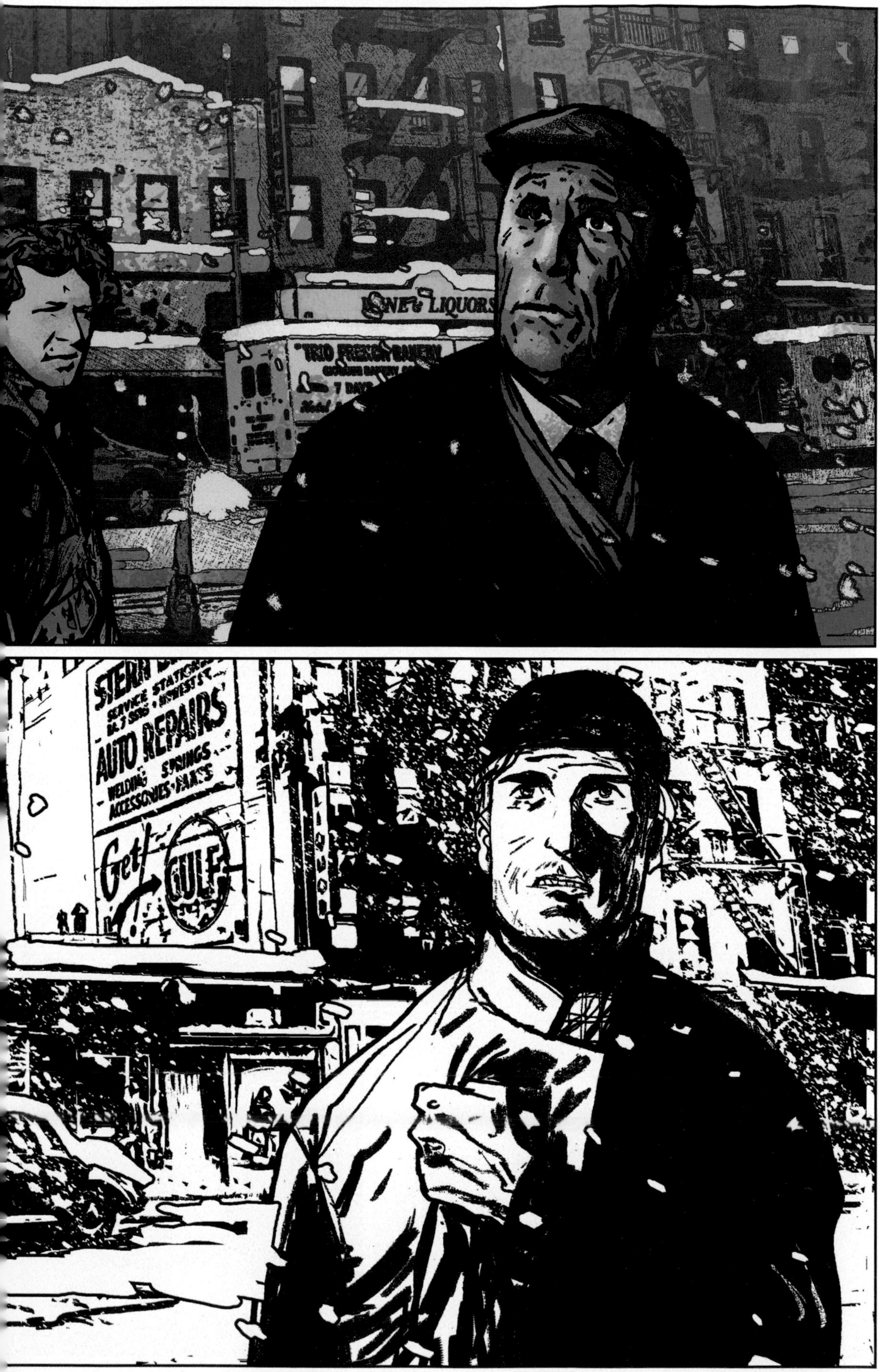
INE & LIQUORS
TRIO FRENCH BAKERY
7 DAYS
SERVICE STATION
AUTO REPAIRS
WELDING SPRINGS
ACCESSORIES • PARTS
Get
GULF

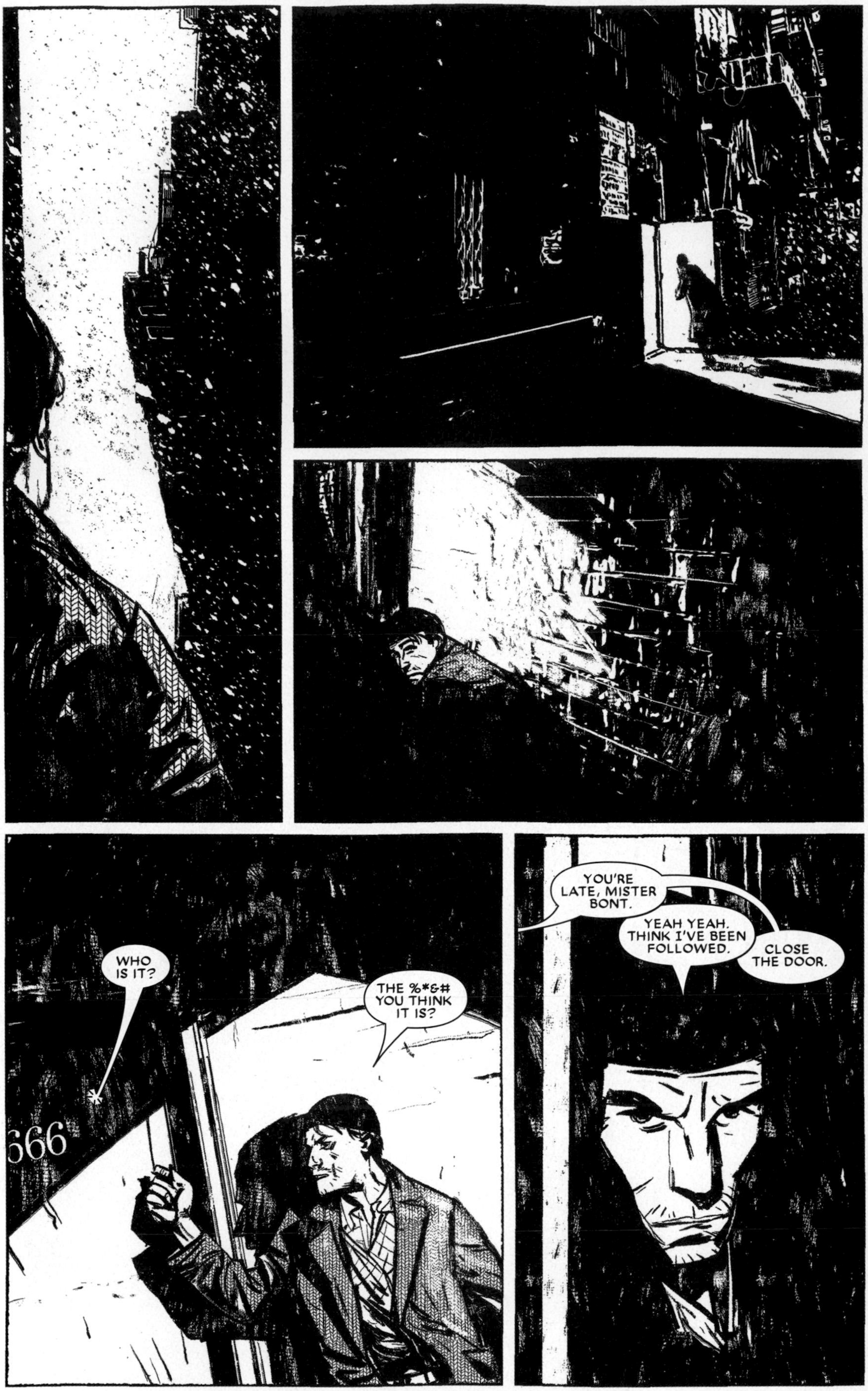
WHO IS IT?
666
THE %*&# YOU THINK IT IS?
YOU'RE LATE, MISTER BONT.
YEAH YEAH. THINK I'VE BEEN FOLLOWED.
CLOSE THE DOOR.

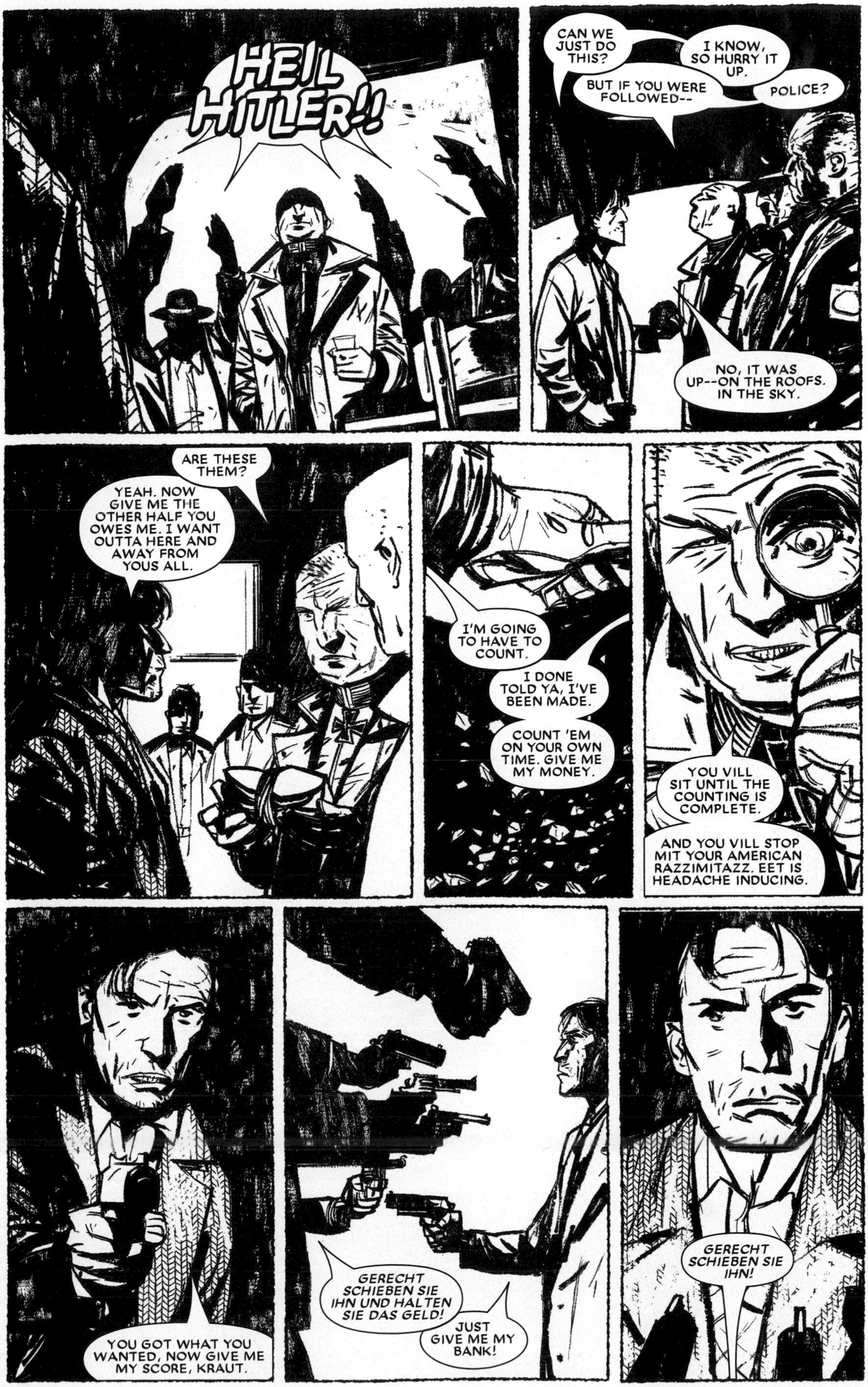
HEIL HITLER!!
CAN WE JUST DO THIS?
BUT IF YOU WERE FOLLOWED--
I KNOW, SO HURRY IT UP.
POLICE?
NO, IT WAS UP--ON THE ROOFS. IN THE SKY.
ARE THESE THEM?
YEAH. NOW GIVE ME THE OTHER HALF YOU OWES ME. I WANT OUTTA HERE AND AWAY FROM YOUS ALL.
I'M GOING TO HAVE TO COUNT.
I DONE TOLD YA, I'VE BEEN MADE.
COUNT 'EM ON YOUR OWN TIME. GIVE ME MY MONEY.
YOU VILL SIT UNTIL THE COUNTING IS COMPLETE.
AND YOU VILL STOP MIT YOUR AMERICAN RAZZIMITAZZ. EET IS HEADACHE INDUCING.
YOU GOT WHAT YOU WANTED, NOW GIVE ME MY SCORE, KRAUT.
GERECHT SCHIEBEN SIE IHN UND HALTEN SIE DAS GELD!
JUST GIVE ME MY BANK!
GERECHT SCHIEBEN SIE IHN!

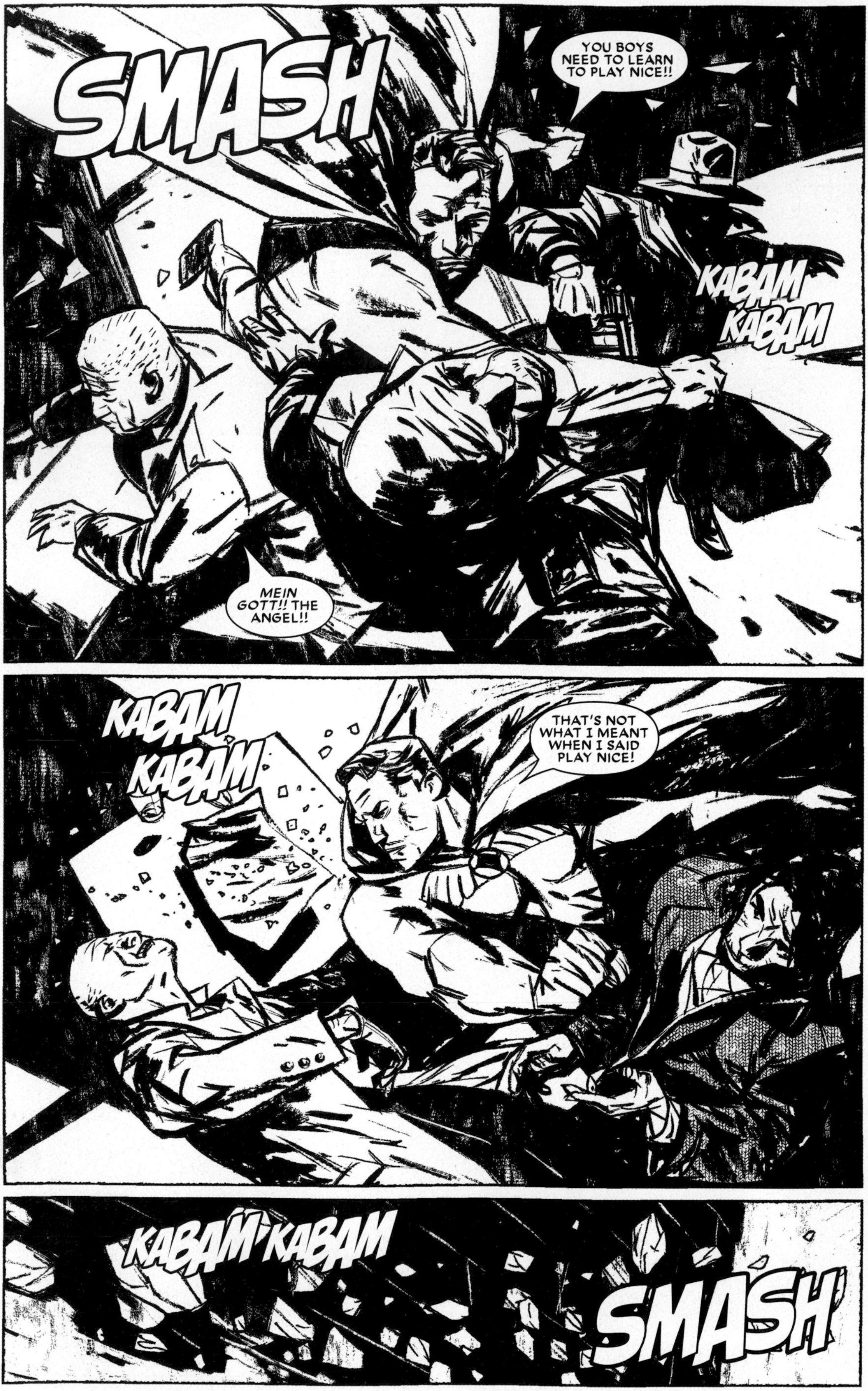
SMASH
YOU BOYS NEED TO LEARN TO PLAY NICE!!
KABAM KABAM
MEIN GOTT!! THE ANGEL!!
KABAM KABAM
THAT'S NOT WHAT I MEANT WHEN I SAID PLAY NICE!
KABAM KABAM
SMASH

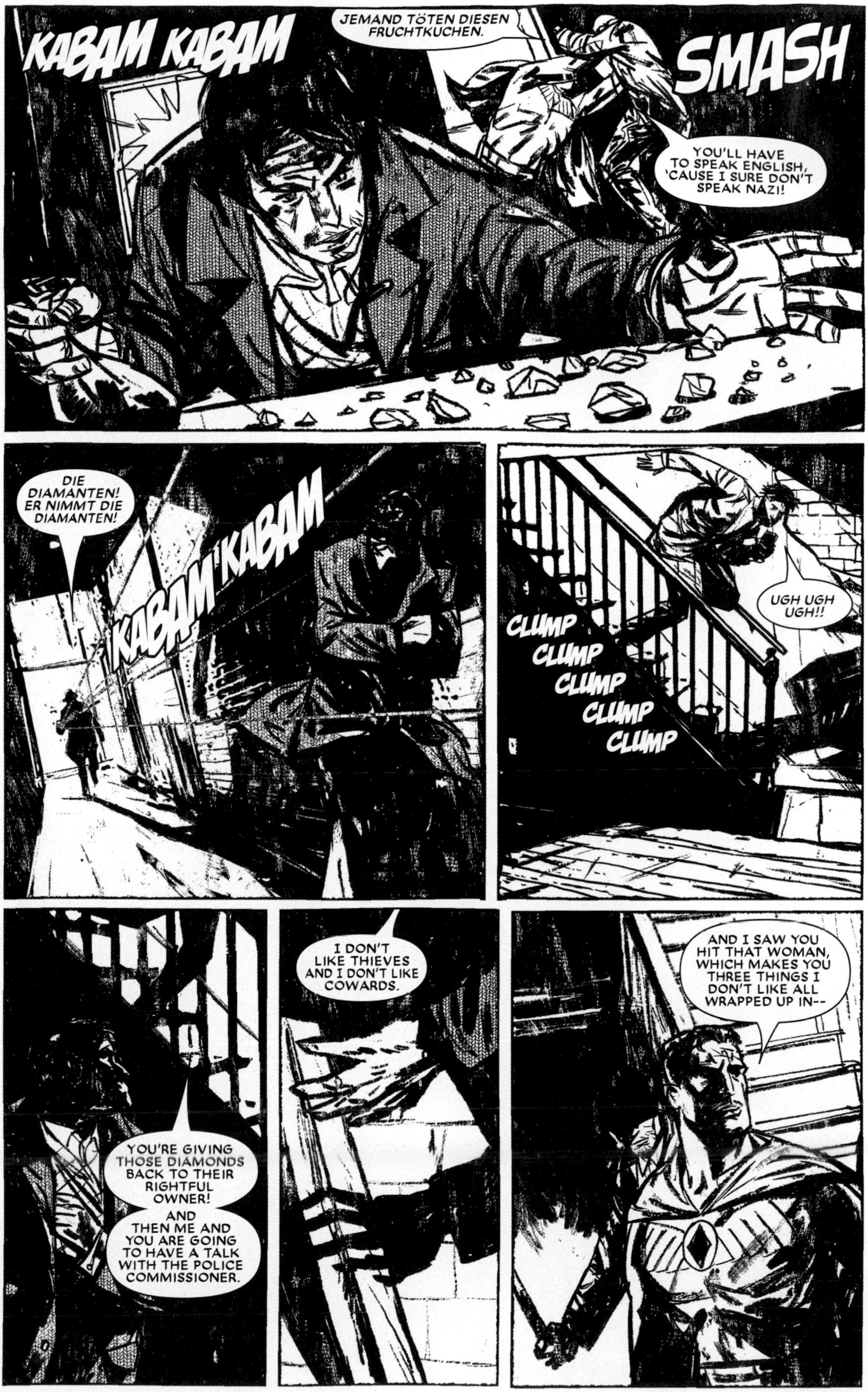
KABAM KABAM
JEMAND TÖTEN DIESEN FRUCHTKUCHEN.
SMASH
YOU'LL HAVE TO SPEAK ENGLISH, 'CAUSE I SURE DON'T SPEAK NAZI!
DIE DIAMANTEN! ER NIMMT DIE DIAMANTEN!
KABAM KABAM
CLUMP CLUMP CLUMP CLUMP CLUMP
UGH UGH UGH!!
YOU'RE GIVING THOSE DIAMONDS BACK TO THEIR RIGHTFUL OWNER!
AND THEN ME AND YOU ARE GOING TO HAVE A TALK WITH THE POLICE COMMISSIONER.
I DON'T LIKE THIEVES AND I DON'T LIKE COWARDS.
AND I SAW YOU HIT THAT WOMAN, WHICH MAKES YOU THREE THINGS I DON'T LIKE ALL WRAPPED UP IN--

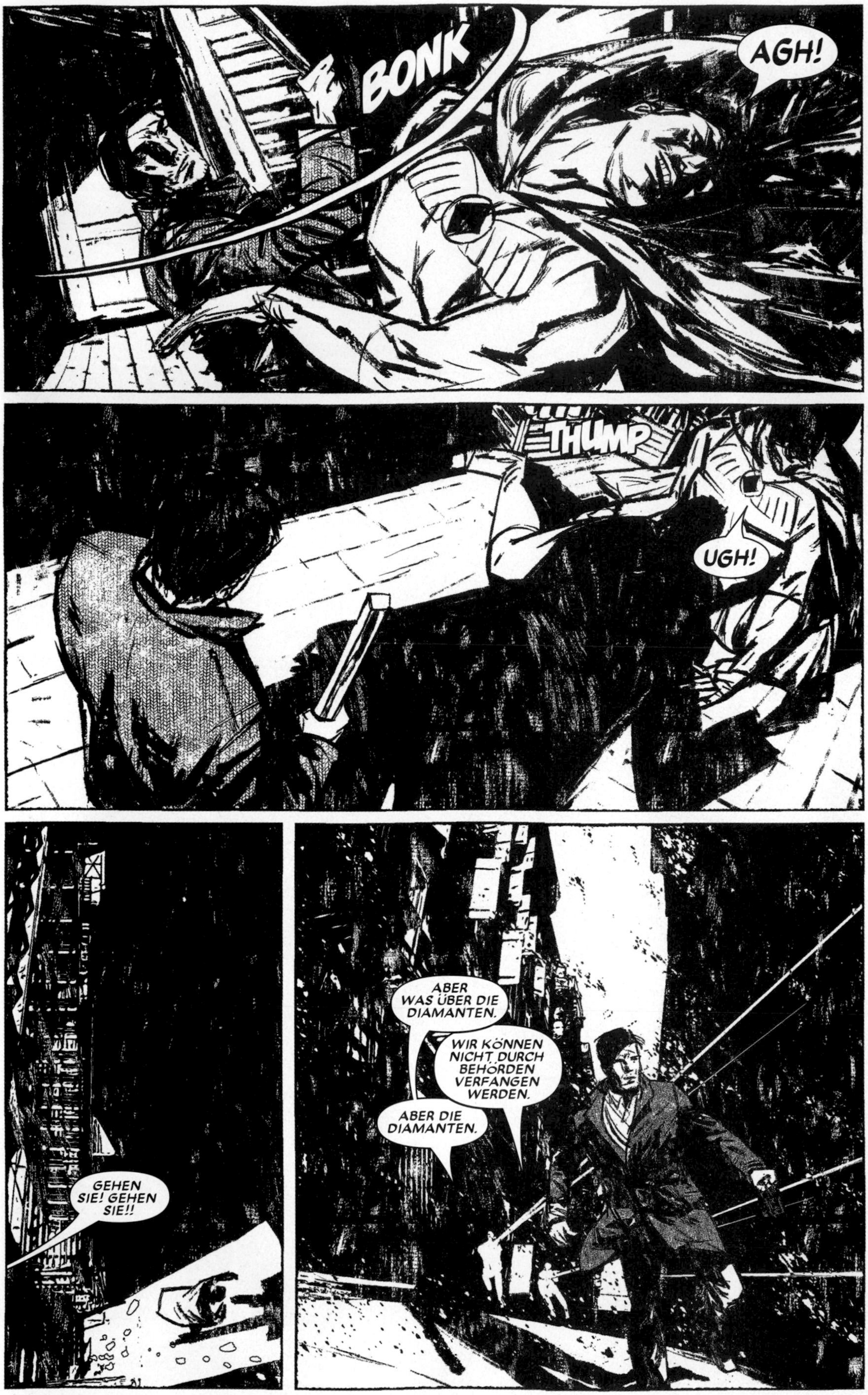
BONK
AGH!
THUMP
UGH!
GEHEN SIE! GEHEN SIE!!
ABER WAS ÜBER DIE DIAMANTEN.
WIR KÖNNEN NICHT DURCH BEHÖRDEN VERFANGEN WERDEN.
ABER DIE DIAMANTEN.

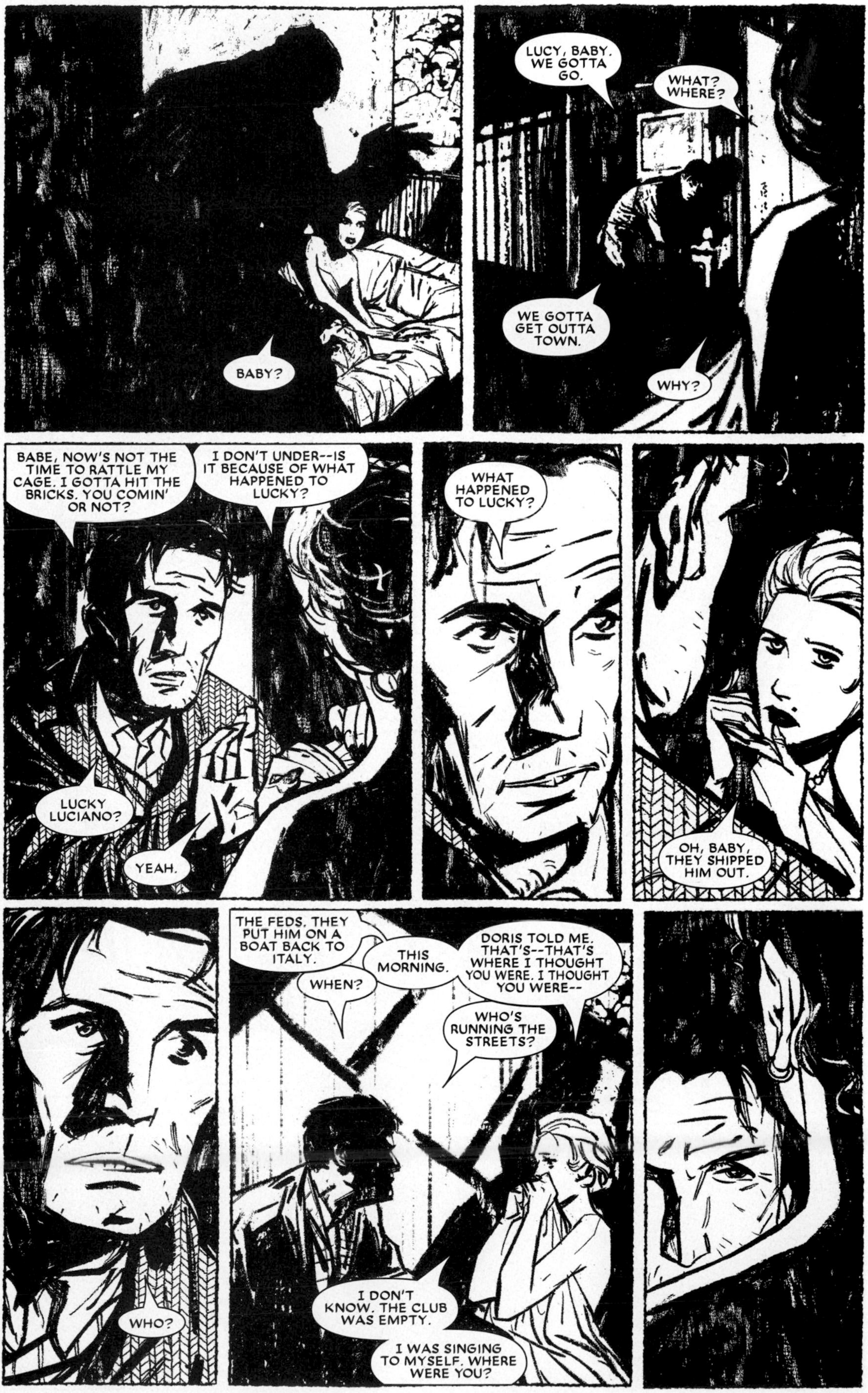
BABY?
LUCY, BABY. WE GOTTA GO.
WHAT? WHERE?
WE GOTTA GET OUTTA TOWN.
WHY?
BABE, NOW'S NOT THE TIME TO RATTLE MY CAGE. I GOTTA HIT THE BRICKS. YOU COMIN' OR NOT?
I DON'T UNDER--IS IT BECAUSE OF WHAT HAPPENED TO LUCKY?
LUCKY LUCIANO?
YEAH.
WHAT HAPPENED TO LUCKY?
OH, BABY, THEY SHIPPED HIM OUT.
WHO?
THE FEDS. THEY PUT HIM ON A BOAT BACK TO ITALY.
WHEN?
THIS MORNING.
DORIS TOLD ME. THAT'S--THAT'S WHERE I THOUGHT YOU WERE. I THOUGHT YOU WERE--
WHO'S RUNNING THE STREETS?
I DON'T KNOW. THE CLUB WAS EMPTY.
I WAS SINGING TO MYSELF. WHERE WERE YOU?

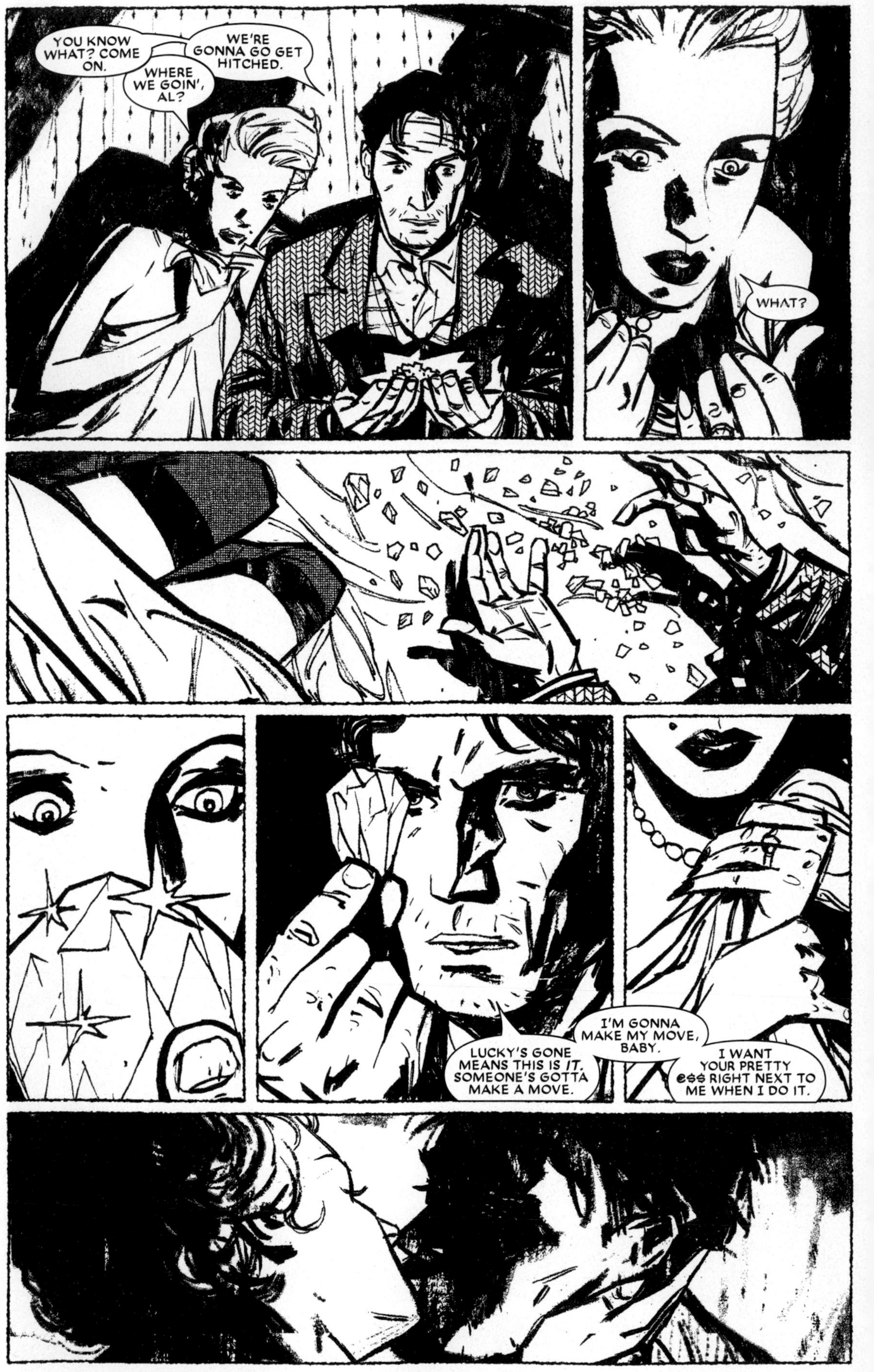
YOU KNOW WHAT? COME ON.
WHERE WE GOIN', AL?
WE'RE GONNA GO GET HITCHED.
WHAT?
LUCKY'S GONE MEANS THIS IS *IT*. SOMEONE'S GOTTA MAKE A MOVE.
I'M GONNA MAKE MY MOVE, BABY.
I WANT YOUR PRETTY @$$ RIGHT NEXT TO ME WHEN I DO IT.

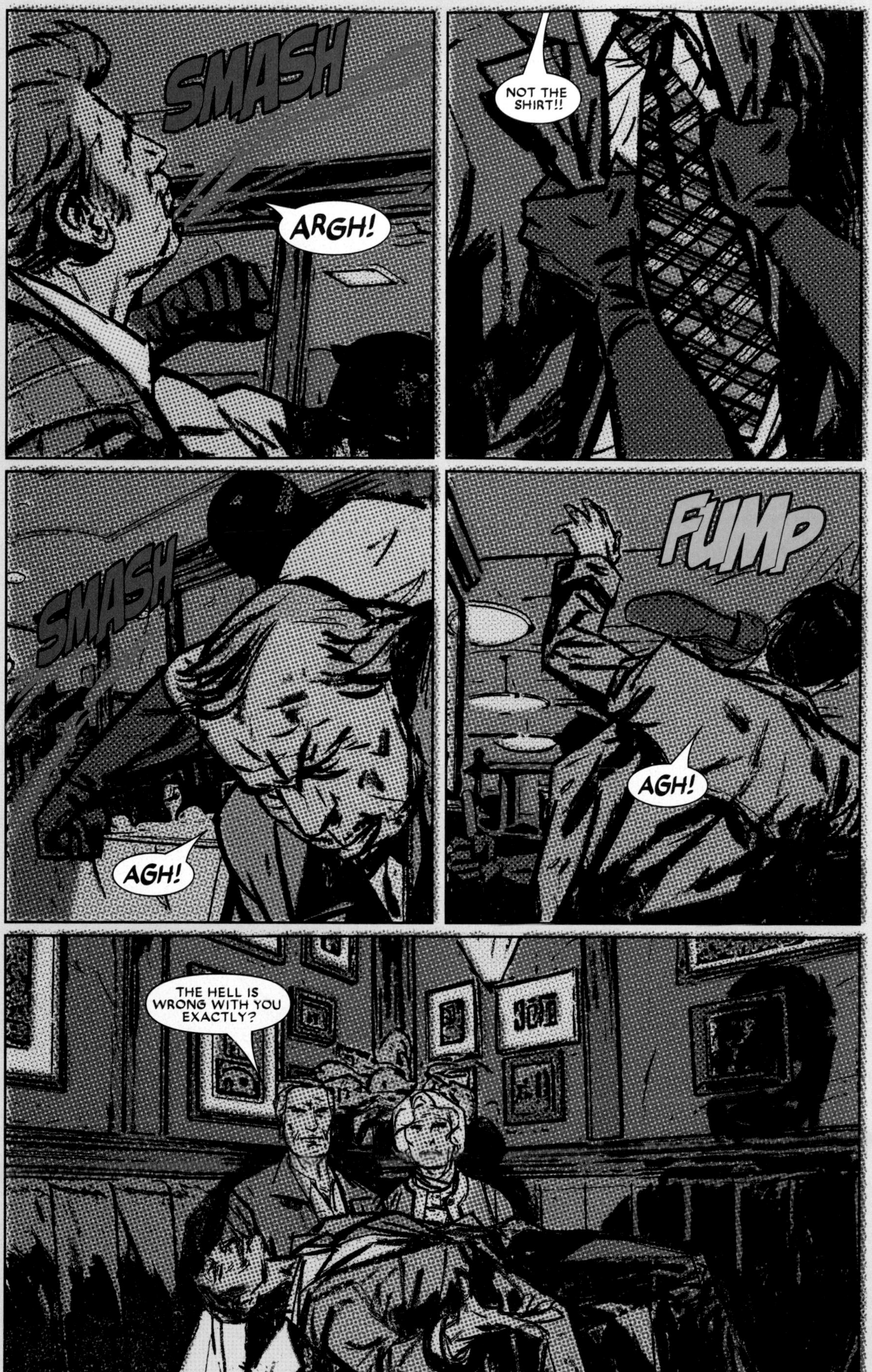
SMASH
ARGH!
NOT THE SHIRT!!
SMASH
AGH!
FUMP
AGH!
THE HELL IS WRONG WITH YOU EXACTLY?

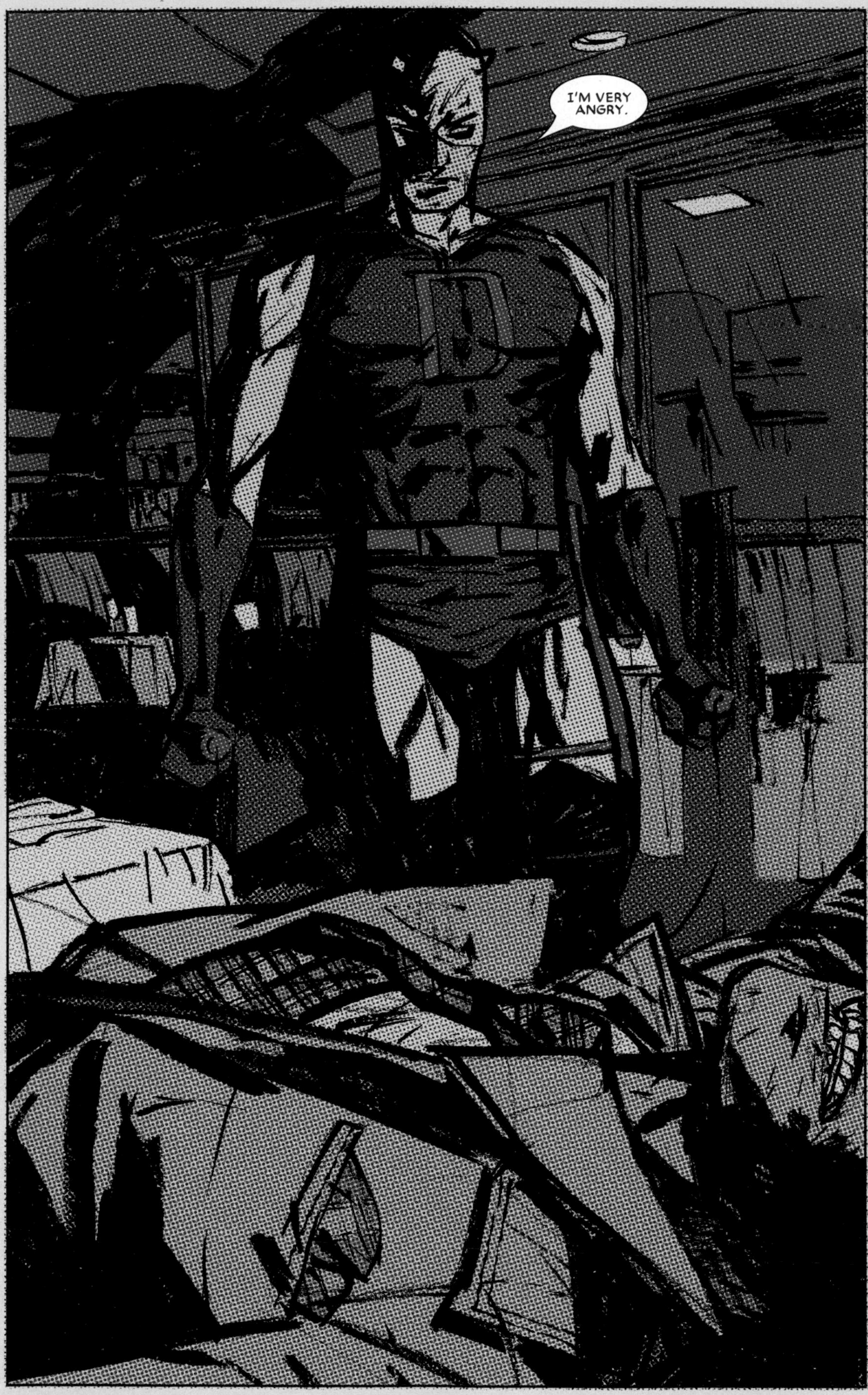
I'M VERY ANGRY.

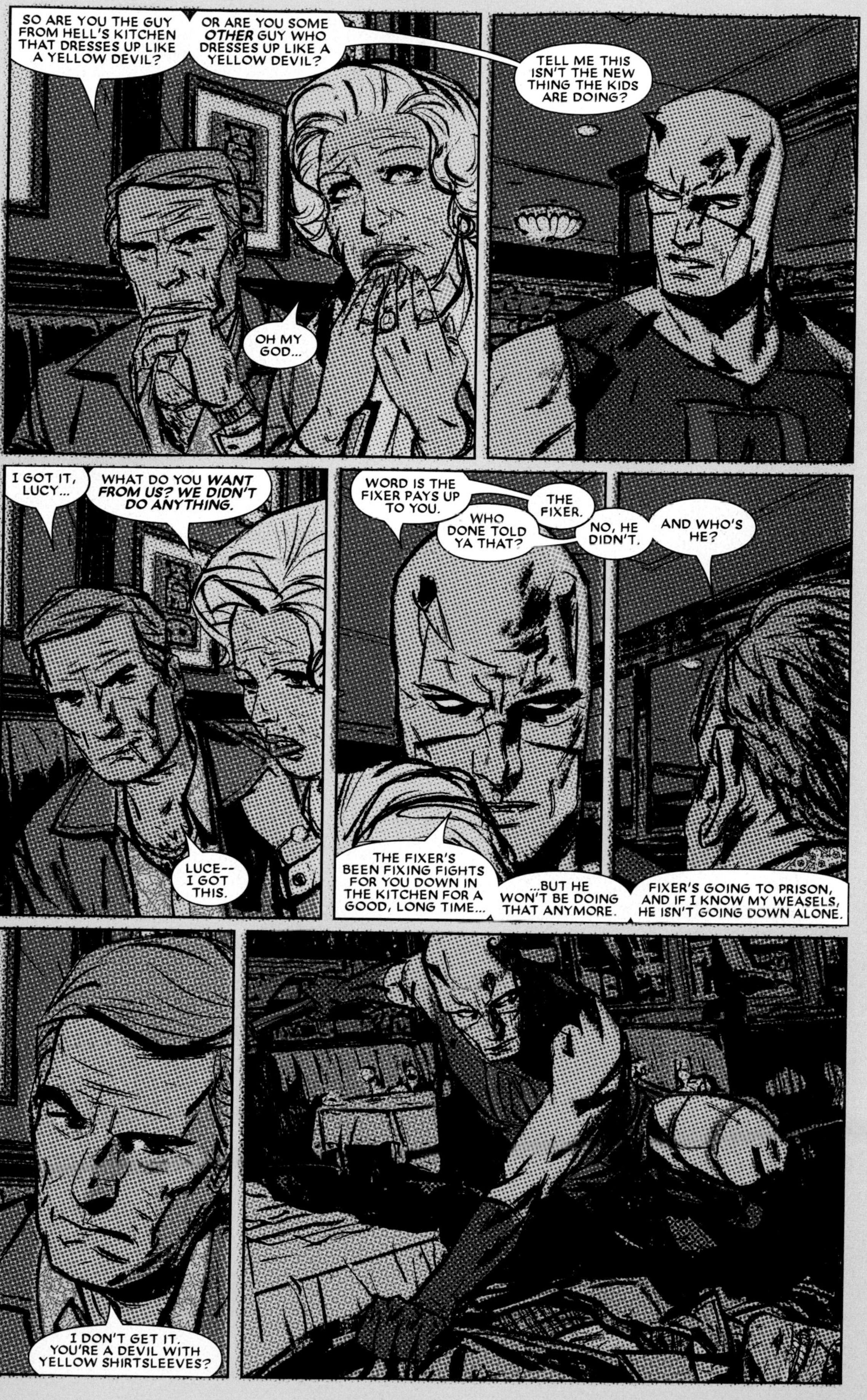
SO ARE YOU THE GUY FROM HELL'S KITCHEN THAT DRESSES UP LIKE A YELLOW DEVIL?
OR ARE YOU SOME *OTHER* GUY WHO DRESSES UP LIKE A YELLOW DEVIL?
OH MY GOD...
TELL ME THIS ISN'T THE NEW THING THE KIDS ARE DOING?
I GOT IT, LUCY...
WHAT DO YOU WANT FROM US? WE DIDN'T DO ANYTHING.
LUCE-- I GOT THIS.
WORD IS THE FIXER PAYS UP TO YOU.
WHO DONE TOLD YA THAT?
THE FIXER.
NO, HE DIDN'T.
AND WHO'S HE?
THE FIXER'S BEEN FIXING FIGHTS FOR YOU DOWN IN THE KITCHEN FOR A GOOD, LONG TIME...
...BUT HE WON'T BE DOING THAT ANYMORE.
FIXER'S GOING TO PRISON, AND IF I KNOW MY WEASELS, HE ISN'T GOING DOWN ALONE.
I DON'T GET IT. YOU'RE A DEVIL WITH YELLOW SHIRTSLEEVES?

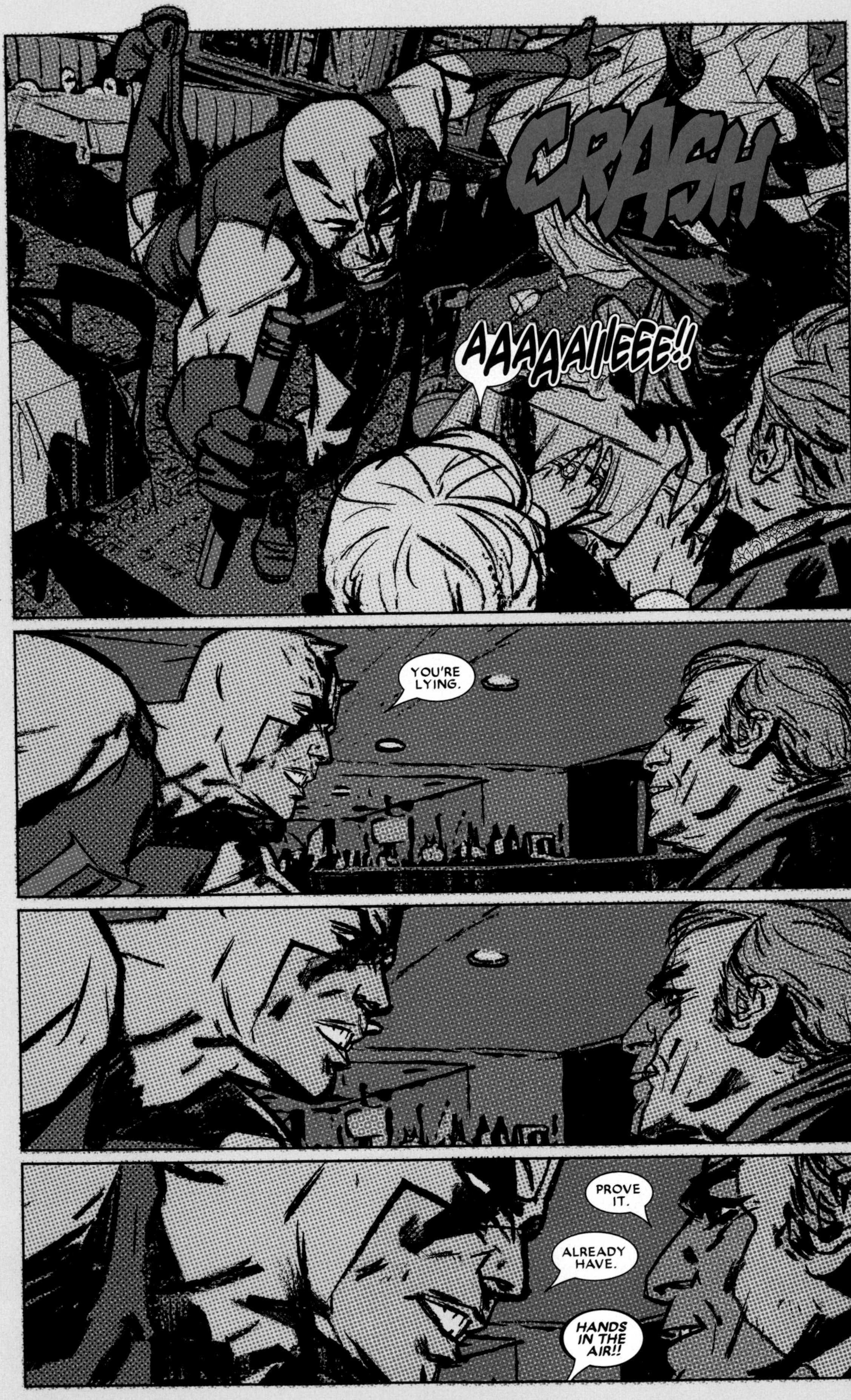
CRASH
AAAAAIIIEEE!!
YOU'RE LYING.
PROVE IT.
ALREADY HAVE.
HANDS IN THE AIR!!

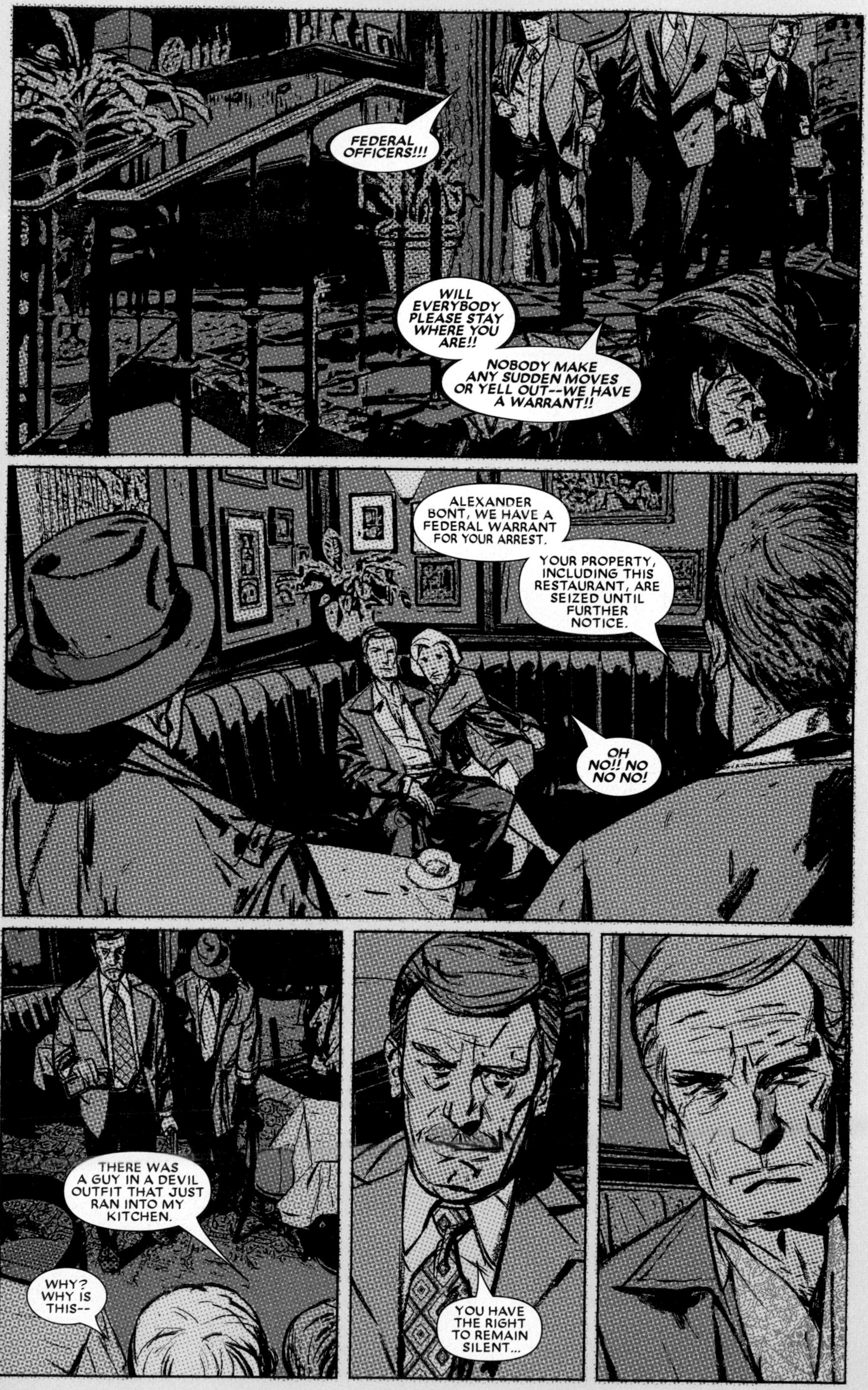
FEDERAL OFFICERS!!!
WILL EVERYBODY PLEASE STAY WHERE YOU ARE!!
NOBODY MAKE ANY SUDDEN MOVES OR YELL OUT--WE HAVE A WARRANT!!
ALEXANDER BONT, WE HAVE A FEDERAL WARRANT FOR YOUR ARREST.
YOUR PROPERTY, INCLUDING THIS RESTAURANT, ARE SEIZED UNTIL FURTHER NOTICE.
OH NO!! NO NO NO!
THERE WAS A GUY IN A DEVIL OUTFIT THAT JUST RAN INTO MY KITCHEN.
WHY? WHY IS THIS--
YOU HAVE THE RIGHT TO REMAIN SILENT...

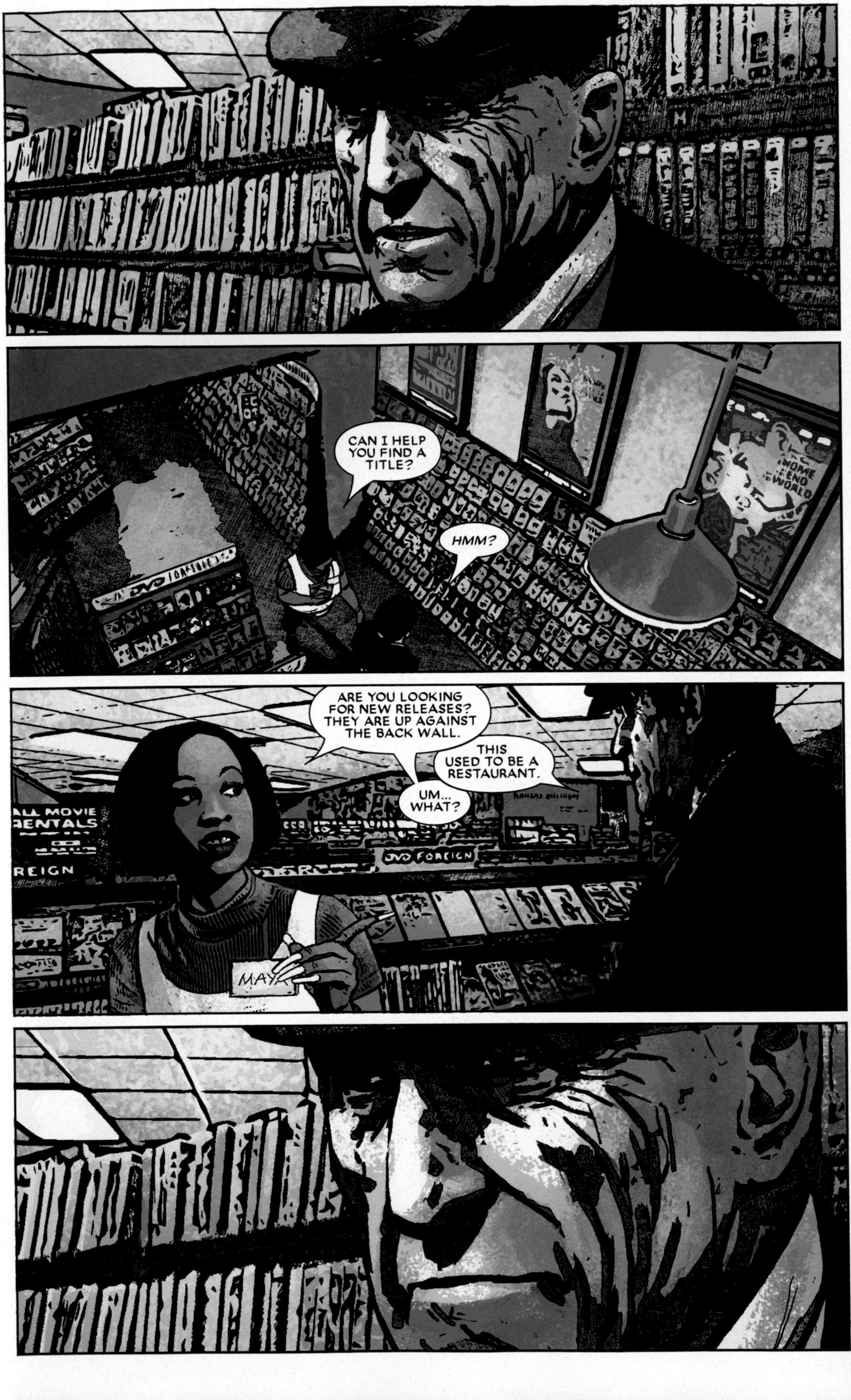
CAN I HELP YOU FIND A TITLE?
HMM?
ARE YOU LOOKING FOR NEW RELEASES? THEY ARE UP AGAINST THE BACK WALL.
THIS USED TO BE A RESTAURANT.
UM... WHAT?
DVD FOREIGN

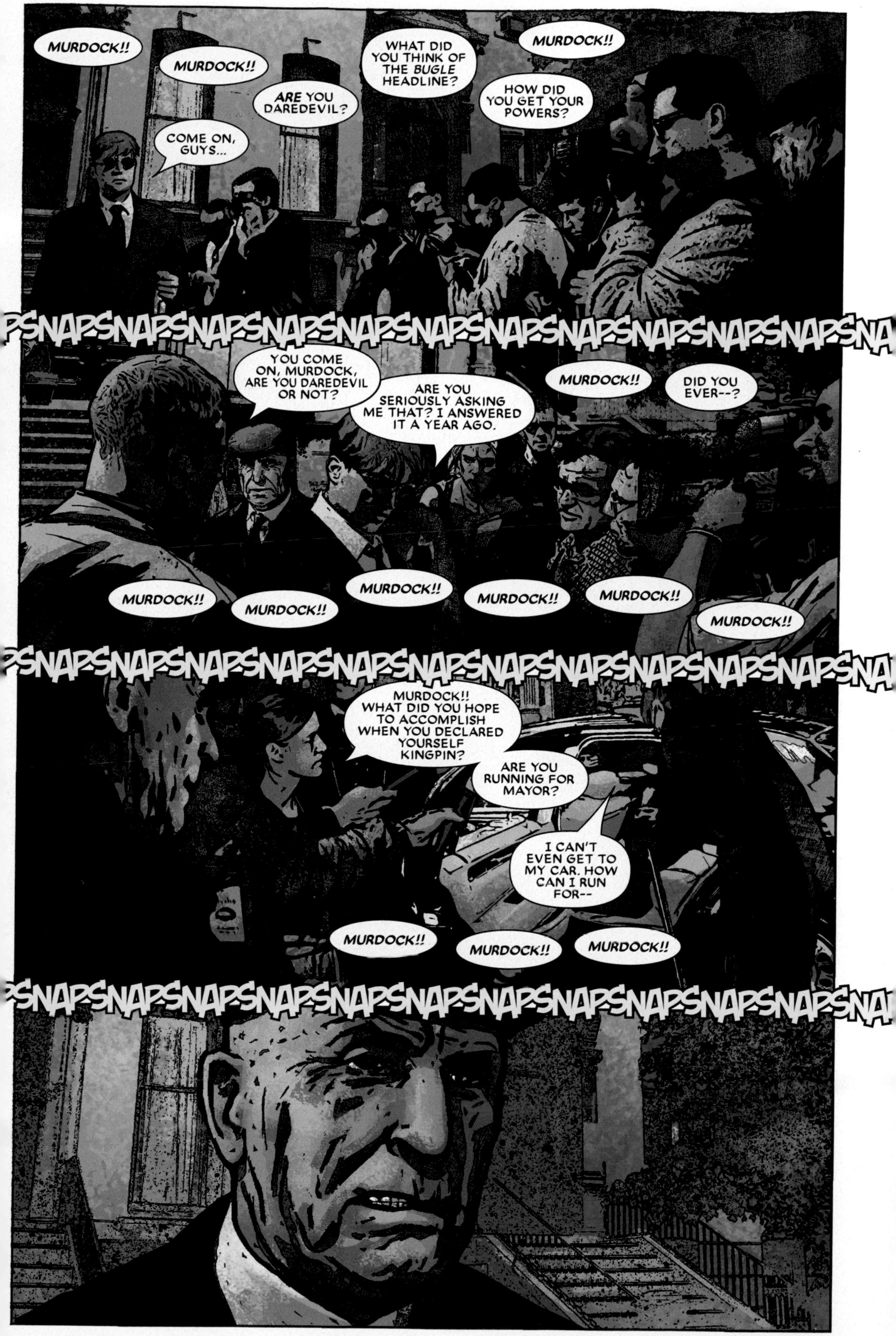
MURDOCK!!
MURDOCK!!
COME ON, GUYS...
ARE YOU DAREDEVIL?
WHAT DID YOU THINK OF THE BUGLE HEADLINE?
MURDOCK!!
HOW DID YOU GET YOUR POWERS?
SNAPSNAPSNAPSNAPSNAPSNAPSNAPSNAPSNAPSNAPSNAPSNAPSNA
YOU COME ON, MURDOCK, ARE YOU DAREDEVIL OR NOT?
ARE YOU SERIOUSLY ASKING ME THAT? I ANSWERED IT A YEAR AGO.
MURDOCK!!
DID YOU EVER--?
MURDOCK!!
MURDOCK!!
MURDOCK!!
MURDOCK!!
MURDOCK!!
MURDOCK!!
SNAPSNAPSNAPSNAPSNAPSNAPSNAPSNAPSNAPSNAPSNAPSNAPSNA
MURDOCK!! WHAT DID YOU HOPE TO ACCOMPLISH WHEN YOU DECLARED YOURSELF KINGPIN?
ARE YOU RUNNING FOR MAYOR?
I CAN'T EVEN GET TO MY CAR. HOW CAN I RUN FOR--
MURDOCK!!
MURDOCK!!
MURDOCK!!
SNAPSNAPSNAPSNAPSNAPSNAPSNAPSNAPSNAPSNAPSNAPSNAPSNA

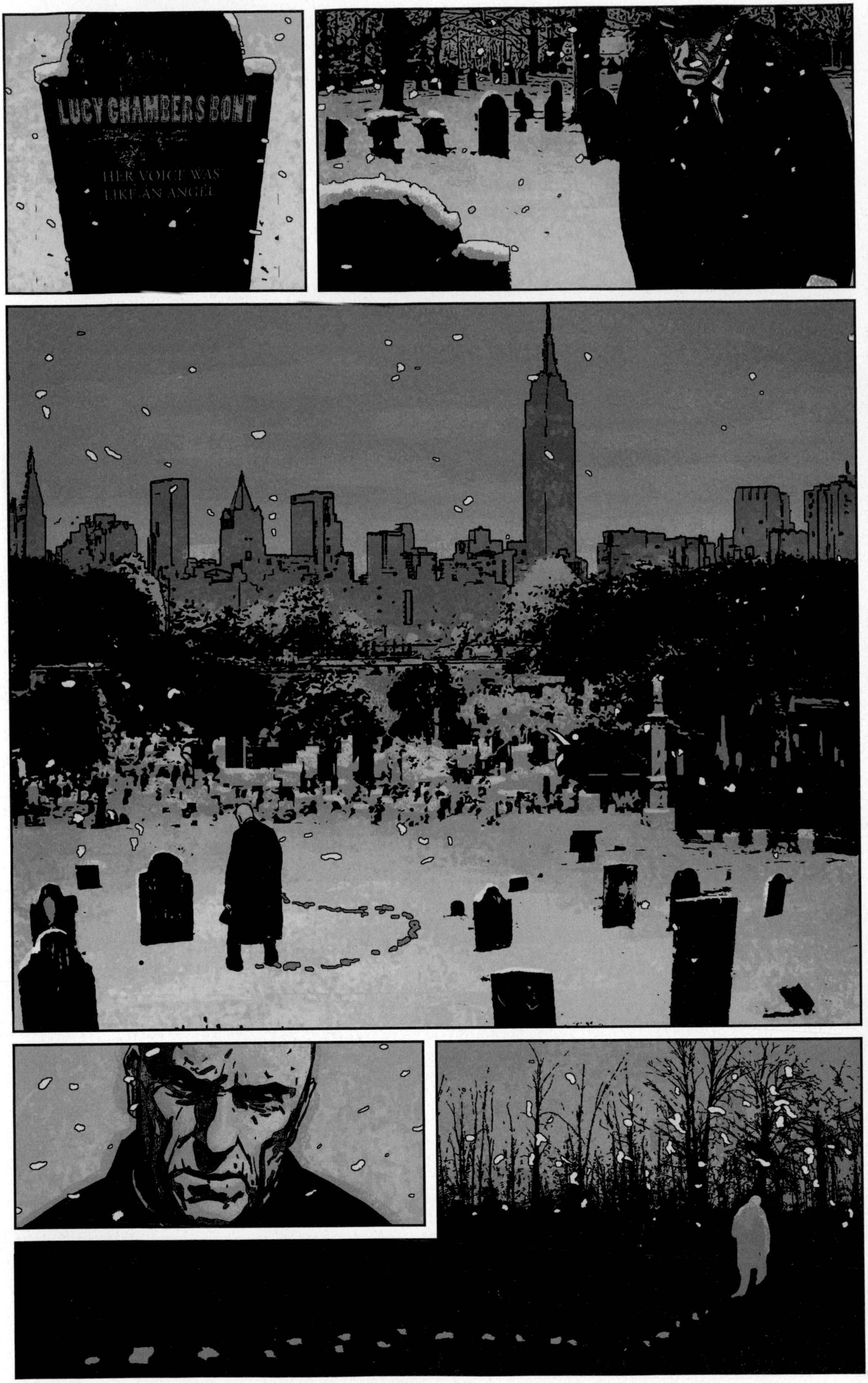
LUCY CHAMBERS BONT
HER VOICE WAS
LIKE AN ANGEL

THERE HE IS!! (I'LL CALL YOU BACK.)

ALEXANDER BONT. THE BIG BONT. THE BIG MAN.

SLICK SAUL.

I DIDN'T KNOWS IT WAS TODAY. IT WAS TODAY? WHAT AM I ASKIN'? HERE YOU ARE. WANT A DRINK?

YES.

HEY, TOOTSIE, A DRINK! (WHAT, GLEN-LIVET? STILL WITH THE--)

YES.

GOT SOME OF THE GOOD STUFF IN HERE.

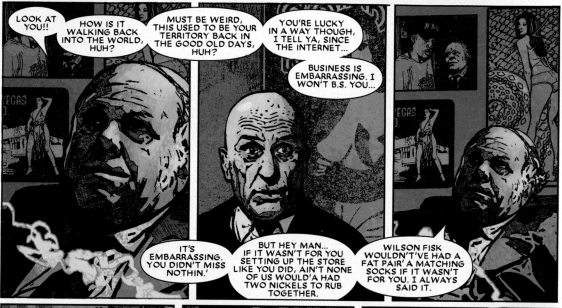

LOOK AT YOU!!

HOW IS IT WALKING BACK INTO THE WORLD, HUH?

MUST BE WEIRD, THIS USED TO BE YOUR TERRITORY BACK IN THE GOOD OLD DAYS, HUH?

YOU'RE LUCKY IN A WAY THOUGH, I TELL YA, SINCE THE INTERNET...

BUSINESS IS EMBARRASSING. I WON'T B.S. YOU...

IT'S EMBARRASSING. YOU DIDN'T MISS NOTHIN.'

BUT HEY MAN... IF IT WASN'T FOR YOU SETTING UP THE STORE LIKE YOU DID, AIN'T NONE OF US WOULD'A HAD TWO NICKELS TO RUB TOGETHER.

WILSON FISK WOULDN'T'VE HAD A FAT PAIR A' MATCHING SOCKS IF IT WASN'T FOR YOU. I ALWAYS SAID IT.

THE CITY HAS CHANGED.

REALLY? SEEMS THE SAME.

HEY!! SO...?

SO, BIG MAN. WHAT'S THE PLAN?

GET YOURSELF A CONDO IN FLORIDA? GET SOME SUN?

NO. I'M NOT DONE HERE.

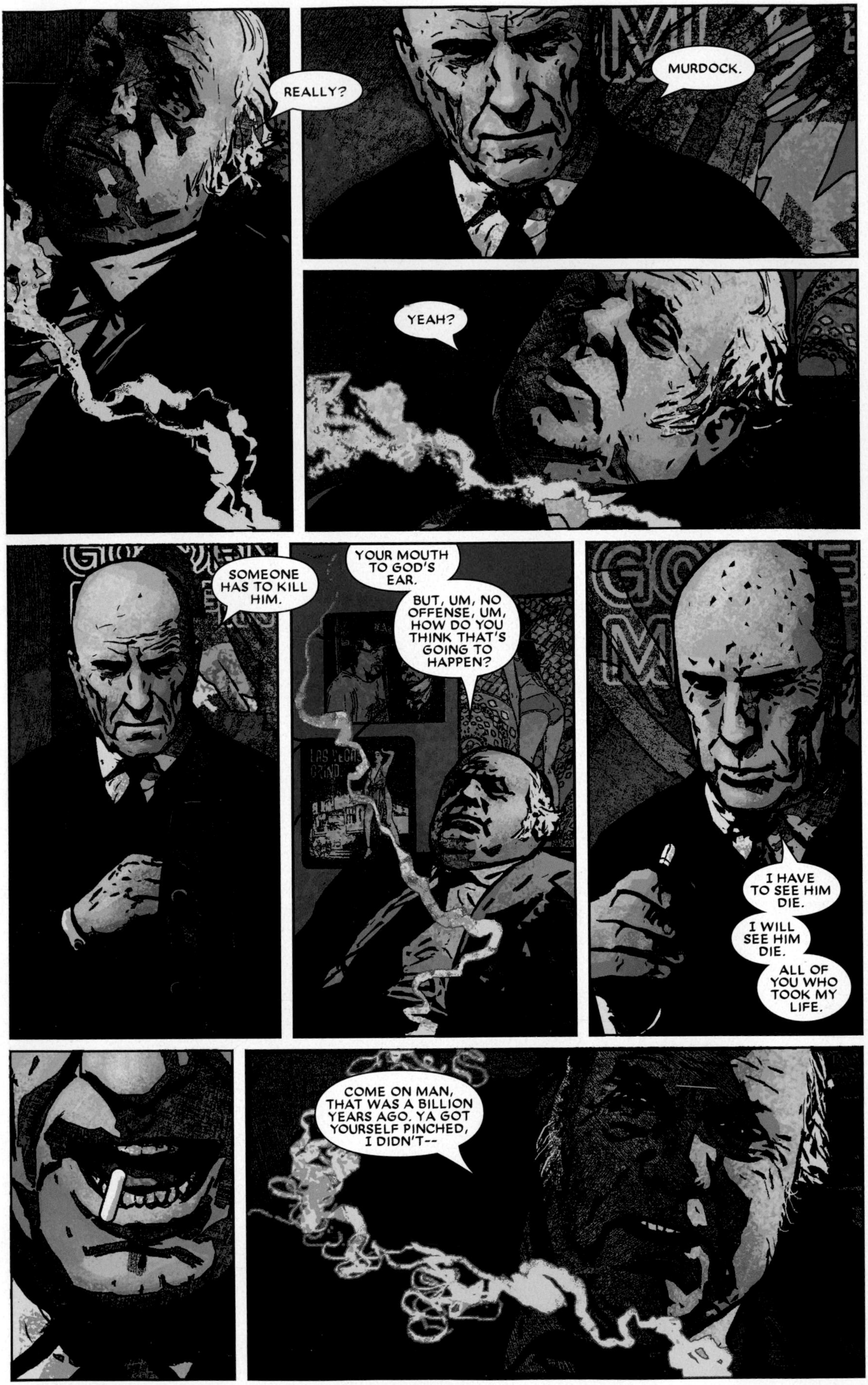
REALLY?
MURDOCK.
YEAH?
SOMEONE HAS TO KILL HIM.
YOUR MOUTH TO GOD'S EAR.
BUT, UM, NO OFFENSE, UM, HOW DO YOU THINK THAT'S GOING TO HAPPEN?
I HAVE TO SEE HIM DIE.
I WILL SEE HIM DIE.
ALL OF YOU WHO TOOK MY LIFE.
COME ON MAN, THAT WAS A BILLION YEARS AGO. YA GOT YOURSELF PINCHED, I DIDN'T--

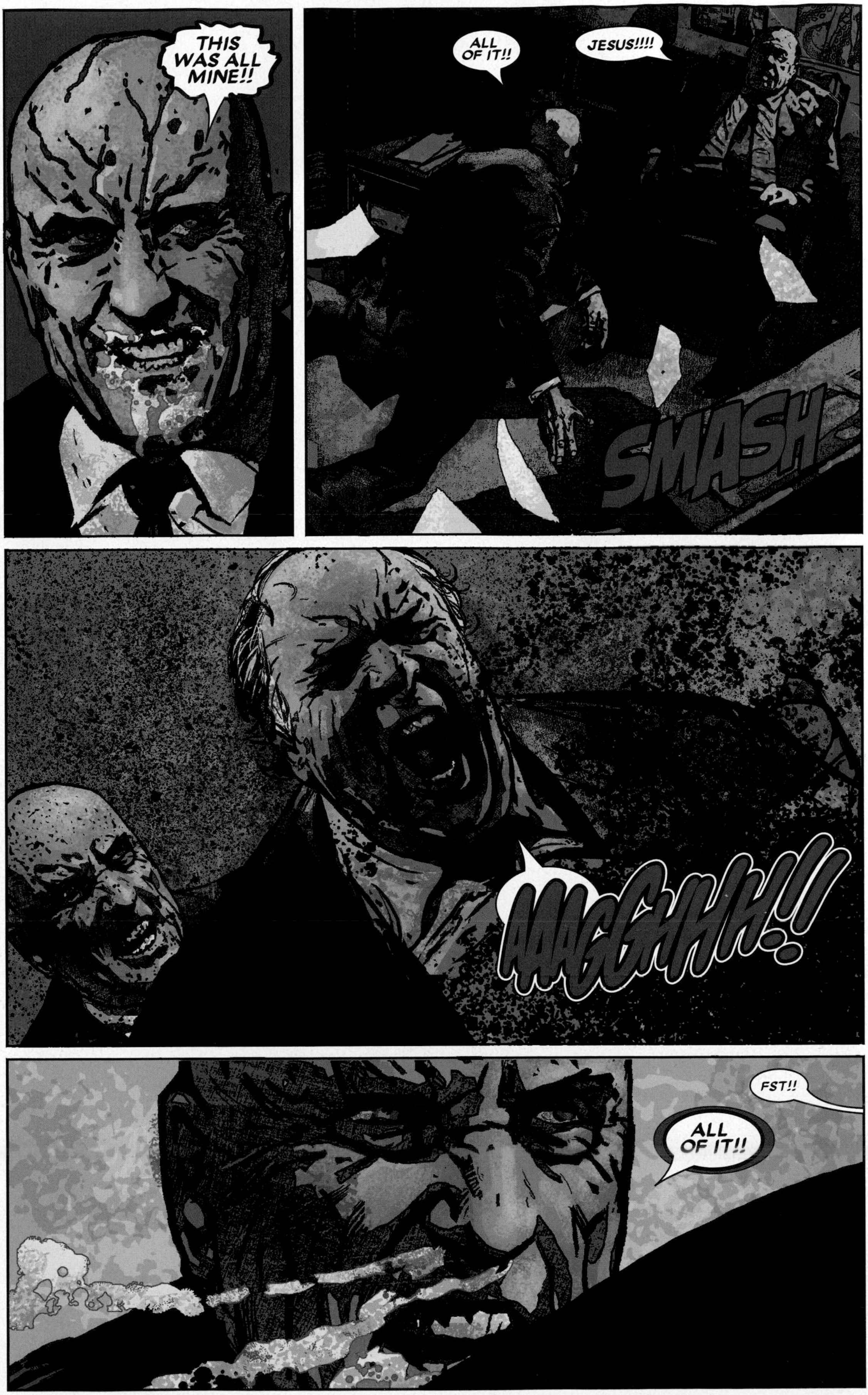
THIS WAS ALL MINE!!
ALL OF IT!!
JESUS!!!!
SMASH
AAAGGHHH!!
FST!!
ALL OF IT!!

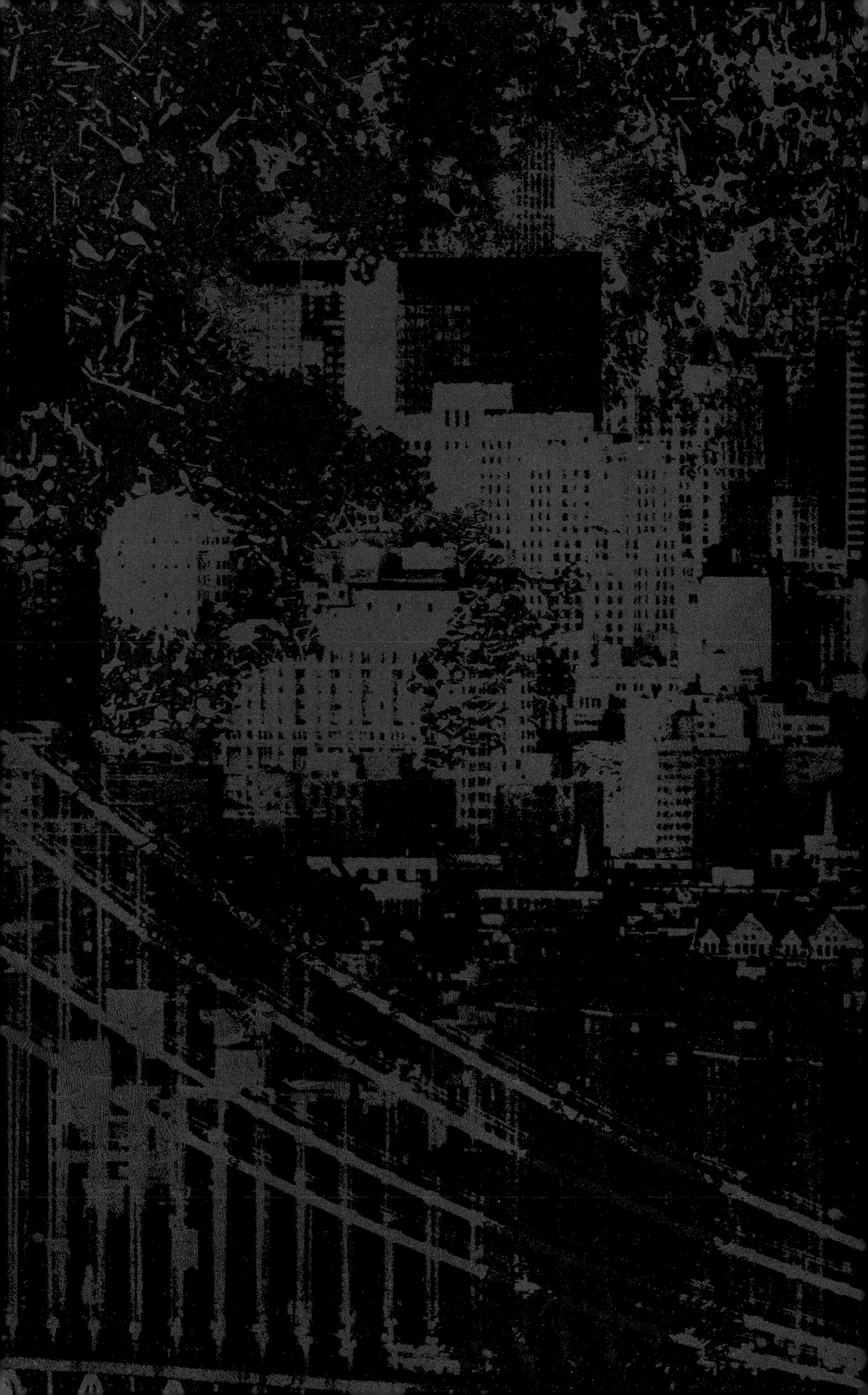

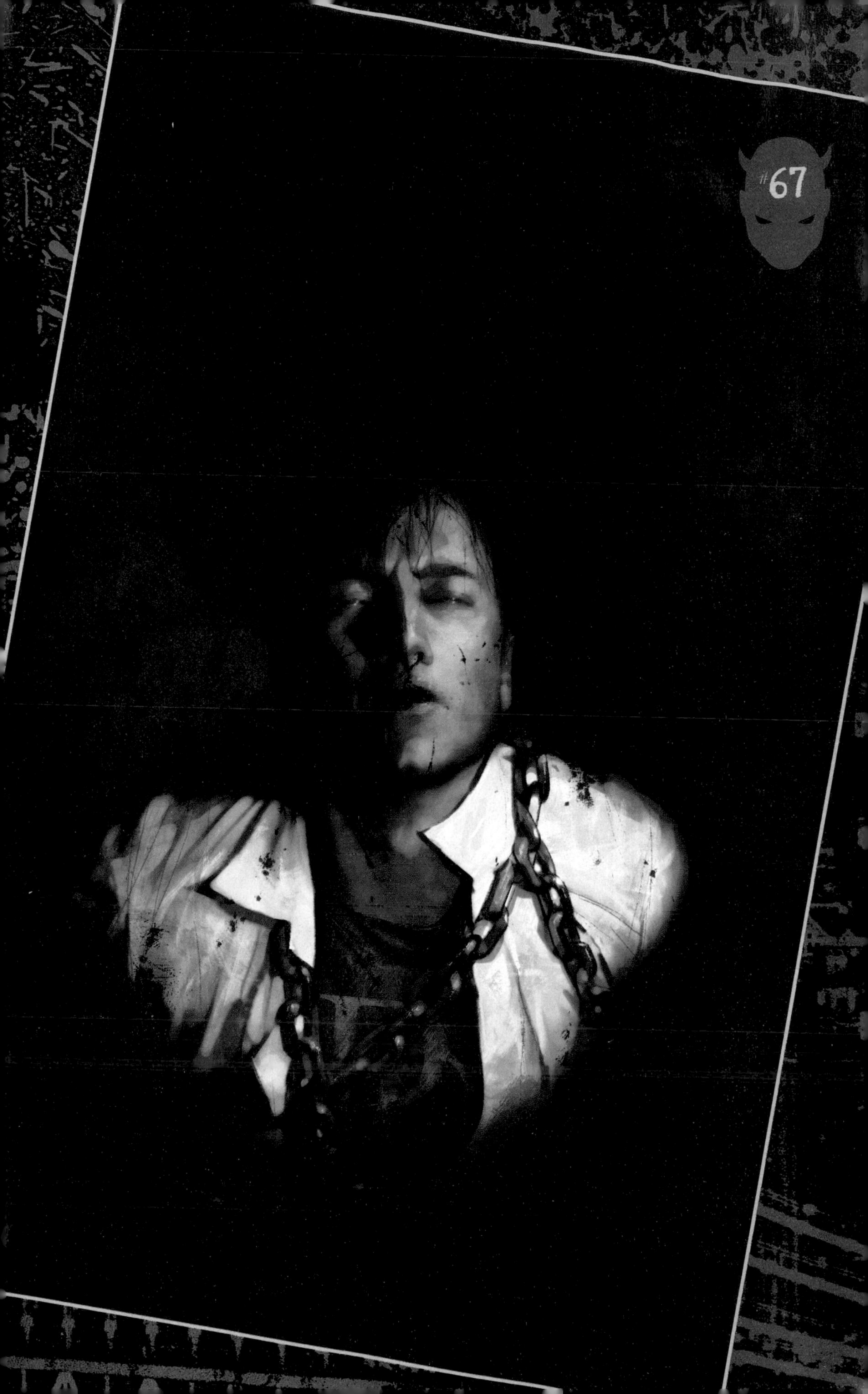
#67

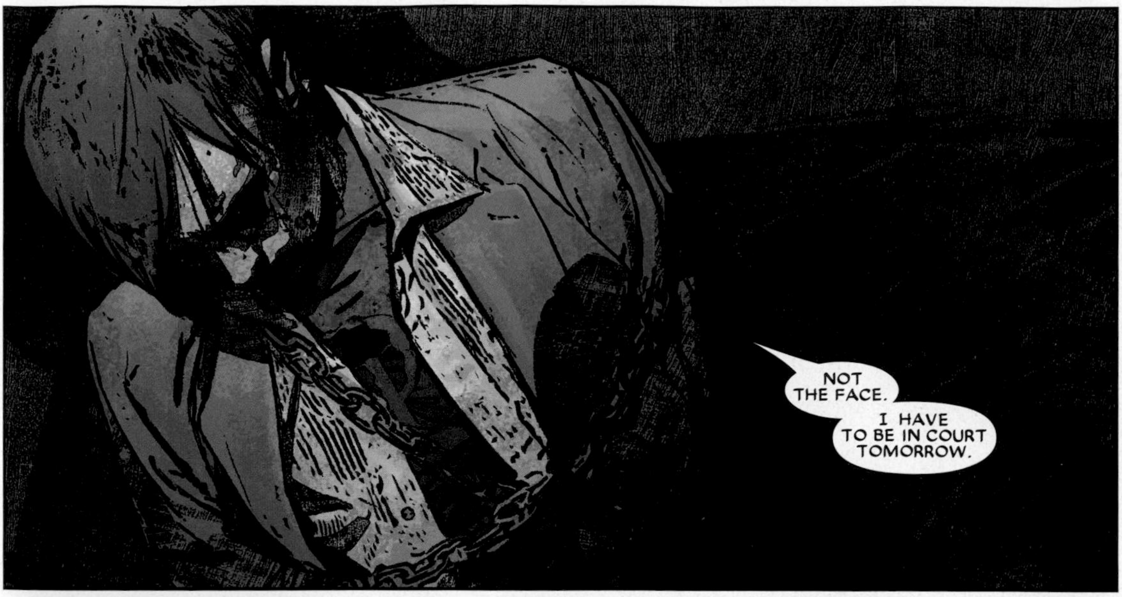
NOT THE FACE.
I HAVE TO BE IN COURT TOMORROW.

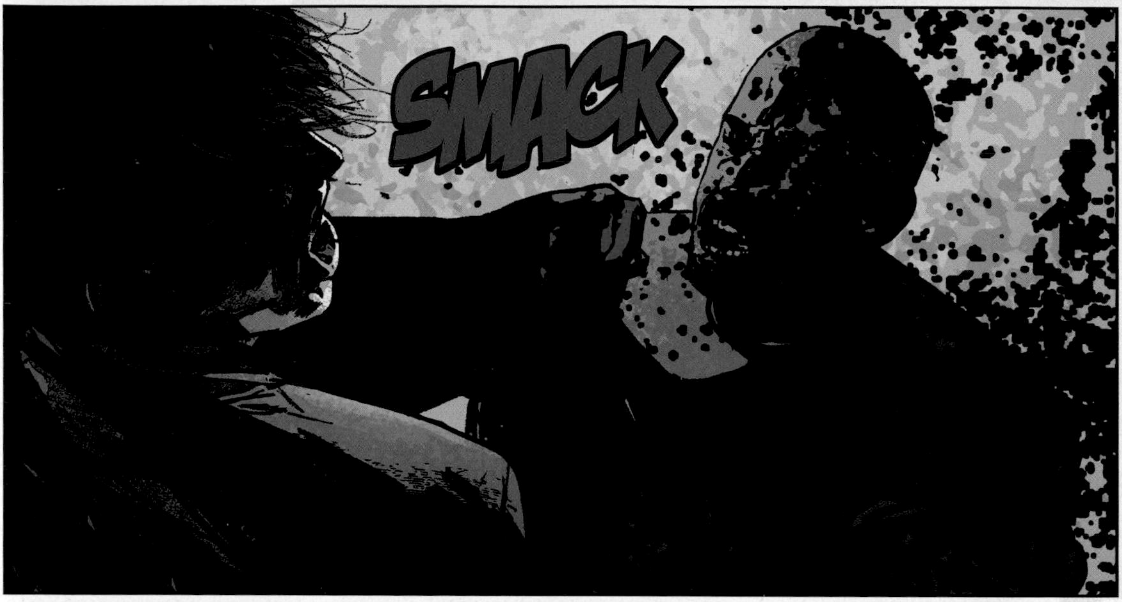
SMACK

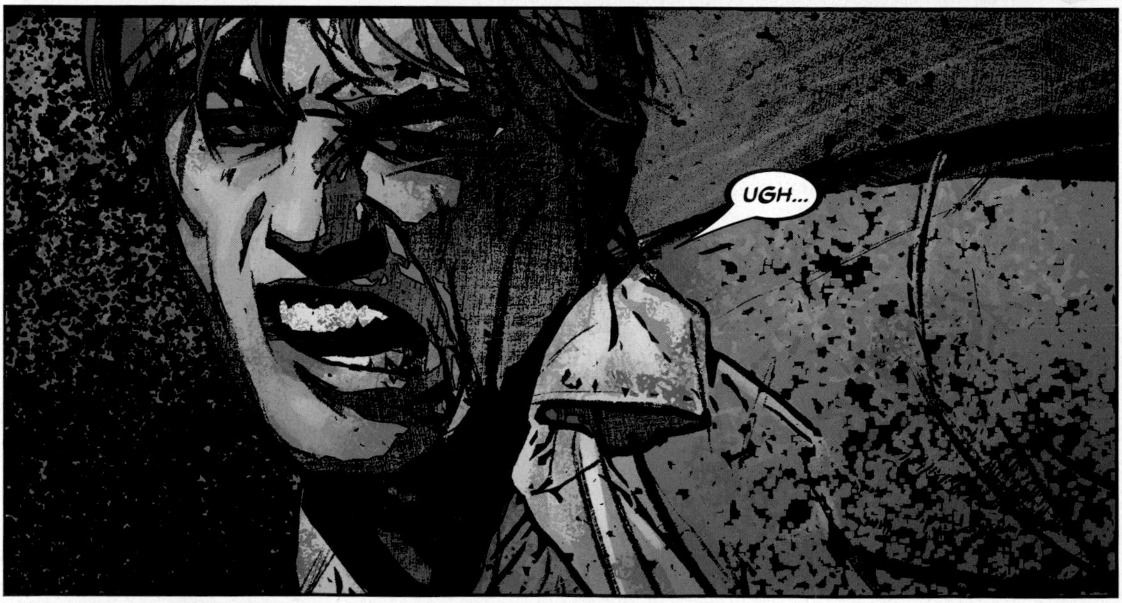
UGH...

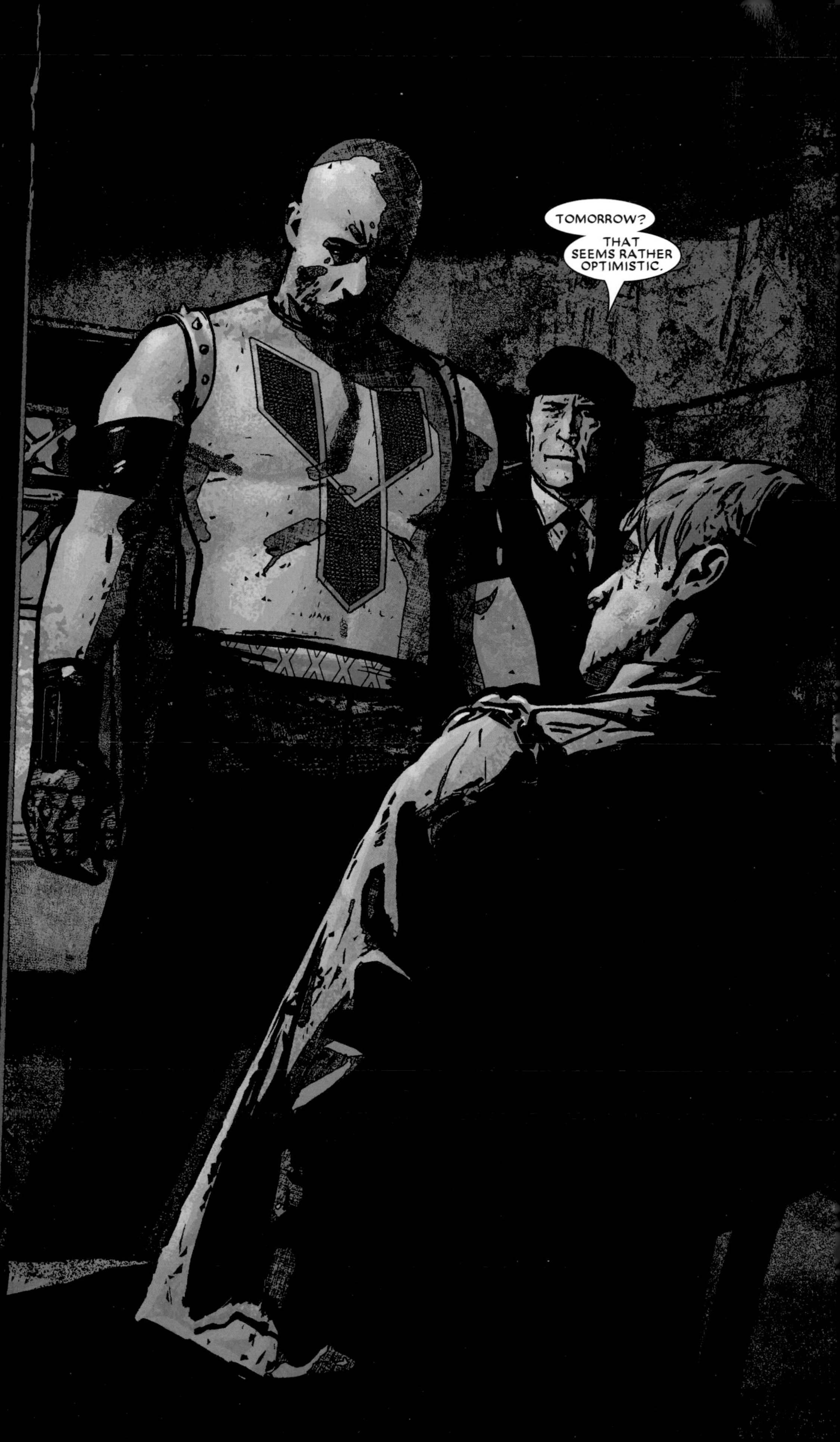
TOMORROW? THAT SEEMS RATHER OPTIMISTIC.

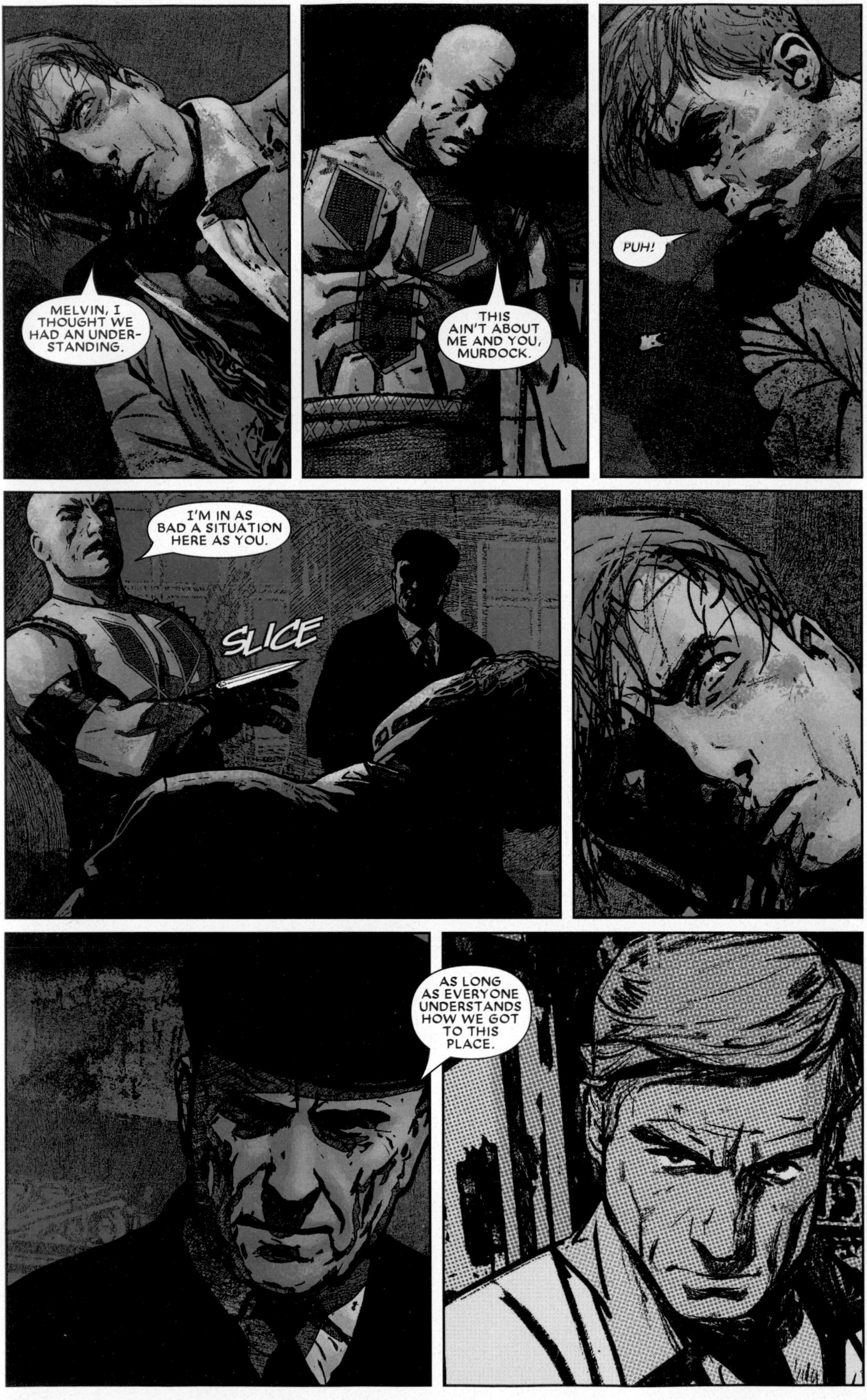
MELVIN, I THOUGHT WE HAD AN UNDER-STANDING.
THIS AIN'T ABOUT ME AND YOU, MURDOCK.
PUH!
I'M IN AS BAD A SITUATION HERE AS YOU.
SLICE
AS LONG AS EVERYONE UNDERSTANDS HOW WE GOT TO THIS PLACE.

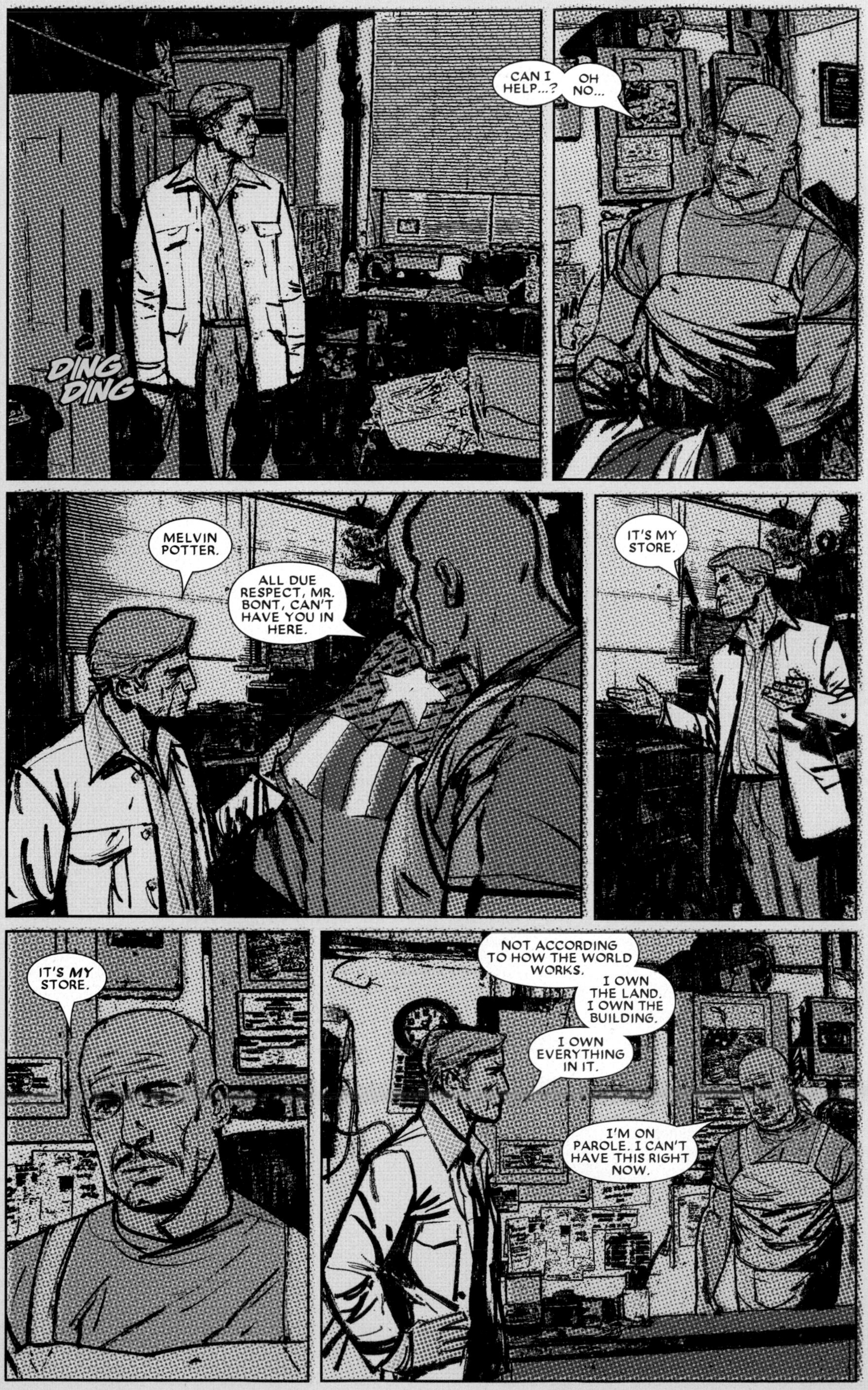
DING DING
CAN I HELP...?
OH NO...
MELVIN POTTER.
ALL DUE RESPECT, MR. BONT, CAN'T HAVE YOU IN HERE.
IT'S MY STORE.
IT'S MY STORE.
NOT ACCORDING TO HOW THE WORLD WORKS.
I OWN THE LAND. I OWN THE BUILDING.
I OWN EVERYTHING IN IT.
I'M ON PAROLE. I CAN'T HAVE THIS RIGHT NOW.

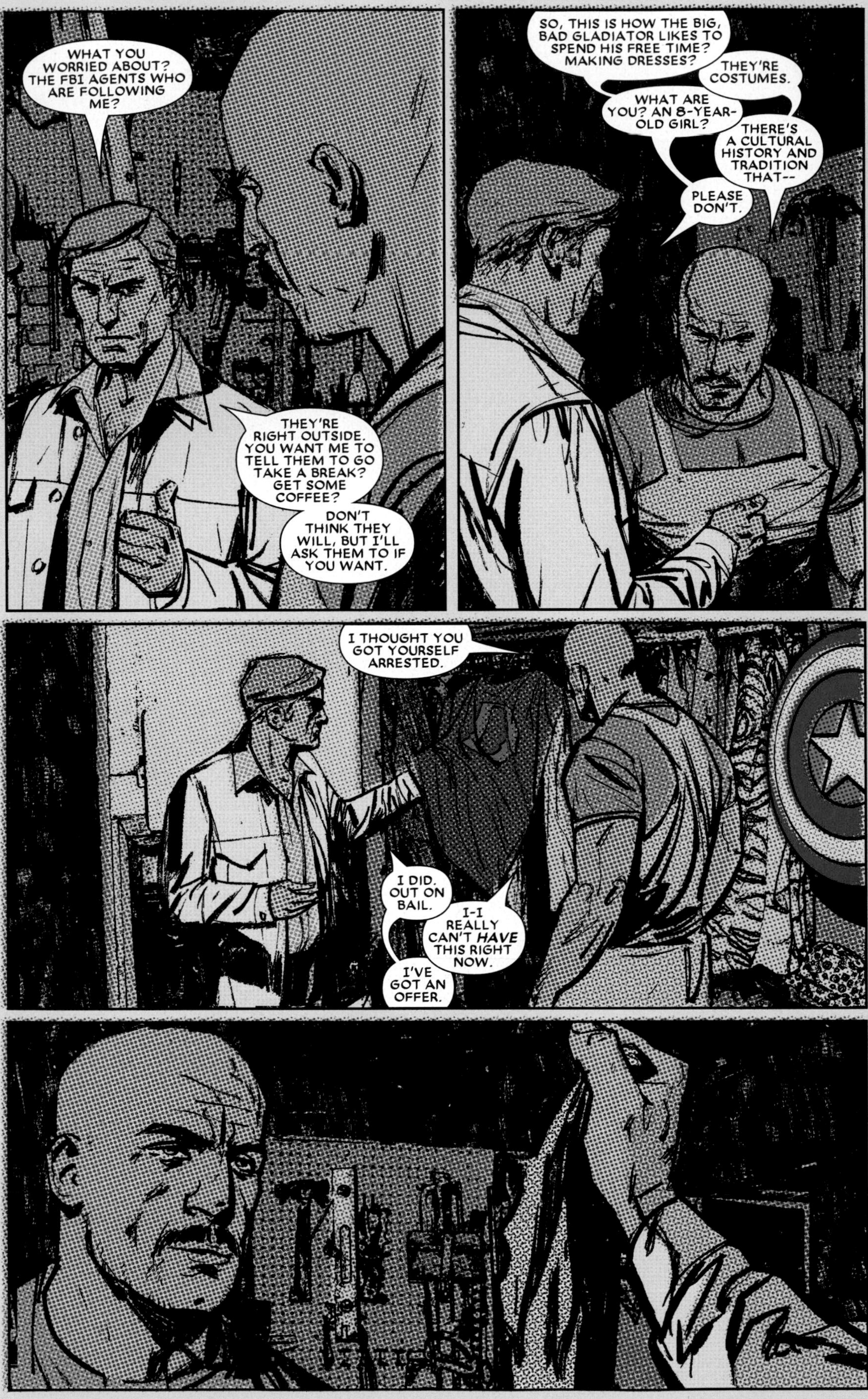
WHAT YOU WORRIED ABOUT? THE FBI AGENTS WHO ARE FOLLOWING ME?
THEY'RE RIGHT OUTSIDE. YOU WANT ME TO TELL THEM TO GO TAKE A BREAK? GET SOME COFFEE?
DON'T THINK THEY WILL, BUT I'LL ASK THEM TO IF YOU WANT.
SO, THIS IS HOW THE BIG, BAD GLADIATOR LIKES TO SPEND HIS FREE TIME? MAKING DRESSES?
THEY'RE COSTUMES.
WHAT ARE YOU? AN 8-YEAR-OLD GIRL?
THERE'S A CULTURAL HISTORY AND TRADITION THAT--
PLEASE DON'T.
I THOUGHT YOU GOT YOURSELF ARRESTED.
I DID. OUT ON BAIL.
I-I REALLY CAN'T HAVE THIS RIGHT NOW.
I'VE GOT AN OFFER.

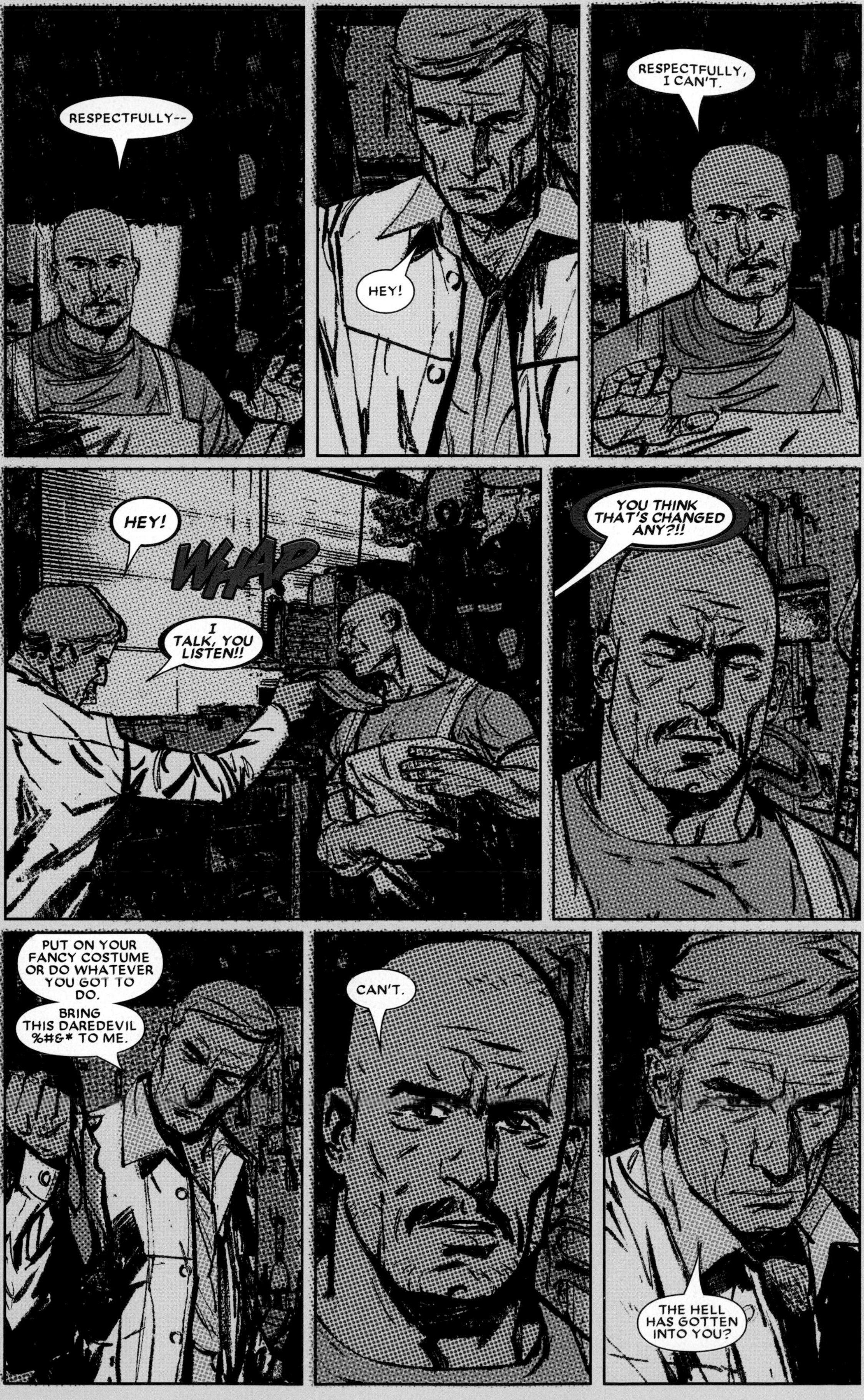
RESPECTFULLY--
HEY!
RESPECTFULLY, I CAN'T.
HEY!
WHAP
I TALK, YOU LISTEN!!
YOU THINK THAT'S CHANGED ANY?!!
PUT ON YOUR FANCY COSTUME OR DO WHATEVER YOU GOT TO DO.
BRING THIS DAREDEVIL %#&* TO ME.
CAN'T.
THE HELL HAS GOTTEN INTO YOU?

DUE RESPECT.

YOU GOT THIS WHOLE SIDE OF THE CITY TO PICK FROM. GET SOMEONE ELSE.

HIRE SOMEONE NEW, FROM OUT OF TOWN.

YOU. I WANT YOU.

YOU'VE GOT A HISTORY WITH THIS IDIOT. FOR YOU IT'S A MATTER OF HONOR.

YOU AND ME--WE BOND ON THIS.

YOU DO THIS FOR ME, YOU OWN YOUR STORE.

IT'S YOURS. THE WHOLE BUILDING.

RESPECT THE FACT THAT I DIDN'T COME IN HERE AND THREATEN YOU.

RESPECT THE FACT THAT I DIDN'T COME IN HERE AND SAY THAT IF YOU DON'T DO THIS FOR ME... I'M GIVING YOU TO THE FEDS.

RESPECT THE FACT THAT I WON'T LIST ALL OF THE THINGS I HIRED YOU TO DO FOR ME--

ALL THE PEOPLE I HAD YOU KILL.

I CAME IN HERE AND OFFERED YOU FAIR TRADE.

I NEED YOU TO BRING DAREDEVIL TO ME.

YOU KNOW HOW I MADE MY REP?

I MADE MY REP ON THE BLOOD OF ONE MASKED MYSTERY MAN...

I'M NOT--I AM NOT GOING TO LOSE IT OVER ANOTHER ONE.

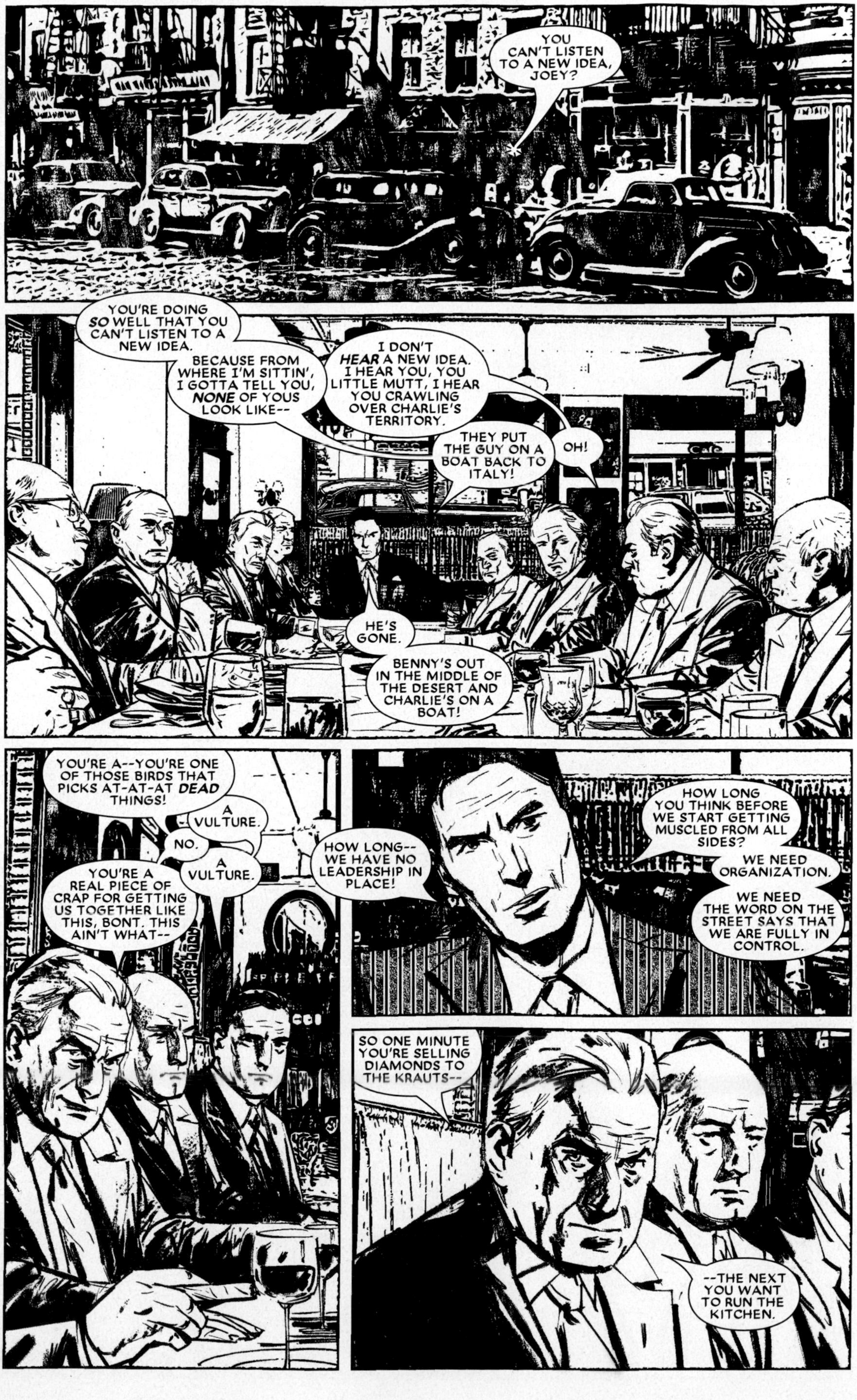
YOU CAN'T LISTEN TO A NEW IDEA, JOEY?
YOU'RE DOING *SO* WELL THAT YOU CAN'T LISTEN TO A NEW IDEA.
BECAUSE FROM WHERE I'M SITTIN', I GOTTA TELL YOU, *NONE* OF YOUS LOOK LIKE--
I DON'T *HEAR* A NEW IDEA. I HEAR YOU, YOU LITTLE MUTT, I HEAR YOU CRAWLING OVER CHARLIE'S TERRITORY.
OH!
THEY PUT THE GUY ON A BOAT BACK TO ITALY!
HE'S GONE.
BENNY'S OUT IN THE MIDDLE OF THE DESERT AND CHARLIE'S ON A BOAT!
YOU'RE A--YOU'RE ONE OF THOSE BIRDS THAT PICKS AT-AT-AT *DEAD* THINGS!
A VULTURE.
NO.
A VULTURE.
YOU'RE A REAL PIECE OF CRAP FOR GETTING US TOGETHER LIKE THIS, BONT. THIS AIN'T WHAT--
HOW LONG-- WE HAVE NO LEADERSHIP IN PLACE!
HOW LONG YOU THINK BEFORE WE START GETTING MUSCLED FROM ALL SIDES?
WE NEED ORGANIZATION.
WE NEED THE WORD ON THE STREET SAYS THAT WE ARE FULLY IN CONTROL.
SO ONE MINUTE YOU'RE SELLING DIAMONDS TO THE KRAUTS--
--THE NEXT YOU WANT TO RUN THE KITCHEN.

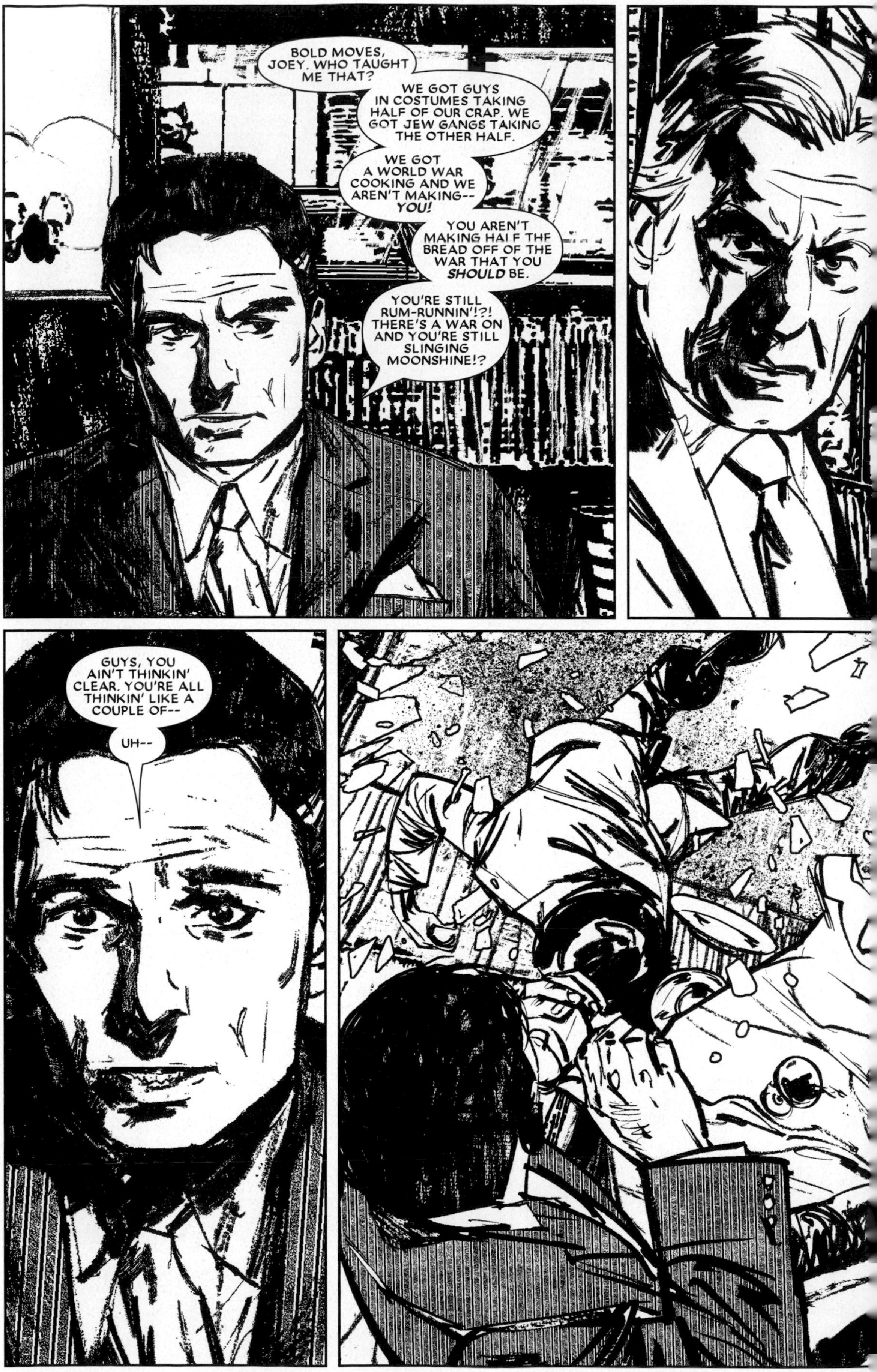
BOLD MOVES, JOEY. WHO TAUGHT ME THAT?
WE GOT GUYS IN COSTUMES TAKING HALF OF OUR CRAP. WE GOT JEW GANGS TAKING THE OTHER HALF.
WE GOT A WORLD WAR COOKING AND WE AREN'T MAKING-- *YOU!*
YOU AREN'T MAKING HALF THE BREAD OFF OF THE WAR THAT YOU *SHOULD* BE.
YOU'RE STILL RUM-RUNNIN'!?! THERE'S A WAR ON AND YOU'RE STILL SLINGING MOONSHINE!?
GUYS, YOU AIN'T THINKIN' CLEAR. YOU'RE ALL THINKIN' LIKE A COUPLE OF--
UH--

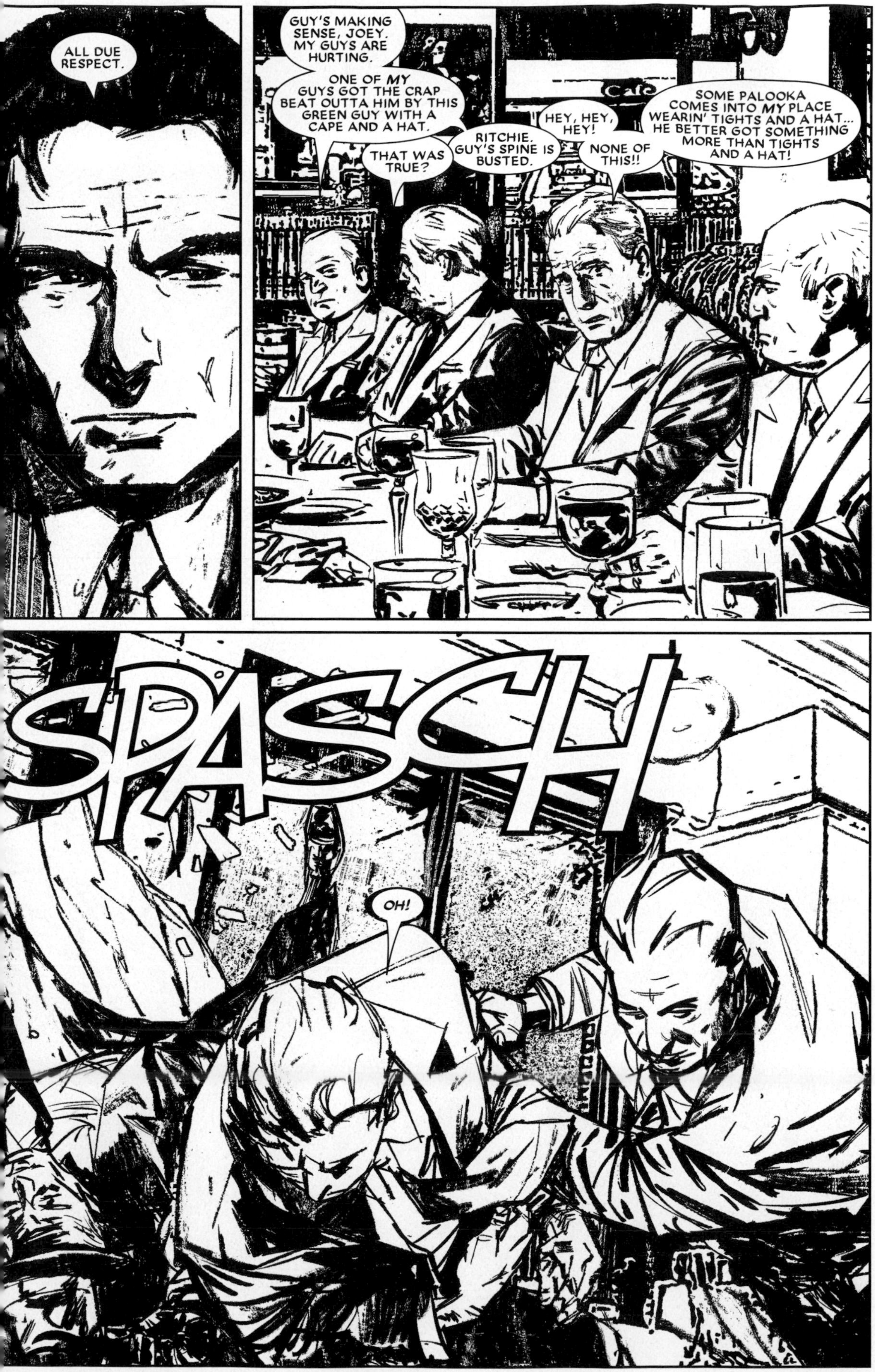
ALL DUE RESPECT.
GUY'S MAKING SENSE, JOEY. MY GUYS ARE HURTING.
ONE OF MY GUYS GOT THE CRAP BEAT OUTTA HIM BY THIS GREEN GUY WITH A CAPE AND A HAT.
THAT WAS TRUE?
RITCHIE. GUY'S SPINE IS BUSTED.
HEY, HEY, HEY!
NONE OF THIS!!
SOME PALOOKA COMES INTO MY PLACE WEARIN' TIGHTS AND A HAT... HE BETTER GOT SOMETHING MORE THAN TIGHTS AND A HAT!
SPASCH
OH!

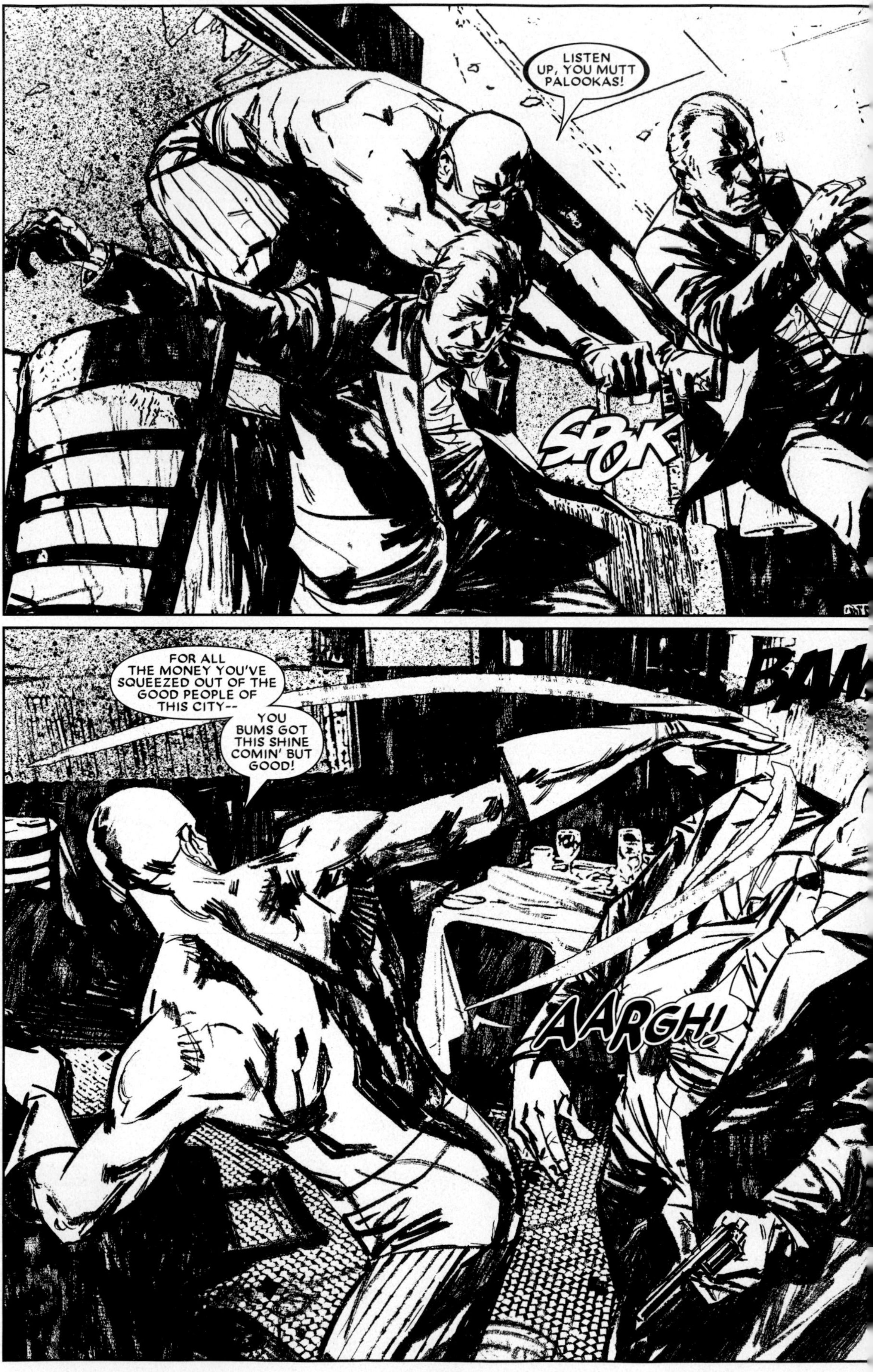
LISTEN UP, YOU MUTT PALOOKAS!
SPOK
FOR ALL THE MONEY YOU'VE SQUEEZED OUT OF THE GOOD PEOPLE OF THIS CITY--
YOU BUMS GOT THIS SHINE COMIN' BUT GOOD!
AARGH!

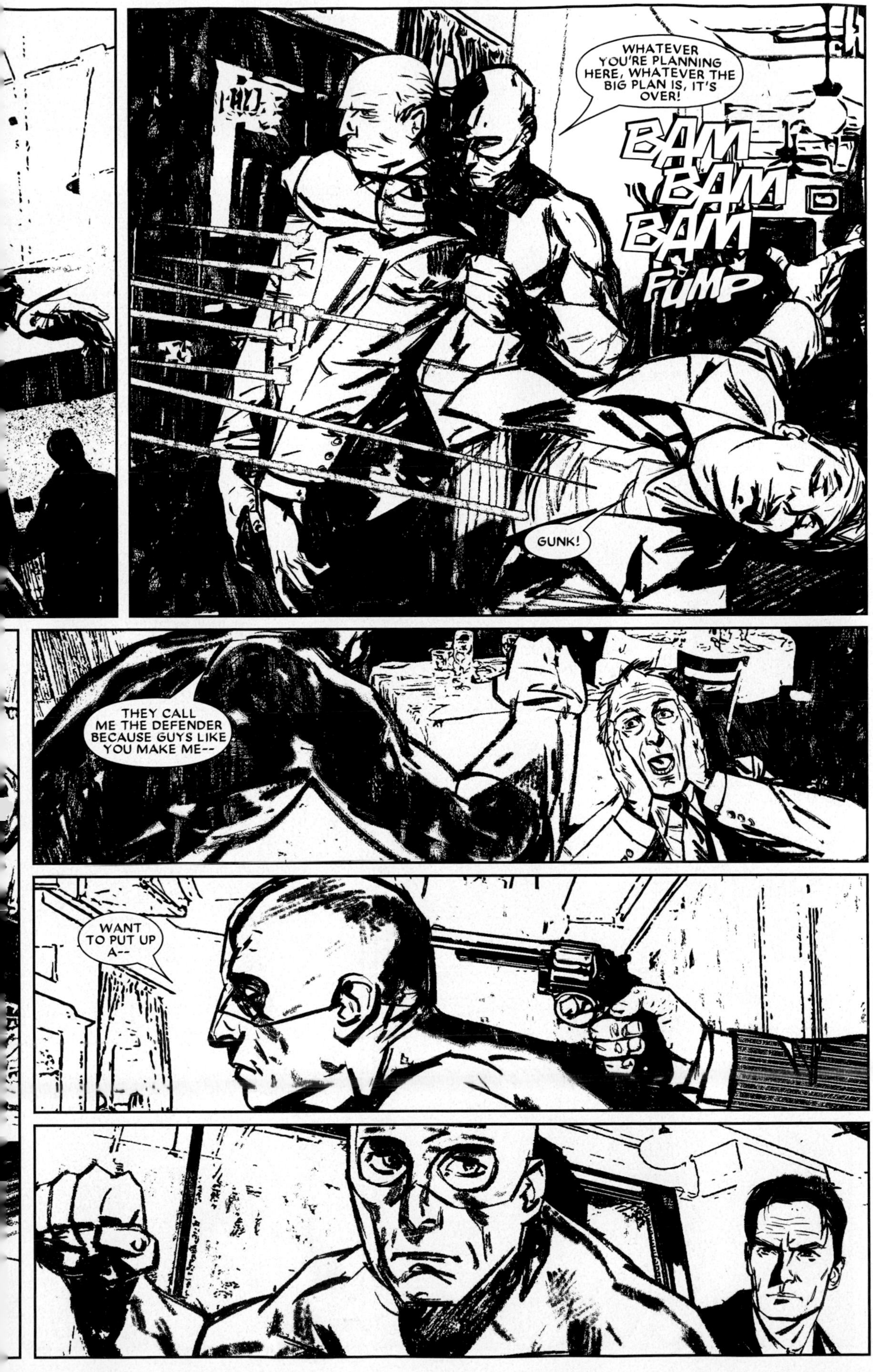

WHATEVER YOU'RE PLANNING HERE, WHATEVER THE BIG PLAN IS, IT'S OVER!
BAM BAM BAM
FUMP
GUNK!
THEY CALL ME THE DEFENDER BECAUSE GUYS LIKE YOU MAKE ME--
WANT TO PUT UP A--

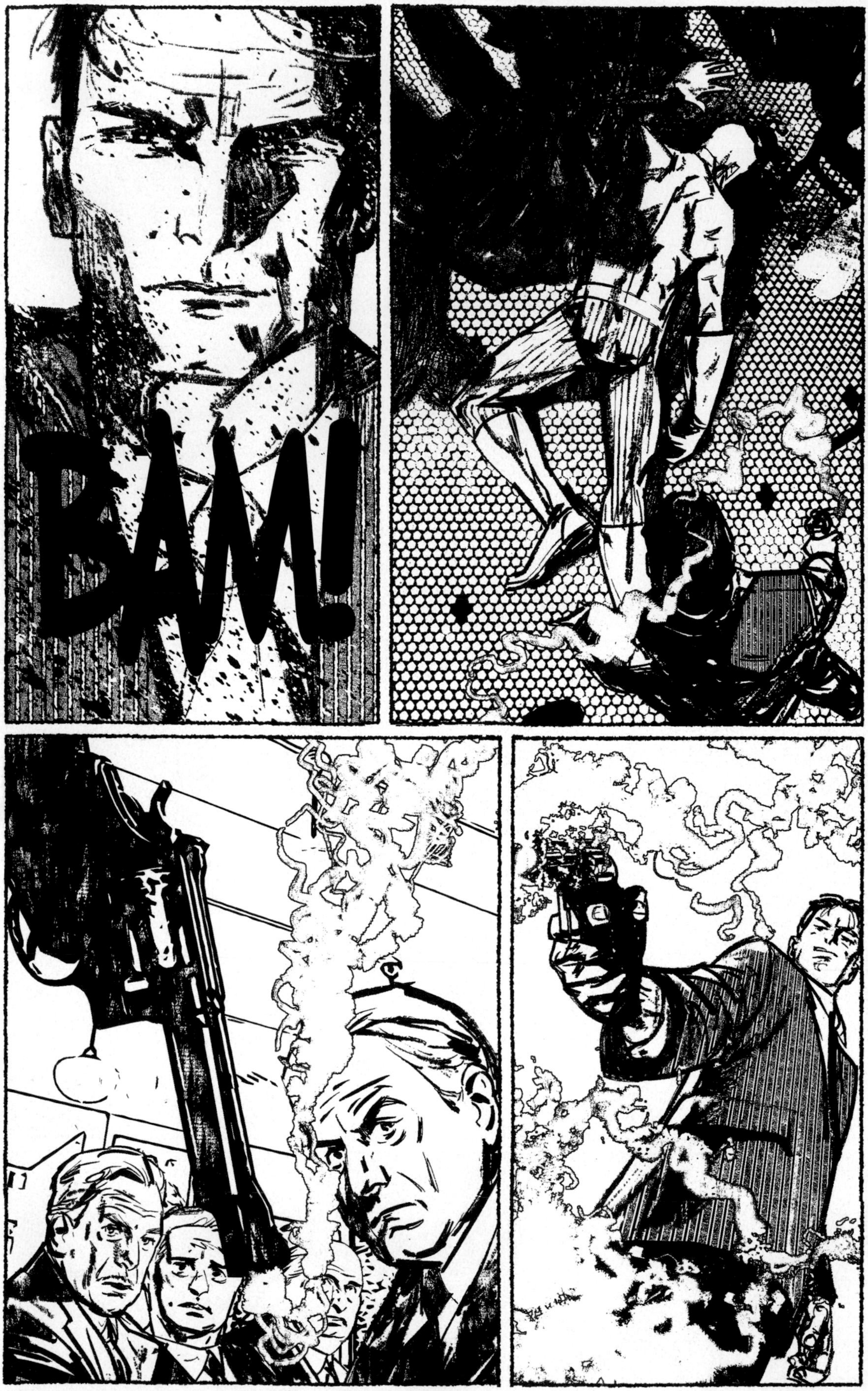
BAM!

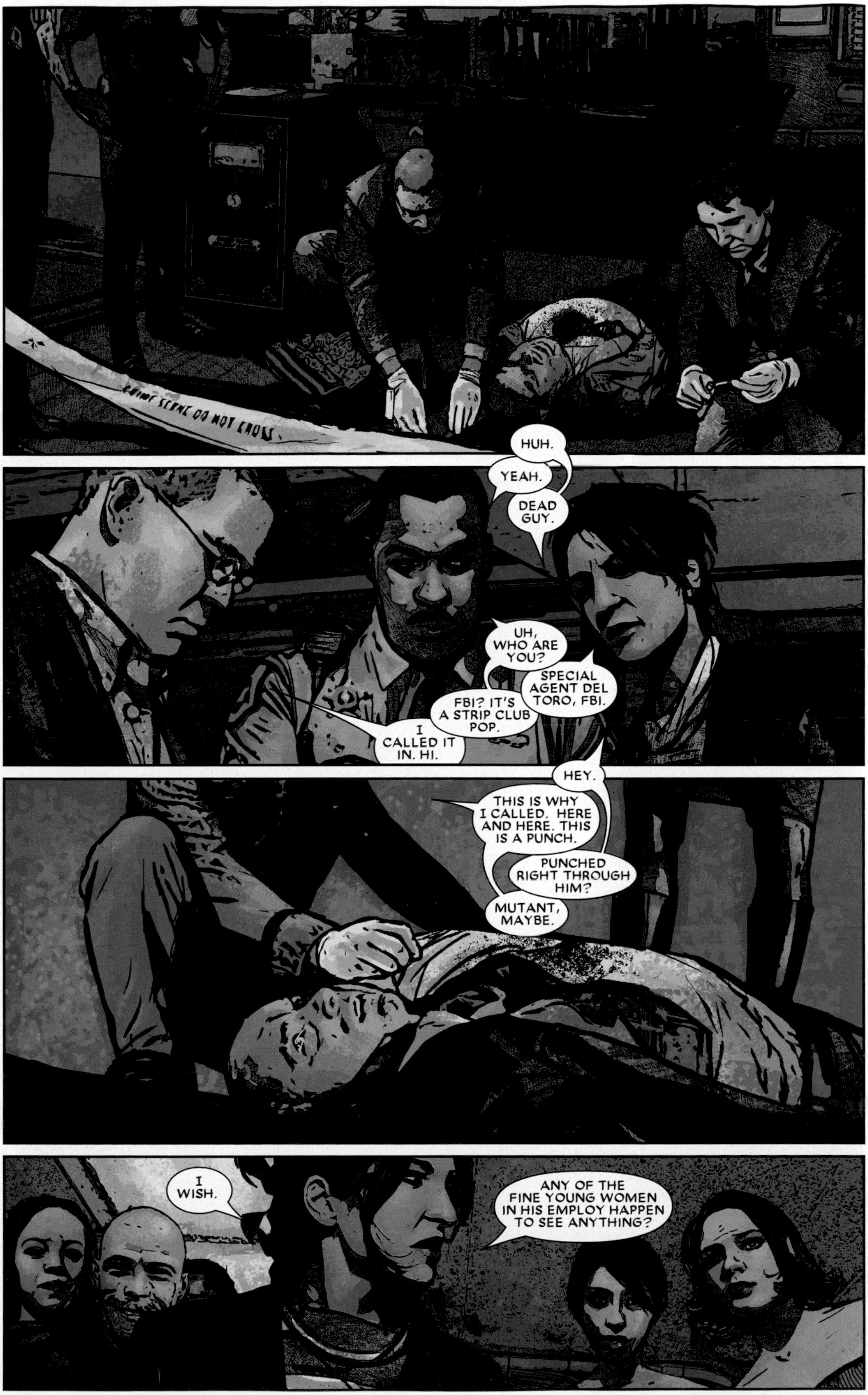
HUH.
YEAH.
DEAD GUY.
UH, WHO ARE YOU?
SPECIAL AGENT DEL TORO, FBI.
FBI? IT'S A STRIP CLUB POP.
I CALLED IT IN. HI.
HEY.
THIS IS WHY I CALLED. HERE AND HERE. THIS IS A PUNCH.
PUNCHED RIGHT THROUGH HIM?
MUTANT, MAYBE.
I WISH.
ANY OF THE FINE YOUNG WOMEN IN HIS EMPLOY HAPPEN TO SEE ANYTHING?

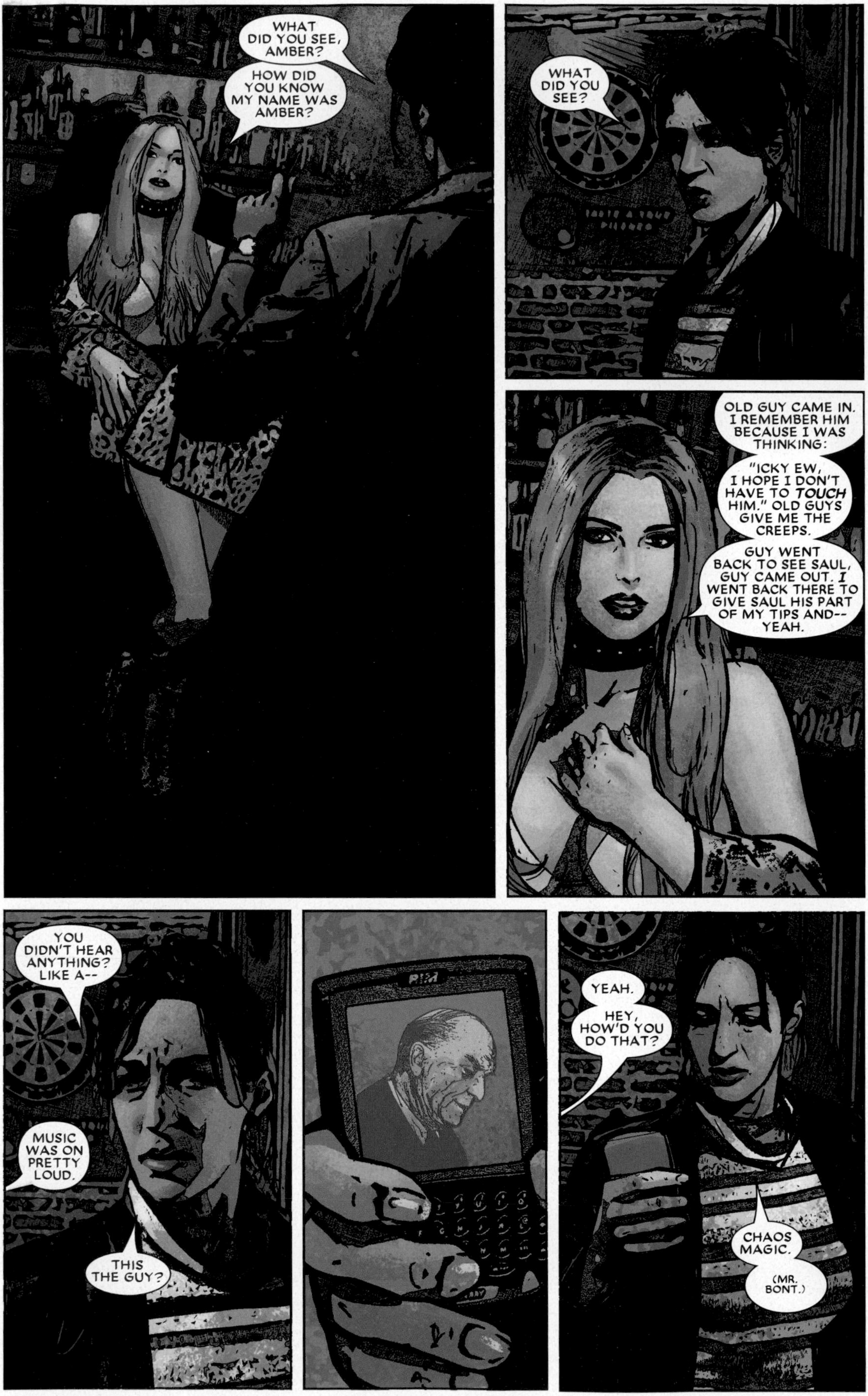
WHAT DID YOU SEE, AMBER?
HOW DID YOU KNOW MY NAME WAS AMBER?
WHAT DID YOU SEE?
OLD GUY CAME IN. I REMEMBER HIM BECAUSE I WAS THINKING:
"ICKY EW, I HOPE I DON'T HAVE TO *TOUCH* HIM." OLD GUYS GIVE ME THE CREEPS.
GUY WENT BACK TO SEE SAUL, GUY CAME OUT. *I* WENT BACK THERE TO GIVE SAUL HIS PART OF MY TIPS AND-- YEAH.
YOU DIDN'T HEAR ANYTHING? LIKE A--
MUSIC WAS ON PRETTY LOUD.
THIS THE GUY?
YEAH.
HEY, HOW'D YOU DO THAT?
CHAOS MAGIC.
(MR. BONT.)

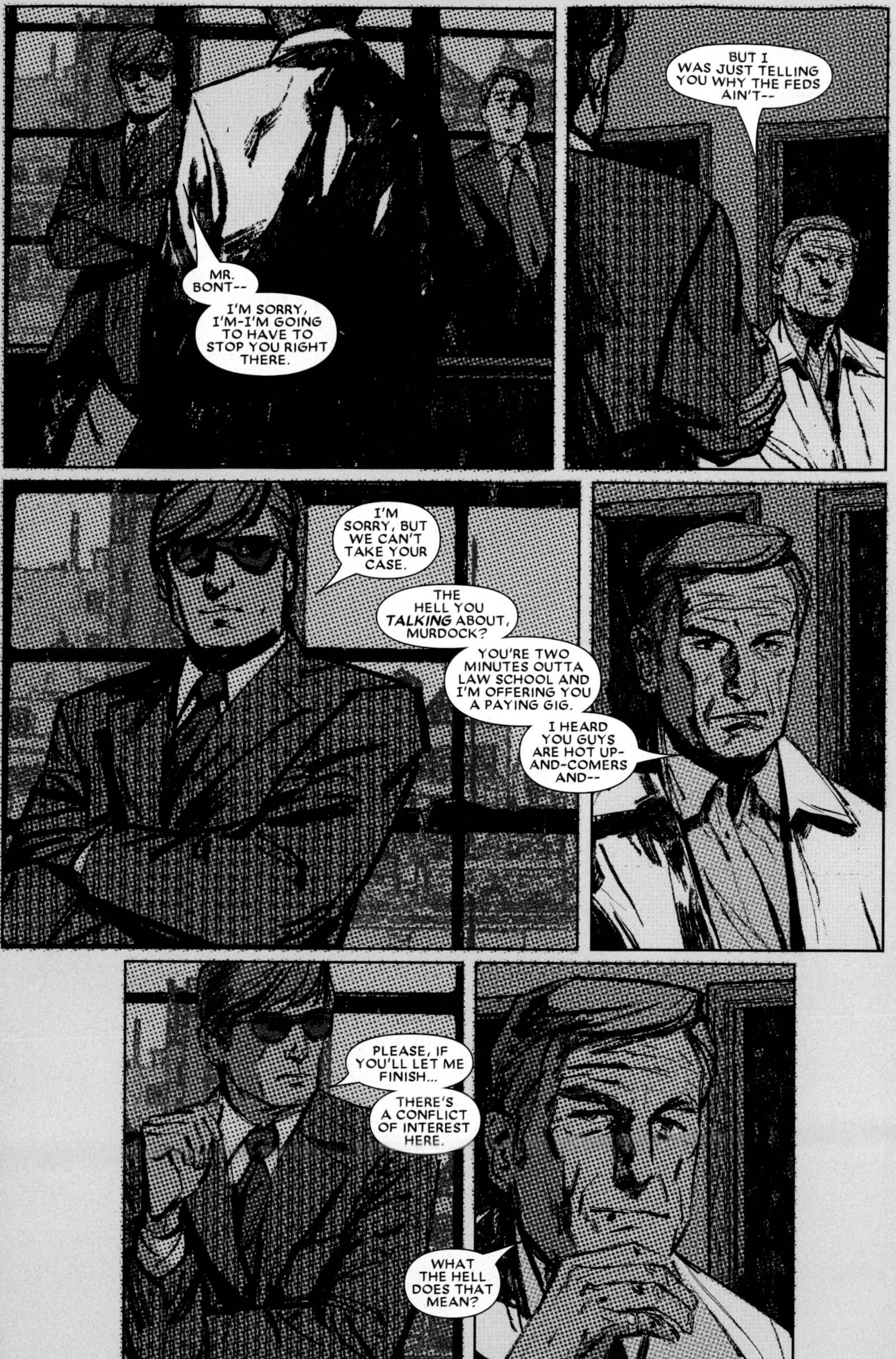
MR. BONT--
I'M SORRY, I'M-I'M GOING TO HAVE TO STOP YOU RIGHT THERE.
BUT I WAS JUST TELLING YOU WHY THE FEDS AIN'T--
I'M SORRY, BUT WE CAN'T TAKE YOUR CASE.
THE HELL YOU *TALKING* ABOUT, MURDOCK?
YOU'RE TWO MINUTES OUTTA LAW SCHOOL AND I'M OFFERING YOU A PAYING GIG.
I HEARD YOU GUYS ARE HOT UP-AND-COMERS AND--
PLEASE, IF YOU'LL LET ME FINISH...
THERE'S A CONFLICT OF INTEREST HERE.
WHAT THE HELL DOES THAT MEAN?

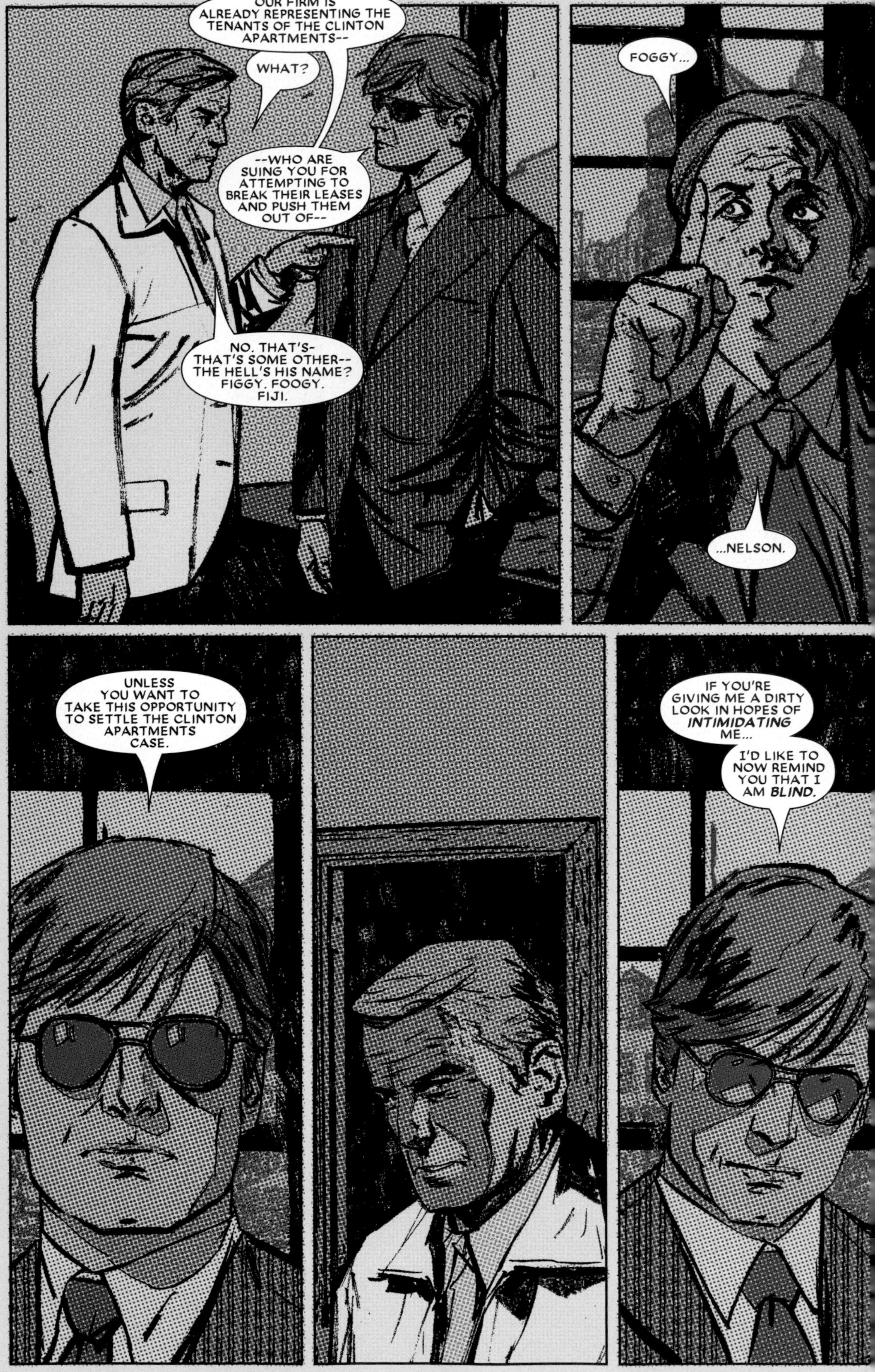
OUR FIRM IS ALREADY REPRESENTING THE TENANTS OF THE CLINTON APARTMENTS--
WHAT?
--WHO ARE SUING YOU FOR ATTEMPTING TO BREAK THEIR LEASES AND PUSH THEM OUT OF--
NO. THAT'S- THAT'S SOME OTHER-- THE HELL'S HIS NAME? FIGGY. FOOGY. FIJI.
FOGGY...
...NELSON.
UNLESS YOU WANT TO TAKE THIS OPPORTUNITY TO SETTLE THE CLINTON APARTMENTS CASE.
IF YOU'RE GIVING ME A DIRTY LOOK IN HOPES OF *INTIMIDATING* ME...
I'D LIKE TO NOW REMIND YOU THAT I AM *BLIND.*

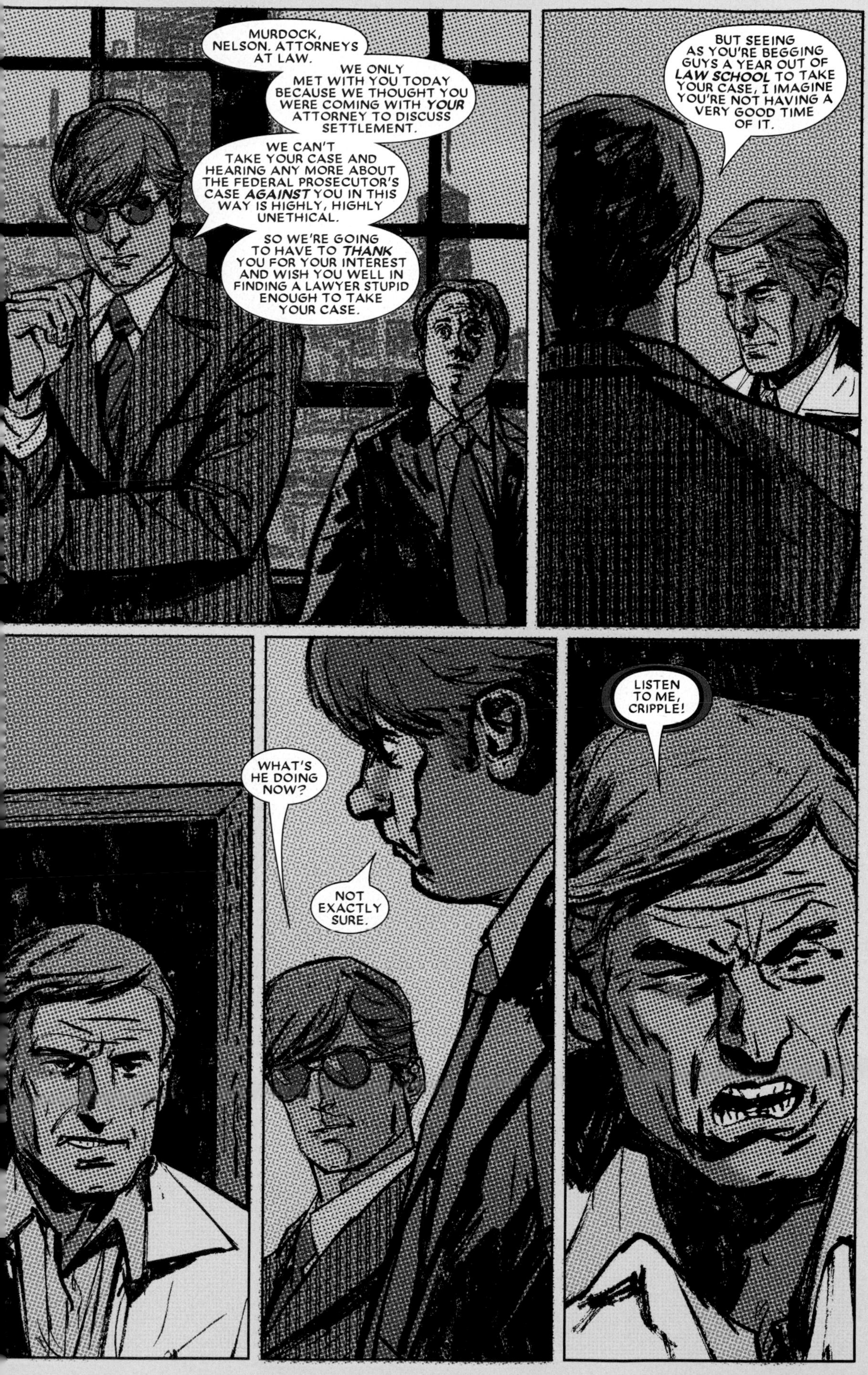
MURDOCK, NELSON, ATTORNEYS AT LAW.
WE ONLY MET WITH YOU TODAY BECAUSE WE THOUGHT YOU WERE COMING WITH *YOUR* ATTORNEY TO DISCUSS SETTLEMENT.
WE CAN'T TAKE YOUR CASE AND HEARING ANY MORE ABOUT THE FEDERAL PROSECUTOR'S CASE *AGAINST* YOU IN THIS WAY IS HIGHLY, HIGHLY UNETHICAL.
SO WE'RE GOING TO HAVE TO *THANK* YOU FOR YOUR INTEREST AND WISH YOU WELL IN FINDING A LAWYER STUPID ENOUGH TO TAKE YOUR CASE.
BUT SEEING AS YOU'RE BEGGING GUYS A YEAR OUT OF *LAW SCHOOL* TO TAKE YOUR CASE, I IMAGINE YOU'RE NOT HAVING A VERY GOOD TIME OF IT.
WHAT'S HE DOING NOW?
NOT EXACTLY SURE.
LISTEN TO ME, CRIPPLE!

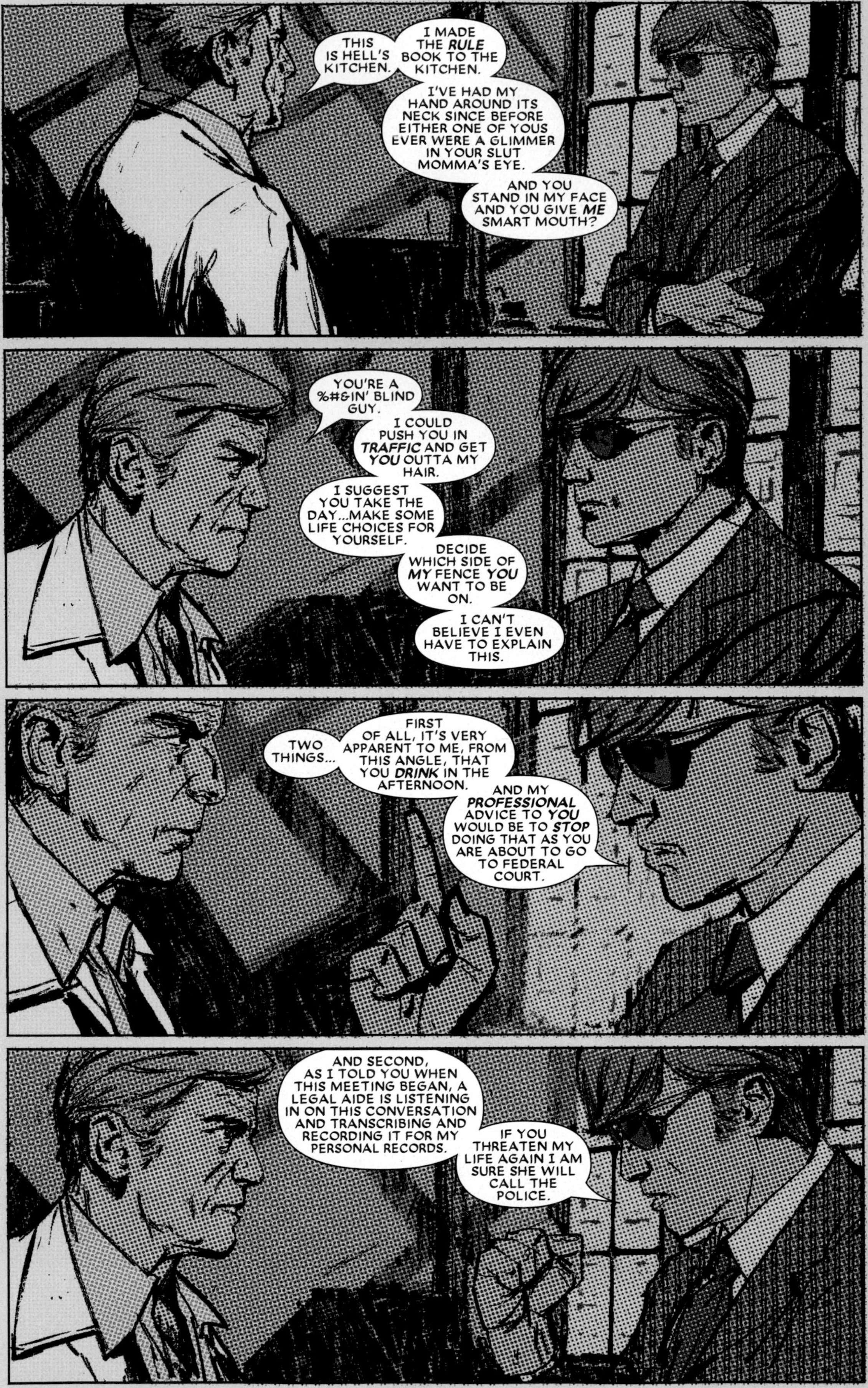
THIS IS HELL'S KITCHEN.
I MADE THE RULE BOOK TO THE KITCHEN.
I'VE HAD MY HAND AROUND ITS NECK SINCE BEFORE EITHER ONE OF YOUS EVER WERE A GLIMMER IN YOUR SLUT MOMMA'S EYE.
AND YOU STAND IN MY FACE AND YOU GIVE ME SMART MOUTH?
YOU'RE A %#&IN' BLIND GUY.
I COULD PUSH YOU IN TRAFFIC AND GET YOU OUTTA MY HAIR.
I SUGGEST YOU TAKE THE DAY...MAKE SOME LIFE CHOICES FOR YOURSELF.
DECIDE WHICH SIDE OF MY FENCE YOU WANT TO BE ON.
I CAN'T BELIEVE I EVEN HAVE TO EXPLAIN THIS.
TWO THINGS...
FIRST OF ALL, IT'S VERY APPARENT TO ME, FROM THIS ANGLE, THAT YOU DRINK IN THE AFTERNOON.
AND MY PROFESSIONAL ADVICE TO YOU WOULD BE TO STOP DOING THAT AS YOU ARE ABOUT TO GO TO FEDERAL COURT.
AND SECOND, AS I TOLD YOU WHEN THIS MEETING BEGAN, A LEGAL AIDE IS LISTENING IN ON THIS CONVERSATION AND TRANSCRIBING AND RECORDING IT FOR MY PERSONAL RECORDS.
IF YOU THREATEN MY LIFE AGAIN I AM SURE SHE WILL CALL THE POLICE.

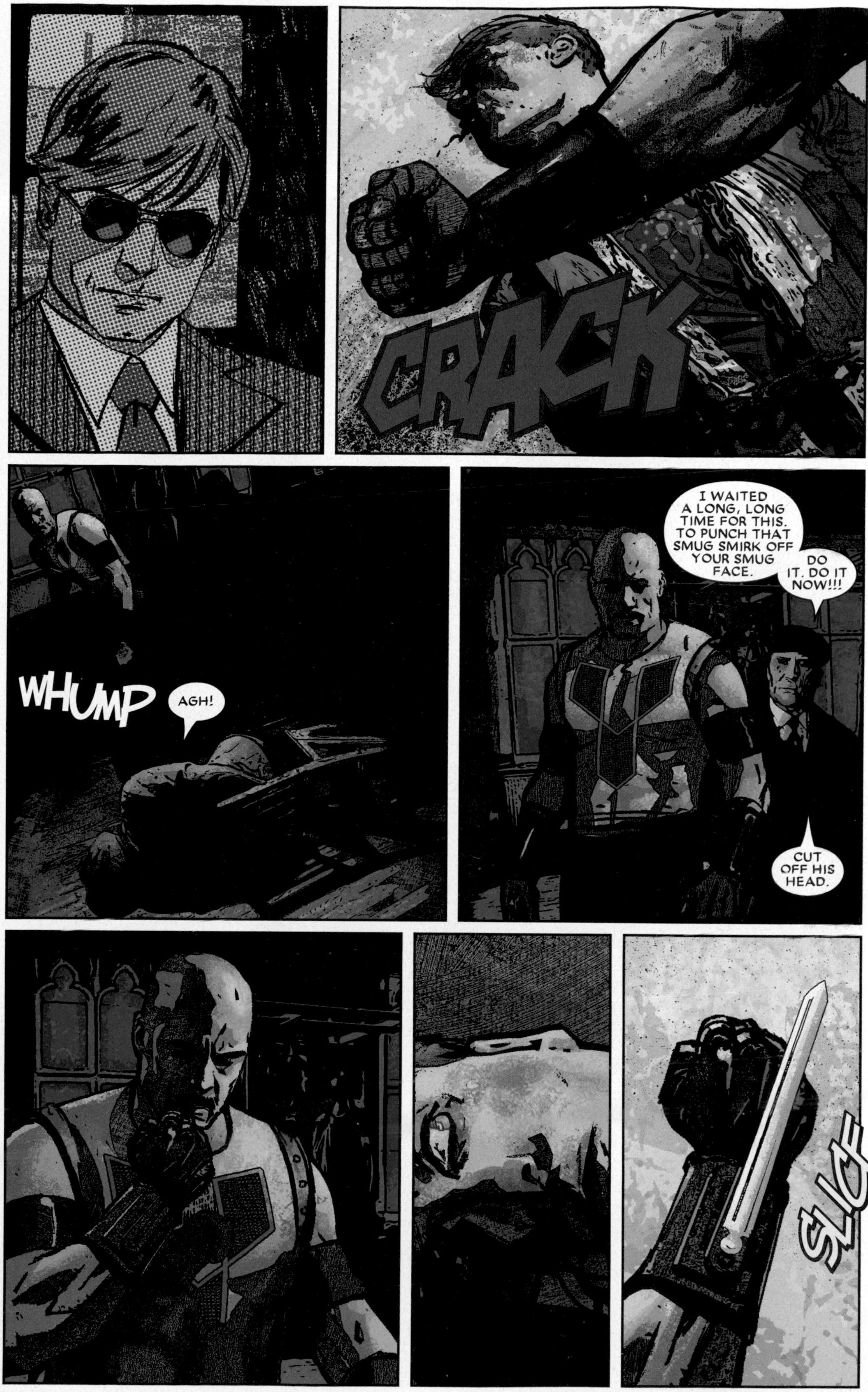
CRACK
WHUMP
AGH!
I WAITED A LONG, LONG TIME FOR THIS. TO PUNCH THAT SMUG SMIRK OFF YOUR SMUG FACE.
DO IT. DO IT NOW!!!
CUT OFF HIS HEAD.
SLICE

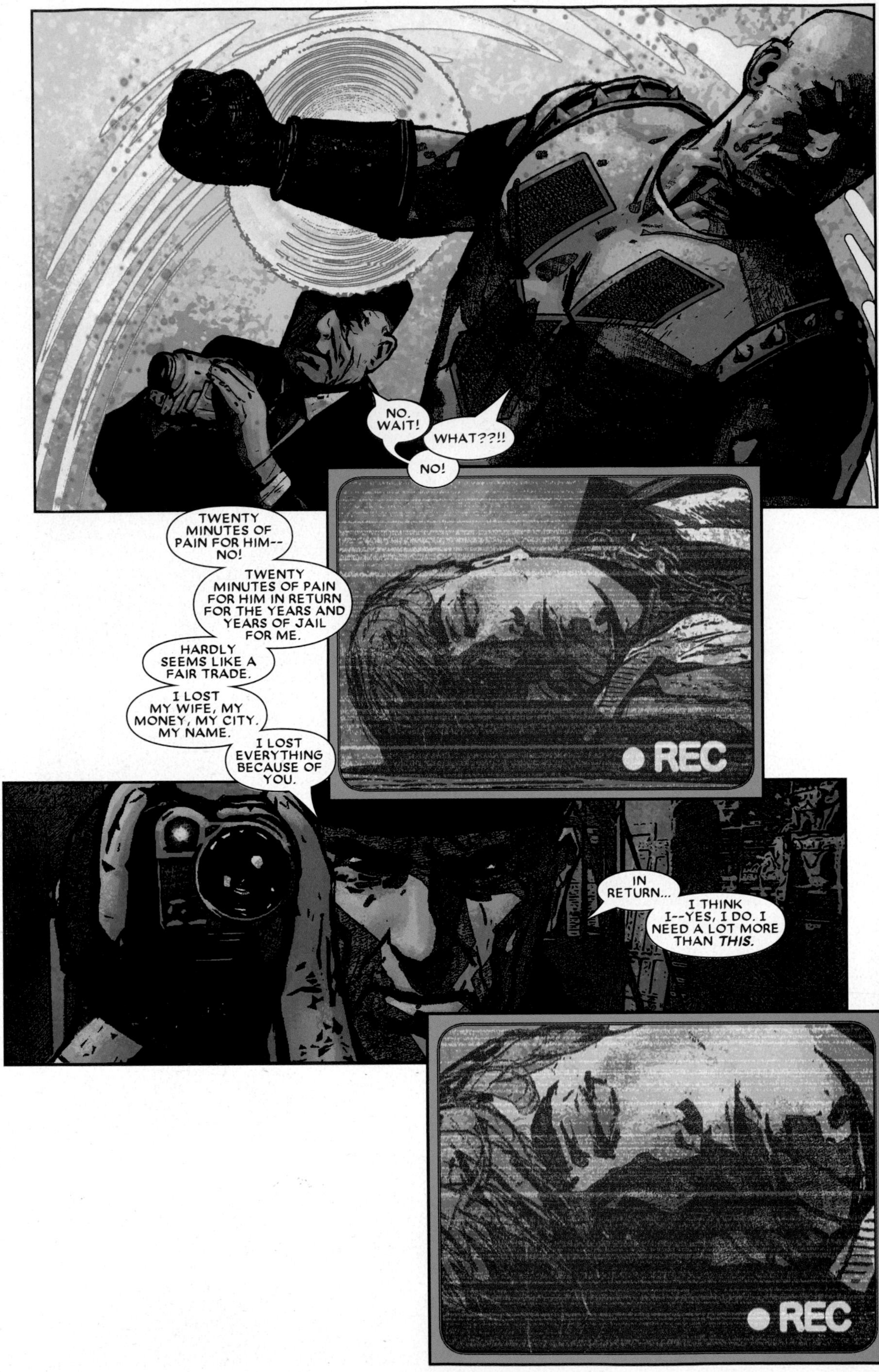
NO. WAIT!
WHAT??!!
NO!
TWENTY MINUTES OF PAIN FOR HIM-- NO!
TWENTY MINUTES OF PAIN FOR HIM IN RETURN FOR THE YEARS AND YEARS OF JAIL FOR ME.
HARDLY SEEMS LIKE A FAIR TRADE.
I LOST MY WIFE, MY MONEY, MY CITY. MY NAME.
I LOST EVERYTHING BECAUSE OF YOU.
REC
IN RETURN...
I THINK I--YES, I DO. I NEED A LOT MORE THAN *THIS.*
REC

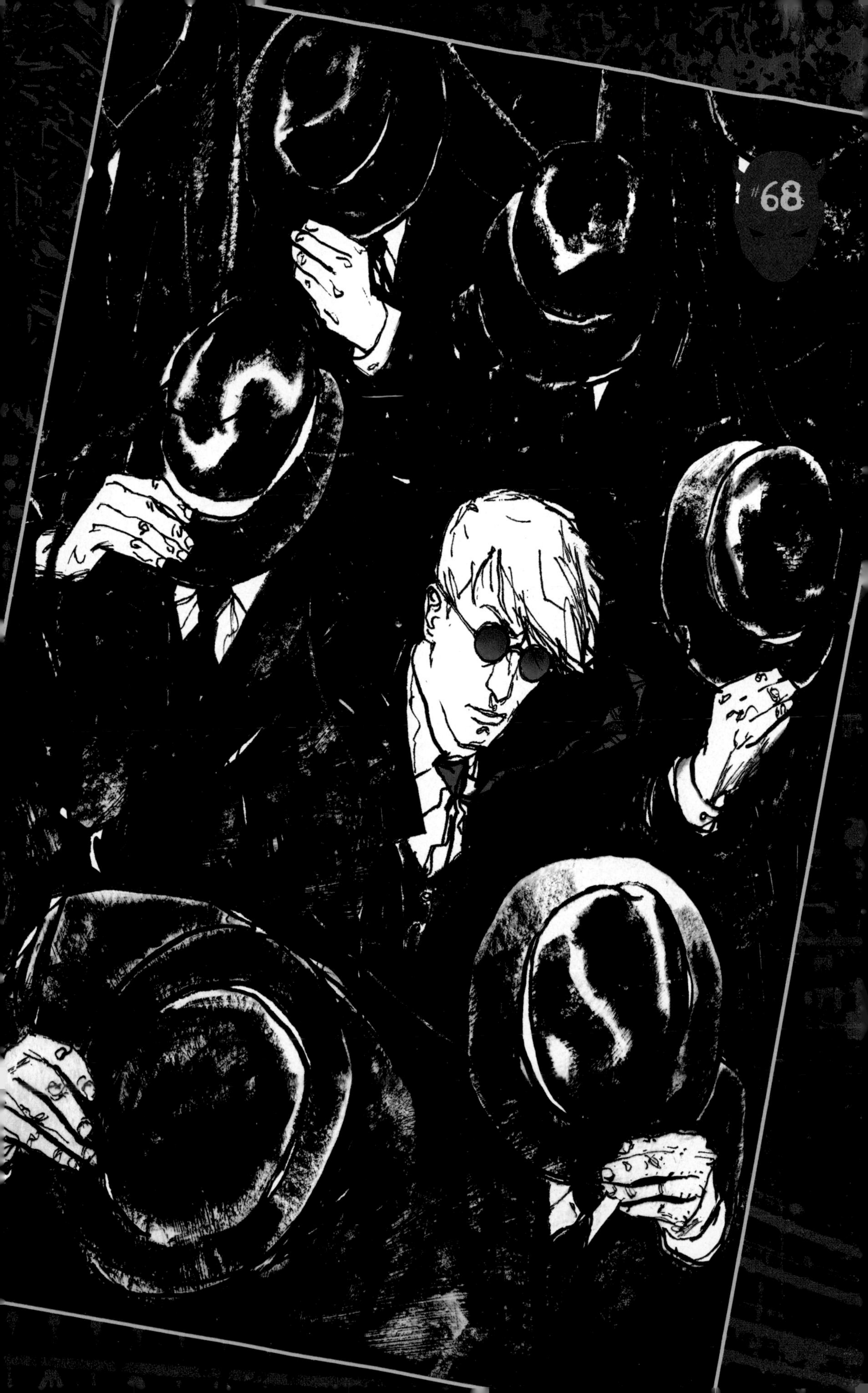
#68

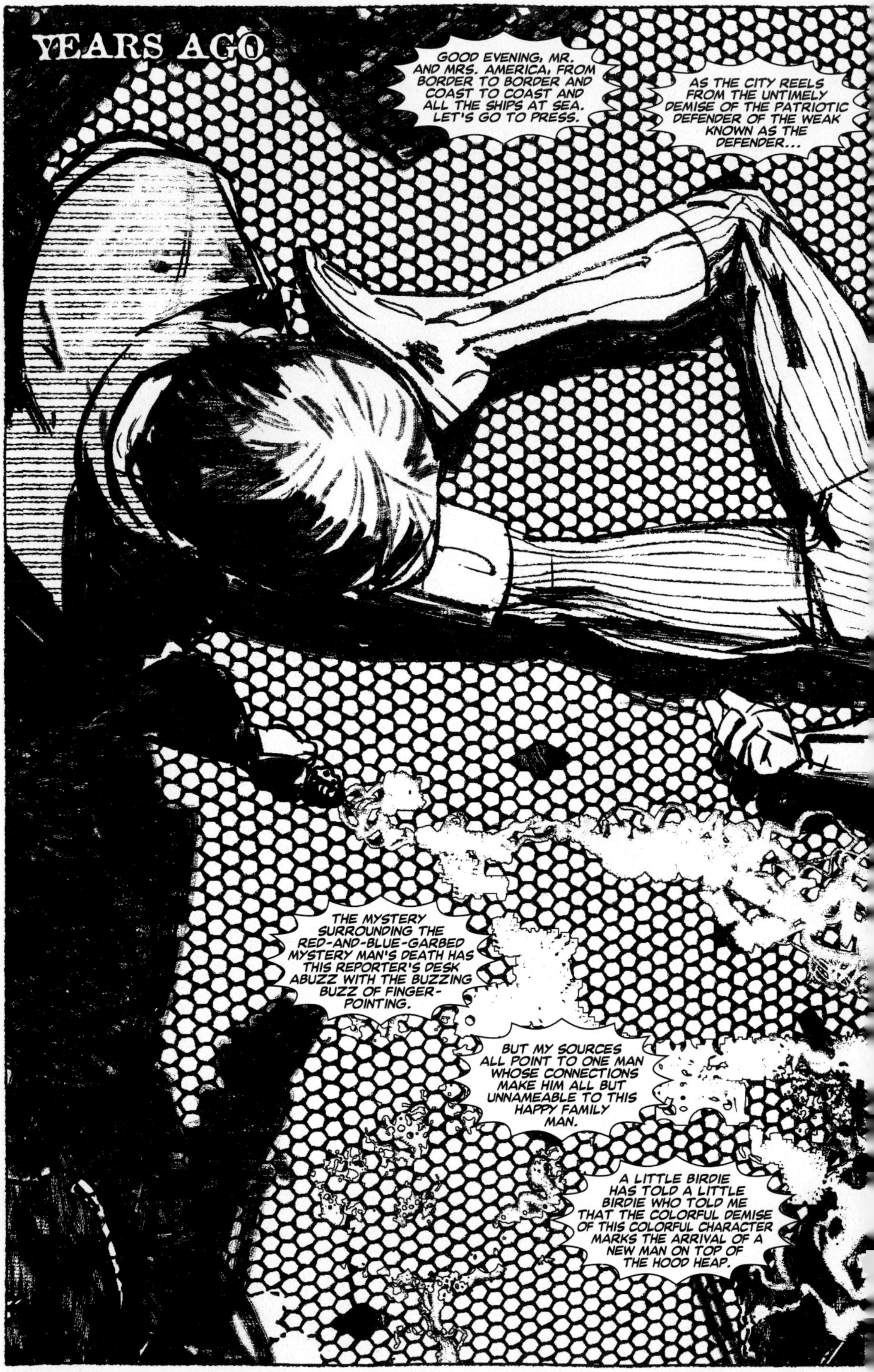
YEARS AGO
GOOD EVENING, MR. AND MRS. AMERICA, FROM BORDER TO BORDER AND COAST TO COAST AND ALL THE SHIPS AT SEA. LET'S GO TO PRESS.
AS THE CITY REELS FROM THE UNTIMELY DEMISE OF THE PATRIOTIC DEFENDER OF THE WEAK KNOWN AS THE DEFENDER...
THE MYSTERY SURROUNDING THE RED-AND-BLUE-GARBED MYSTERY MAN'S DEATH HAS THIS REPORTER'S DESK ABUZZ WITH THE BUZZING BUZZ OF FINGER-POINTING.
BUT MY SOURCES ALL POINT TO ONE MAN WHOSE CONNECTIONS MAKE HIM ALL BUT UNNAMEABLE TO THIS HAPPY FAMILY MAN.
A LITTLE BIRDIE HAS TOLD A LITTLE BIRDIE WHO TOLD ME THAT THE COLORFUL DEMISE OF THIS COLORFUL CHARACTER MARKS THE ARRIVAL OF A NEW MAN ON TOP OF THE HOOD HEAP.

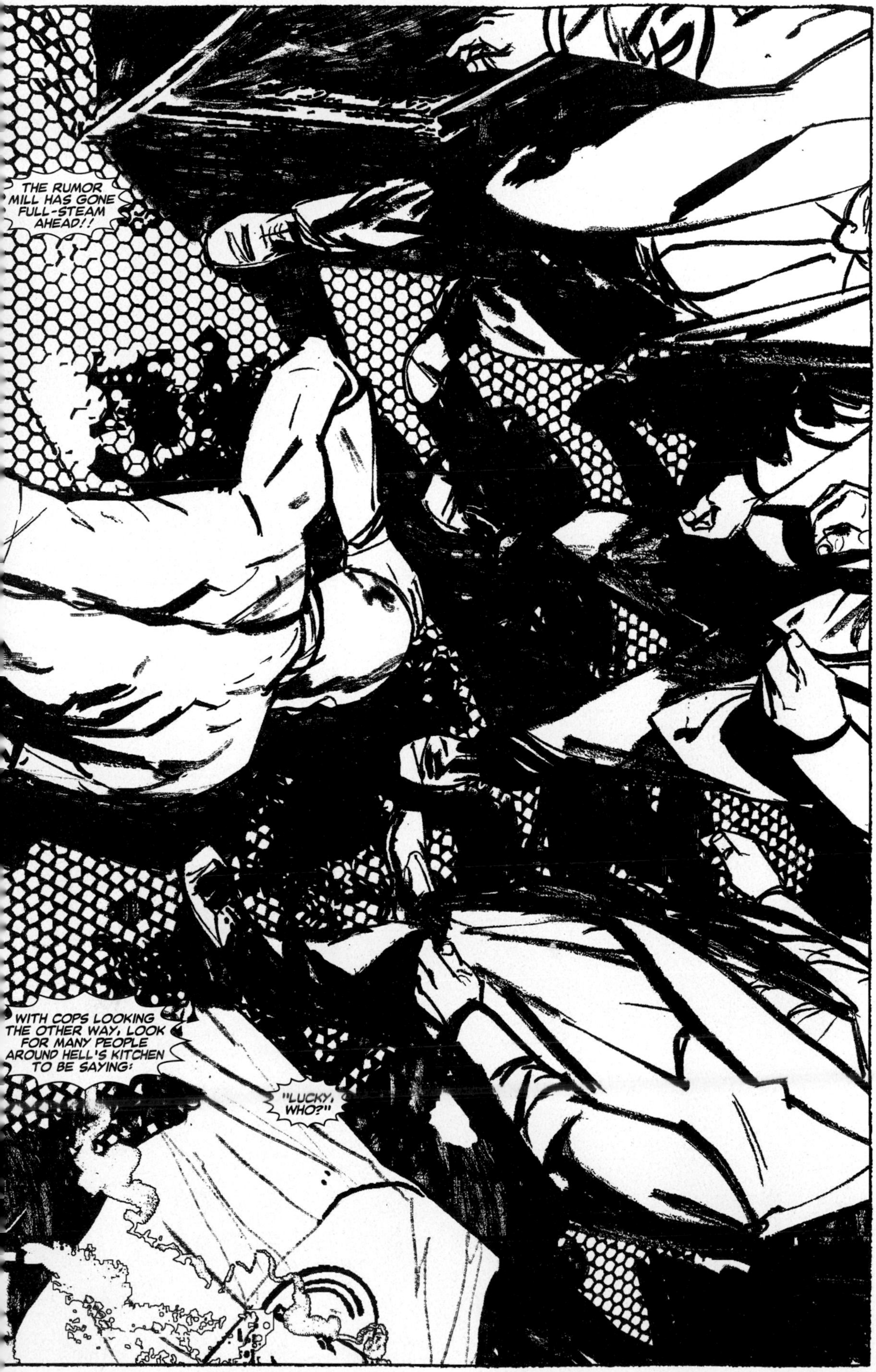
THE RUMOR MILL HAS GONE FULL-STEAM AHEAD!!
WITH COPS LOOKING THE OTHER WAY, LOOK FOR MANY PEOPLE AROUND HELL'S KITCHEN TO BE SAYING:
"LUCKY, WHO?"

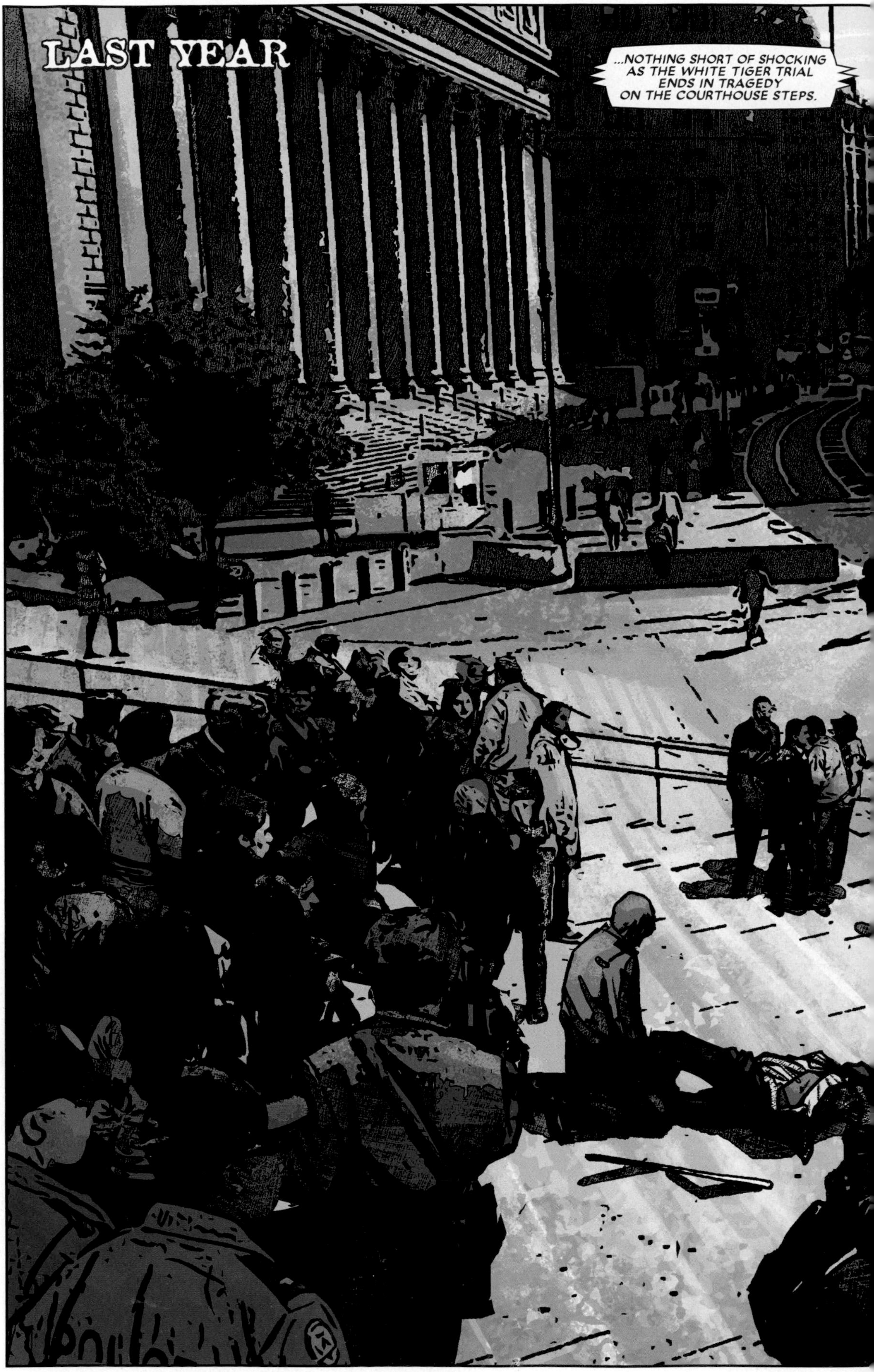
LAST YEAR
...NOTHING SHORT OF SHOCKING AS THE WHITE TIGER TRIAL ENDS IN TRAGEDY ON THE COURTHOUSE STEPS.

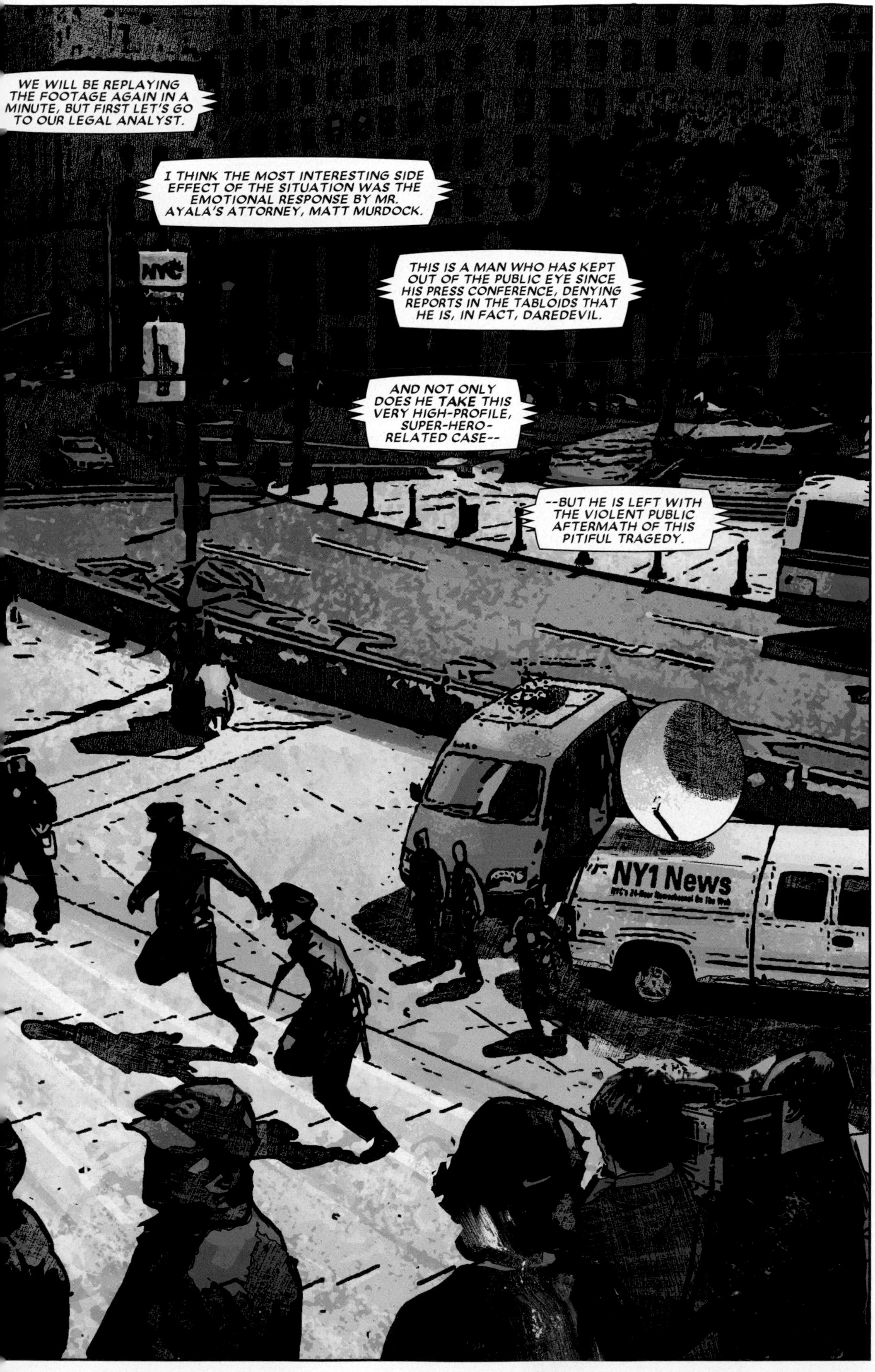
WE WILL BE REPLAYING THE FOOTAGE AGAIN IN A MINUTE, BUT FIRST LET'S GO TO OUR LEGAL ANALYST.
I THINK THE MOST INTERESTING SIDE EFFECT OF THE SITUATION WAS THE EMOTIONAL RESPONSE BY MR. AYALA'S ATTORNEY, MATT MURDOCK.
THIS IS A MAN WHO HAS KEPT OUT OF THE PUBLIC EYE SINCE HIS PRESS CONFERENCE, DENYING REPORTS IN THE TABLOIDS THAT HE IS, IN FACT, DAREDEVIL.
AND NOT ONLY DOES HE TAKE THIS VERY HIGH-PROFILE, SUPER-HERO-RELATED CASE--
--BUT HE IS LEFT WITH THE VIOLENT PUBLIC AFTERMATH OF THIS PITIFUL TRAGEDY.
NYC
NY1 News

TODAY

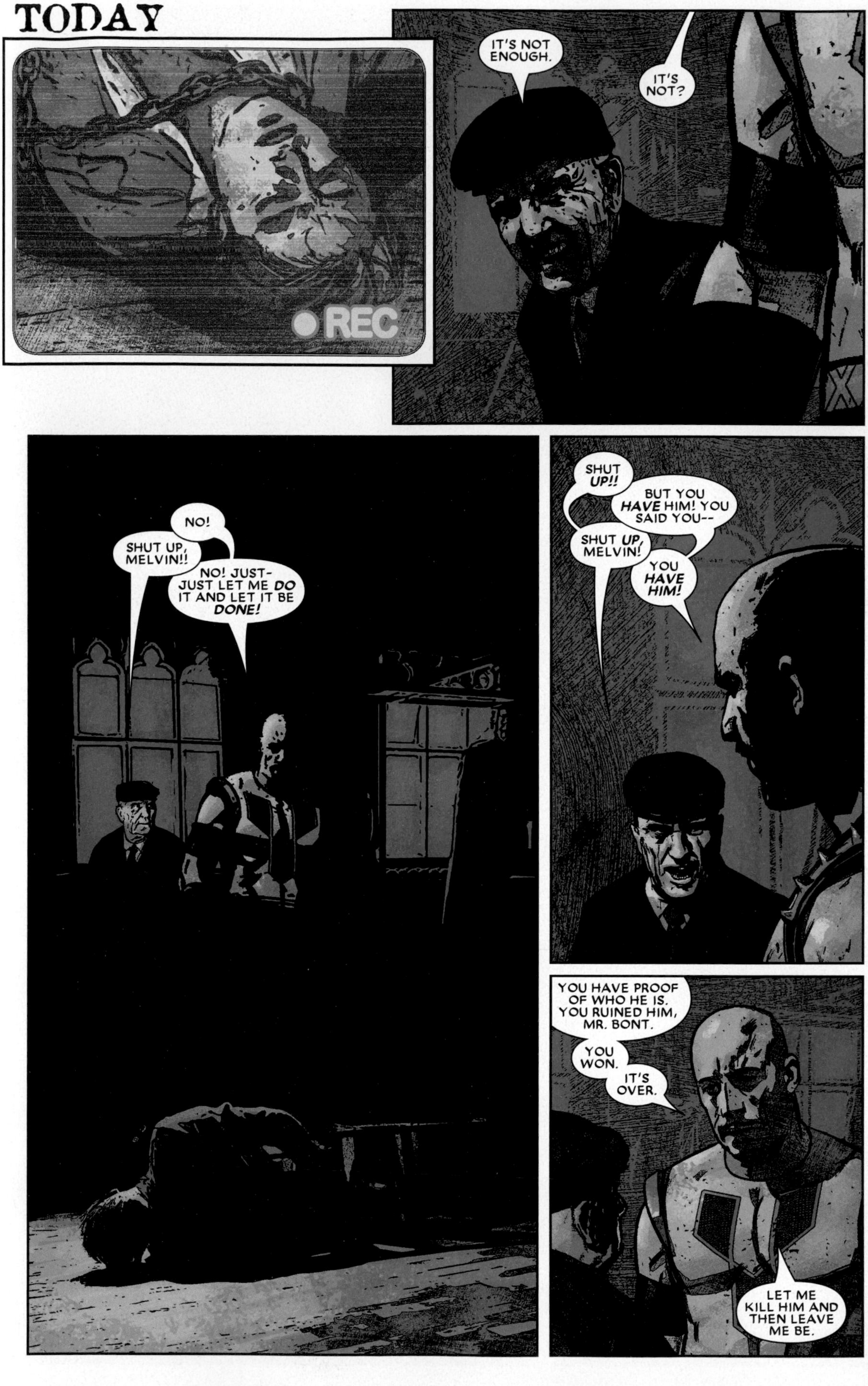
REC
IT'S NOT ENOUGH.
IT'S NOT?
NO!
SHUT UP, MELVIN!!
NO! JUST-JUST LET ME DO IT AND LET IT BE DONE!
SHUT UP!!
BUT YOU HAVE HIM! YOU SAID YOU--
SHUT UP, MELVIN!
YOU HAVE HIM!
YOU HAVE PROOF OF WHO HE IS. YOU RUINED HIM, MR. BONT.
YOU WON.
IT'S OVER.
LET ME KILL HIM AND THEN LEAVE ME BE.

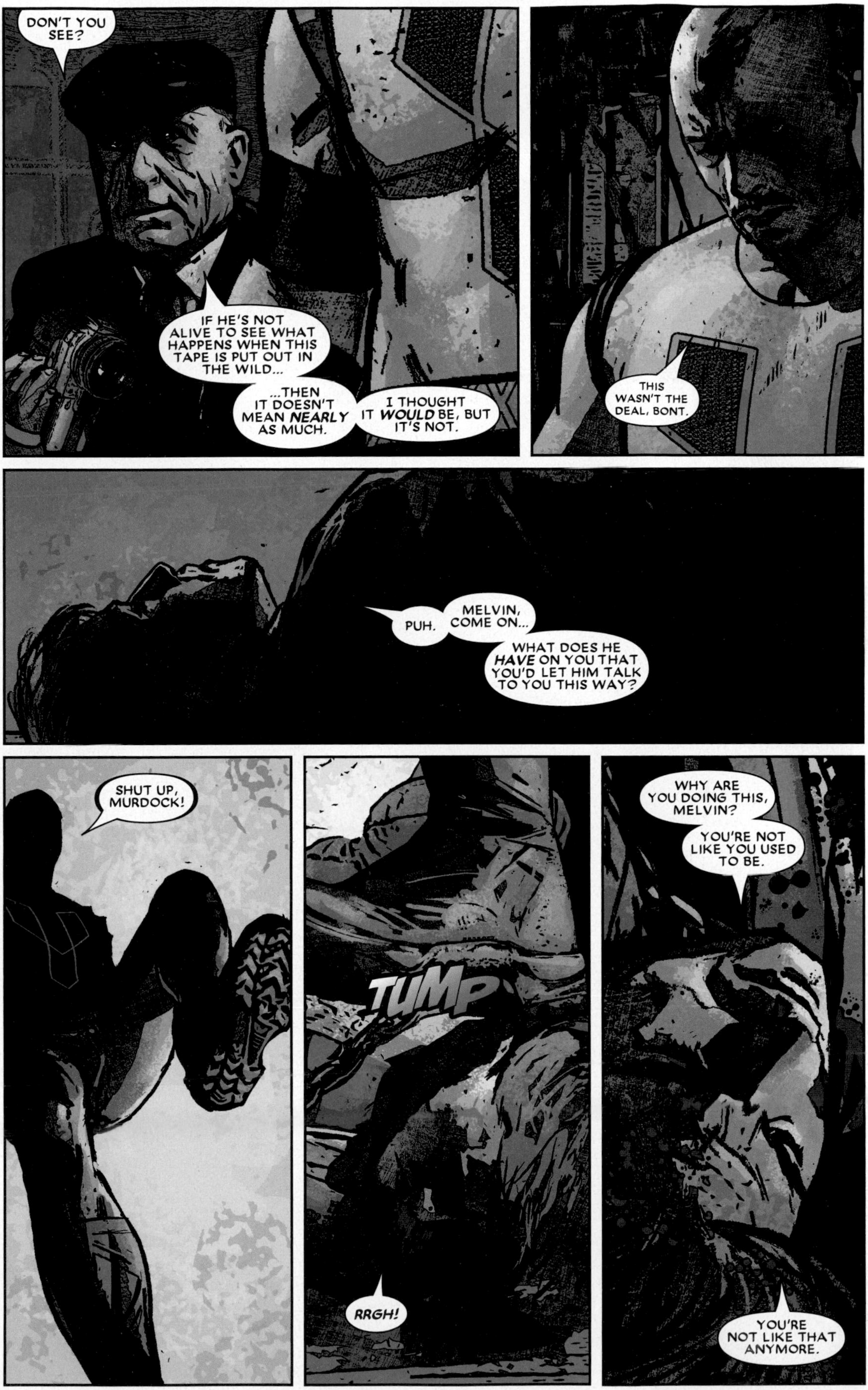
DON'T YOU SEE?
IF HE'S NOT ALIVE TO SEE WHAT HAPPENS WHEN THIS TAPE IS PUT OUT IN THE WILD...
...THEN IT DOESN'T MEAN NEARLY AS MUCH.
I THOUGHT IT WOULD BE, BUT IT'S NOT.
THIS WASN'T THE DEAL, BONT.
PUH.
MELVIN, COME ON...
WHAT DOES HE HAVE ON YOU THAT YOU'D LET HIM TALK TO YOU THIS WAY?
SHUT UP, MURDOCK!
TUMP
RRGH!
WHY ARE YOU DOING THIS, MELVIN?
YOU'RE NOT LIKE YOU USED TO BE.
YOU'RE NOT LIKE THAT ANYMORE.

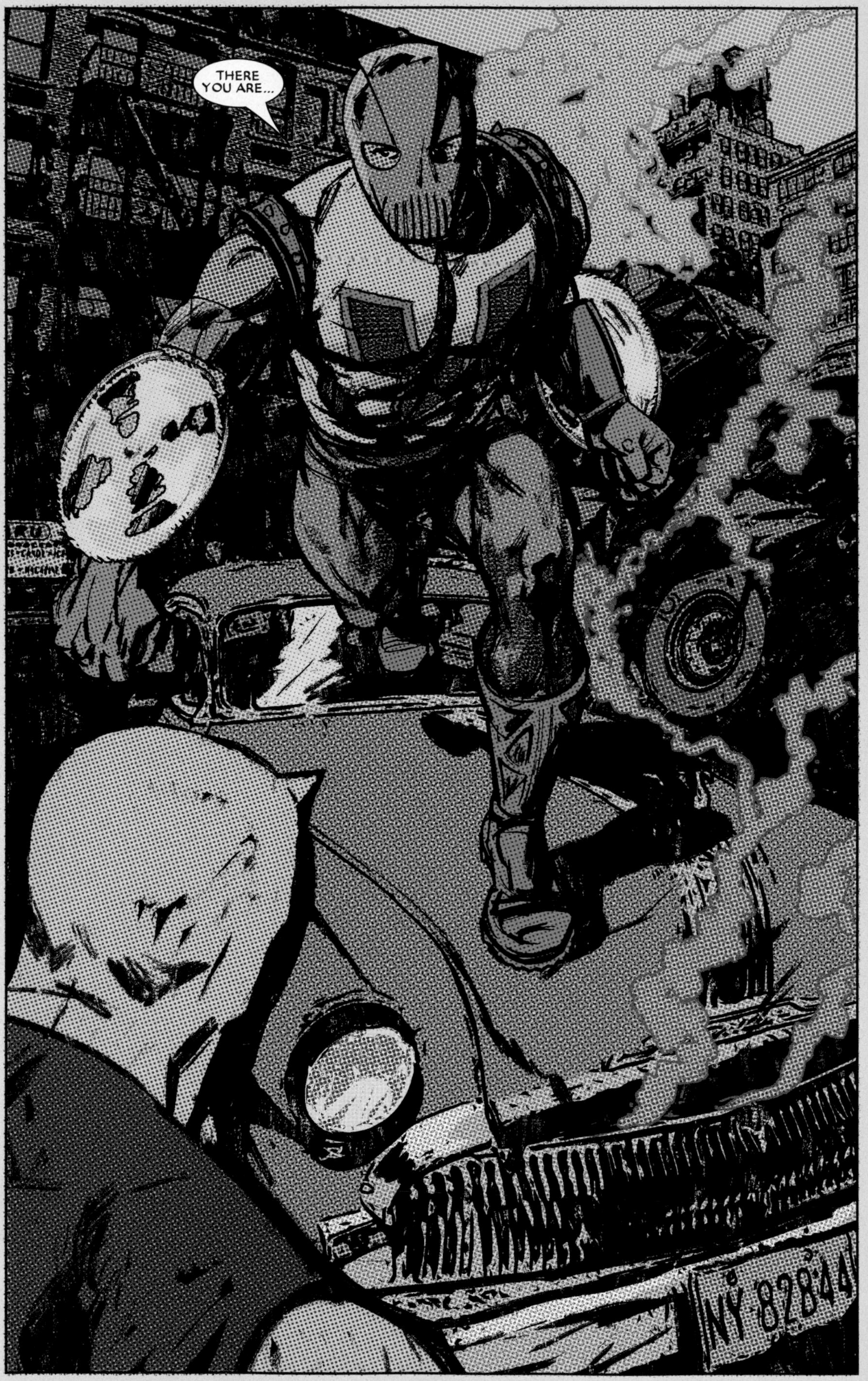
THERE YOU ARE...
NY 82844

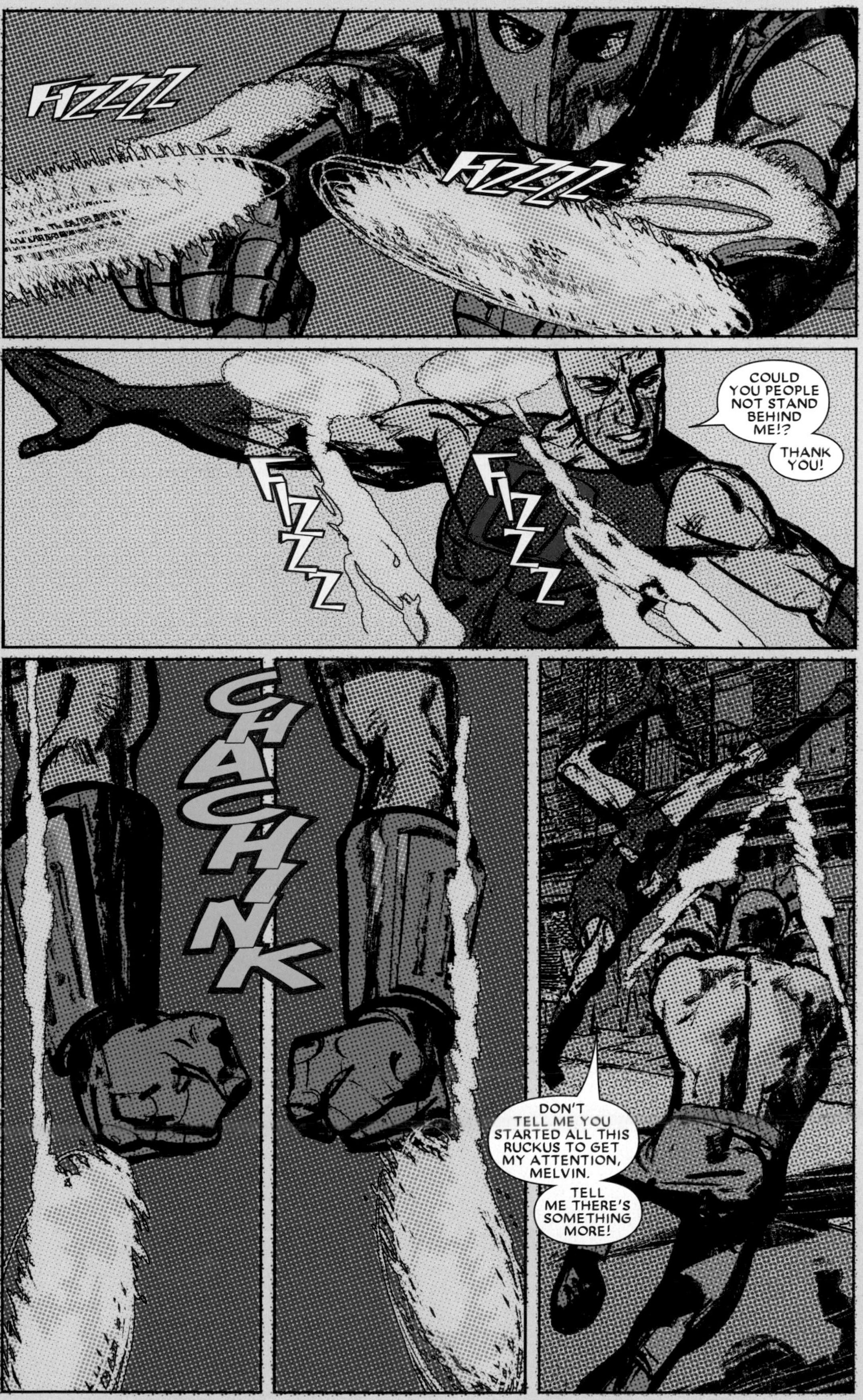
FIZZZZ
FIZZZZ
COULD YOU PEOPLE NOT STAND BEHIND ME!?
THANK YOU!
FIZZZZ
FIZZZZ
CHACHINK
DON'T TELL ME YOU STARTED ALL THIS RUCKUS TO GET MY ATTENTION, MELVIN.
TELL ME THERE'S SOMETHING MORE!

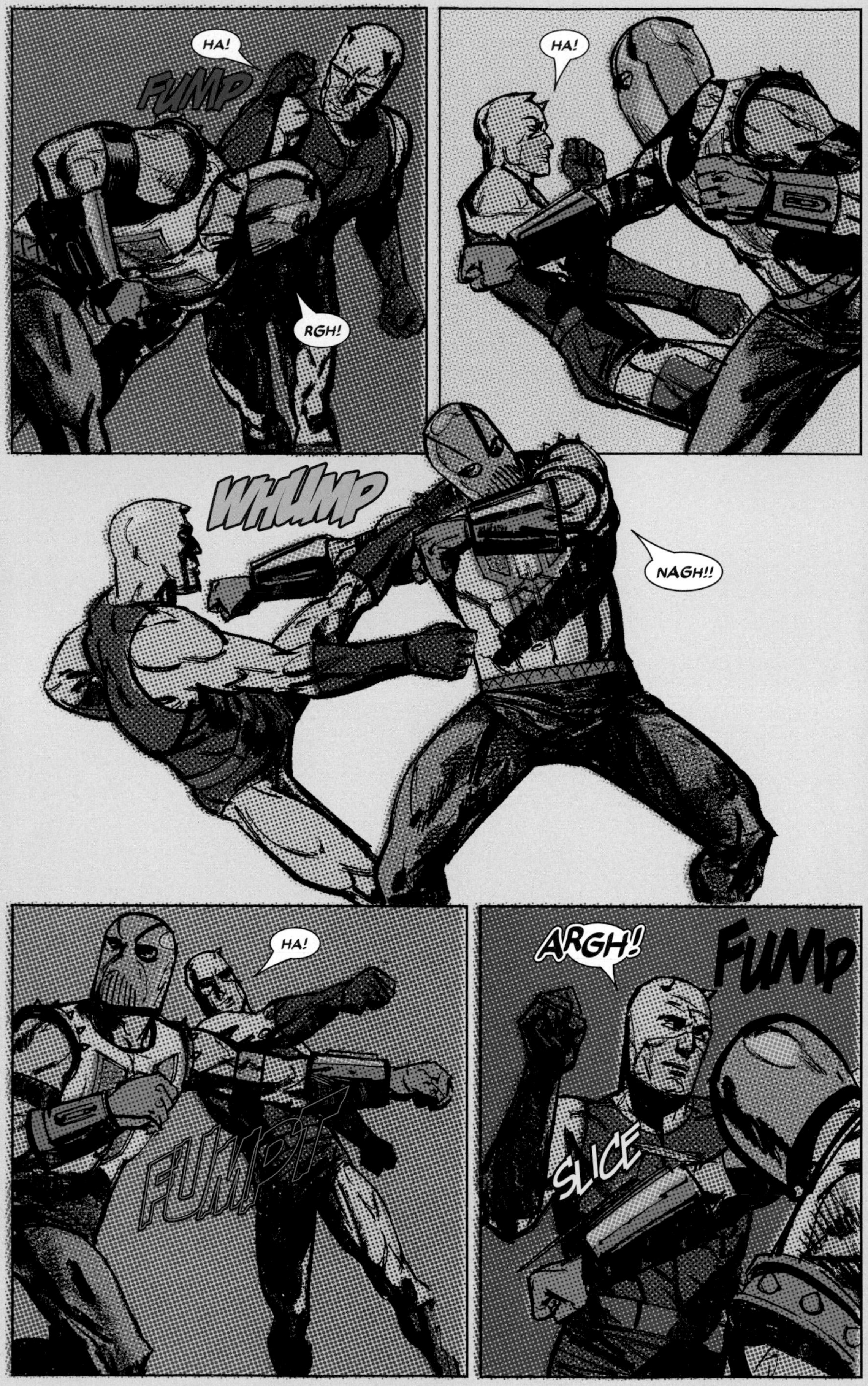
HA!
FUMP
RGH!
HA!
WHUMP
NAGH!!
HA!
FUMPT
ARGH!
FUMP
SLICE

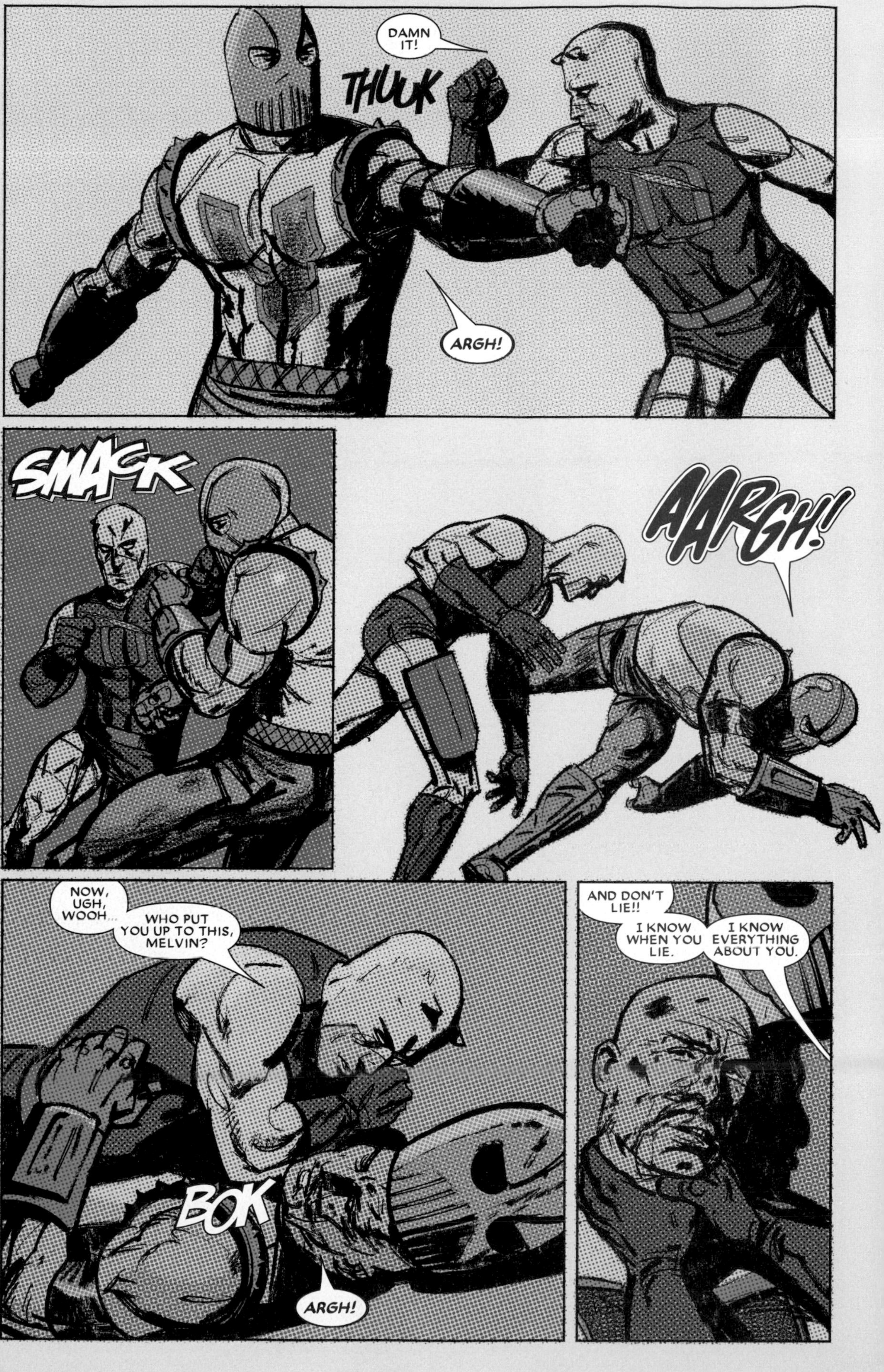
DAMN IT!
THUUK
ARGH!
SMACK
AARGH!
NOW, UGH, WOOH...
WHO PUT YOU UP TO THIS, MELVIN?
BOK
ARGH!
AND DON'T LIE!!
I KNOW WHEN YOU LIE.
I KNOW EVERYTHING ABOUT YOU.

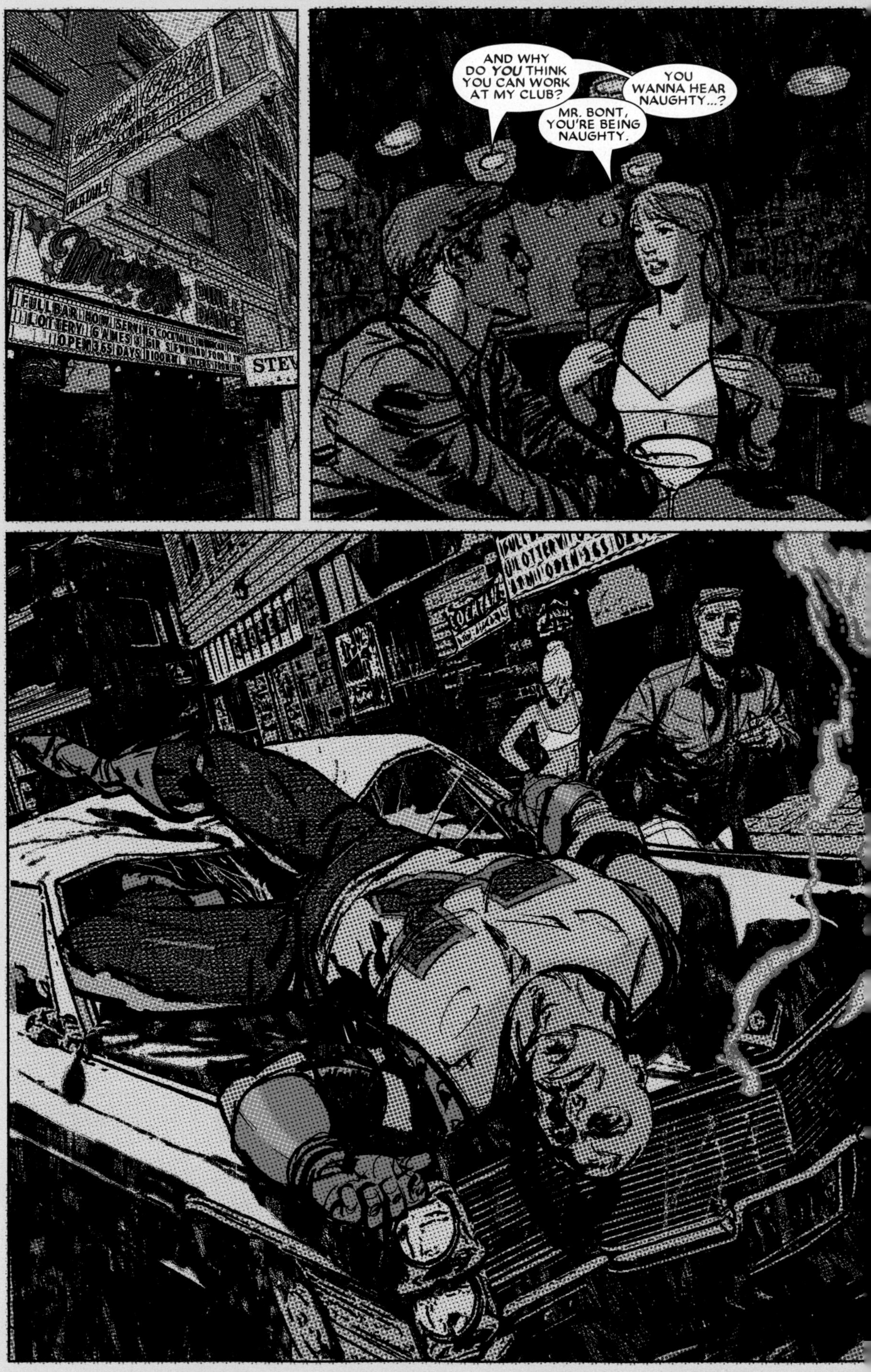
AND WHY DO *YOU* THINK YOU CAN WORK AT MY CLUB?
YOU WANNA HEAR NAUGHTY...?
MR. BONT, YOU'RE BEING NAUGHTY.
COCKTAILS
DINE & DANCE

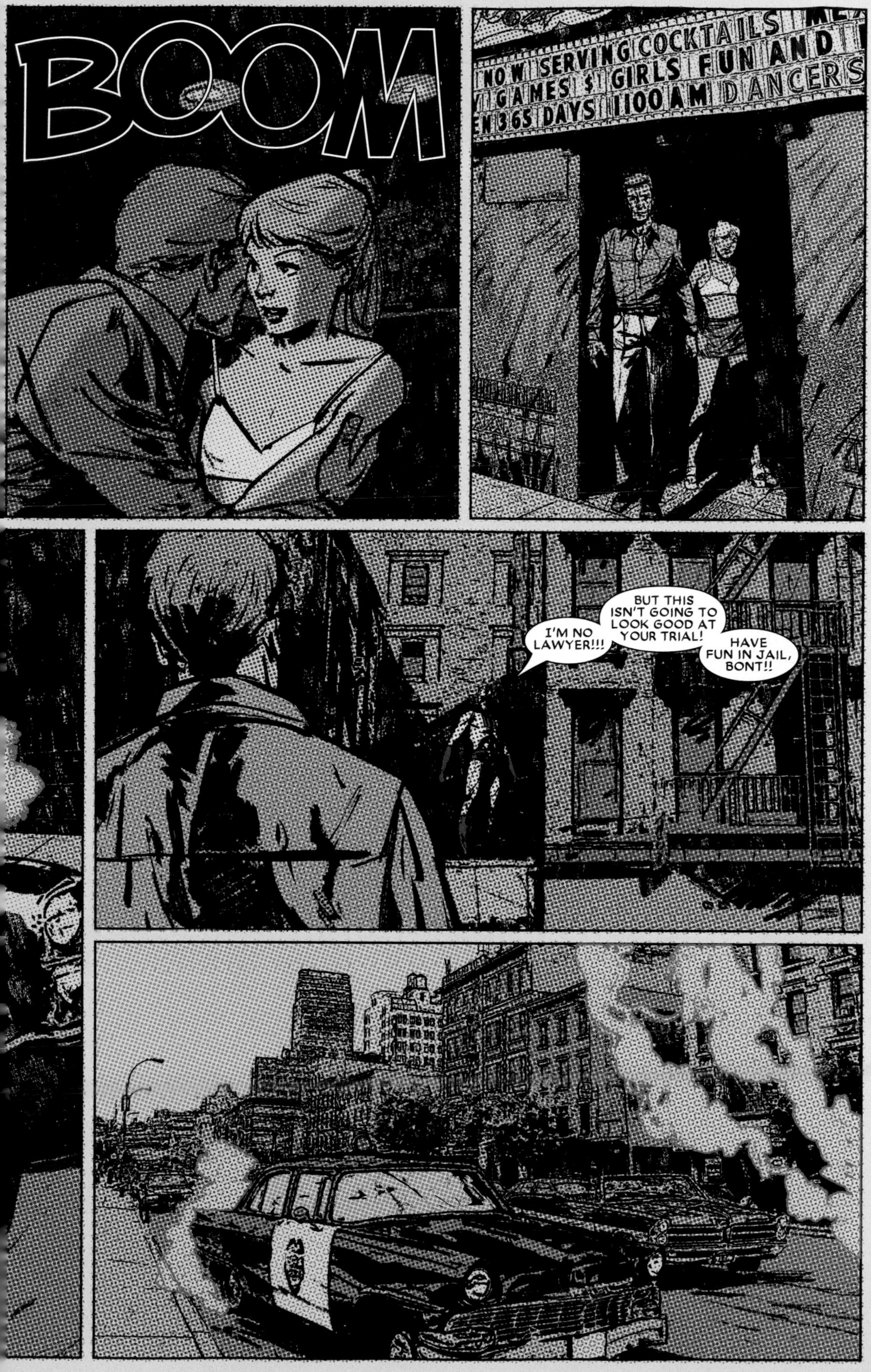
BOOM
NOW SERVING COCKTAILS
GAMES $ GIRLS FUN AND
DANCERS
365 DAYS 1100 AM
I'M NO LAWYER!!!
BUT THIS ISN'T GOING TO LOOK GOOD AT YOUR TRIAL!
HAVE FUN IN JAIL, BONT!!

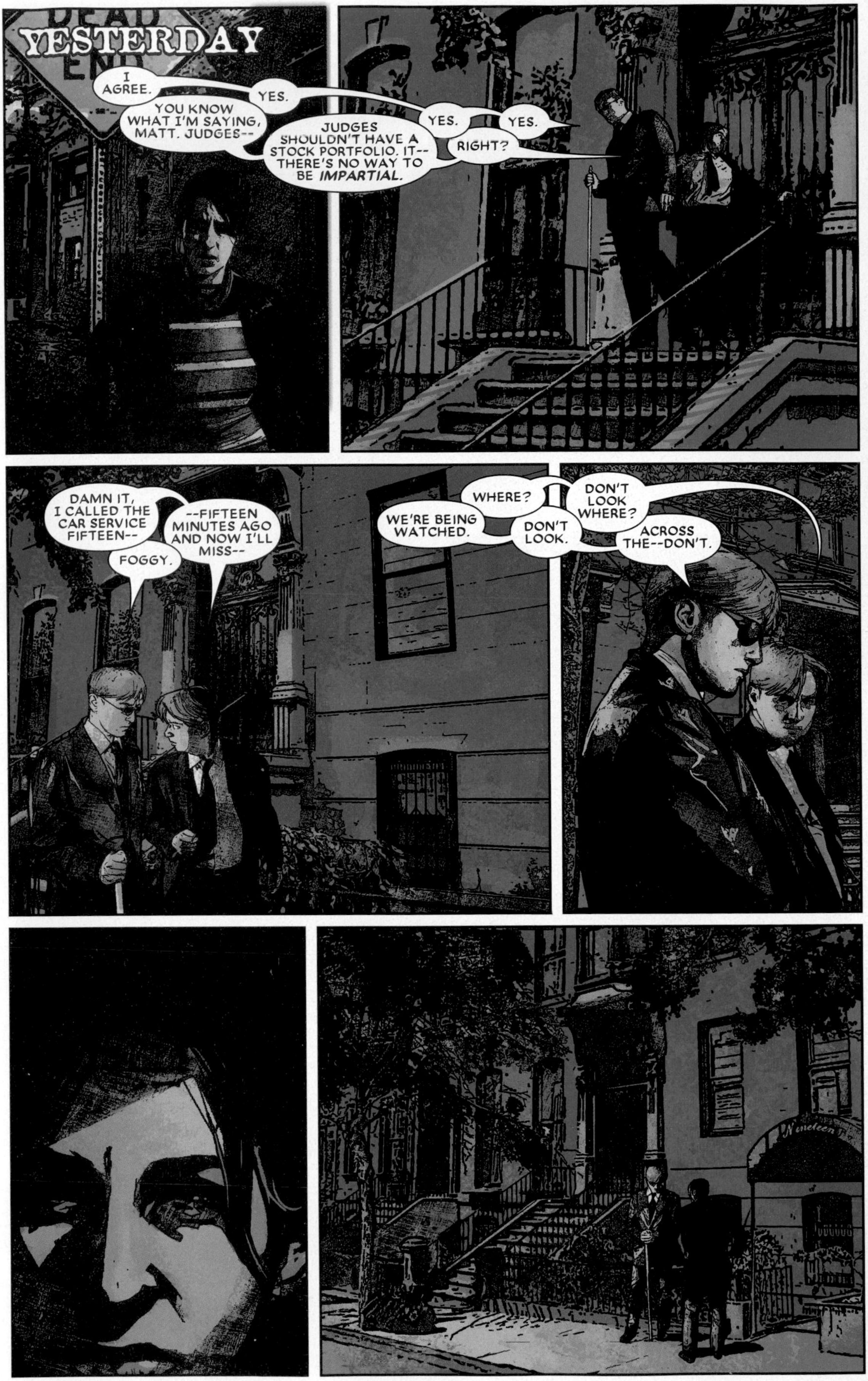
YESTERDAY
I AGREE.
YES.
YOU KNOW WHAT I'M SAYING, MATT. JUDGES--
YES.
YES.
JUDGES SHOULDN'T HAVE A STOCK PORTFOLIO. IT-- THERE'S NO WAY TO BE IMPARTIAL.
RIGHT?
DAMN IT, I CALLED THE CAR SERVICE FIFTEEN--
FOGGY.
--FIFTEEN MINUTES AGO AND NOW I'LL MISS--
WE'RE BEING WATCHED.
WHERE?
DON'T LOOK.
DON'T LOOK WHERE?
ACROSS THE--DON'T.
Nineteen

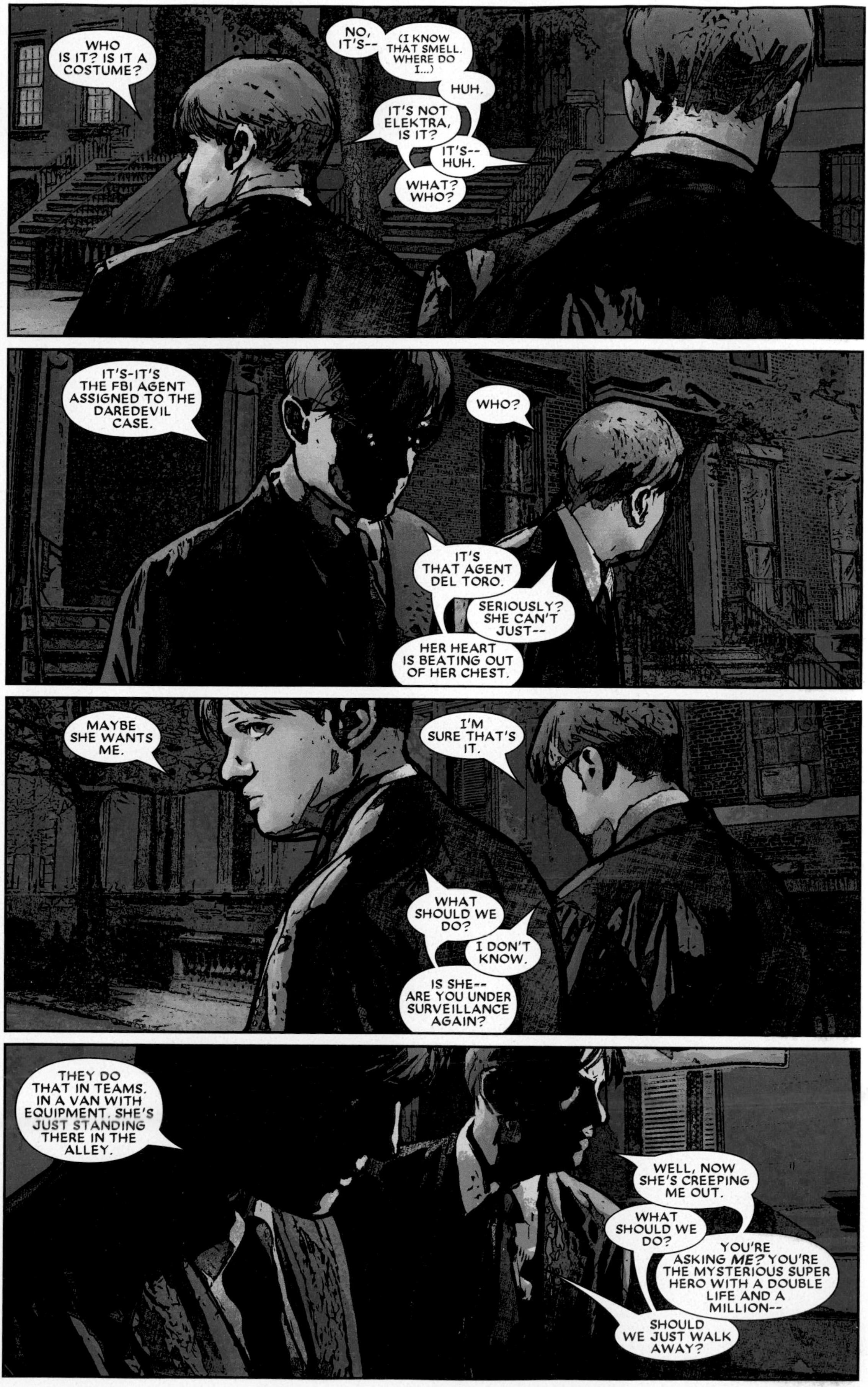
WHO IS IT? IS IT A COSTUME?
NO, IT'S--
(I KNOW THAT SMELL. WHERE DO I...)
HUH.
IT'S NOT ELEKTRA, IS IT?
IT'S-- HUH.
WHAT? WHO?
IT'S-IT'S THE FBI AGENT ASSIGNED TO THE DAREDEVIL CASE.
WHO?
IT'S THAT AGENT DEL TORO.
SERIOUSLY? SHE CAN'T JUST--
HER HEART IS BEATING OUT OF HER CHEST.
MAYBE SHE WANTS ME.
I'M SURE THAT'S IT.
WHAT SHOULD WE DO?
I DON'T KNOW.
IS SHE-- ARE YOU UNDER SURVEILLANCE AGAIN?
THEY DO THAT IN TEAMS. IN A VAN WITH EQUIPMENT. SHE'S JUST STANDING THERE IN THE ALLEY.
WELL, NOW SHE'S CREEPING ME OUT.
WHAT SHOULD WE DO?
YOU'RE ASKING *ME?* YOU'RE THE MYSTERIOUS SUPER HERO WITH A DOUBLE LIFE AND A MILLION--
SHOULD WE JUST WALK AWAY?

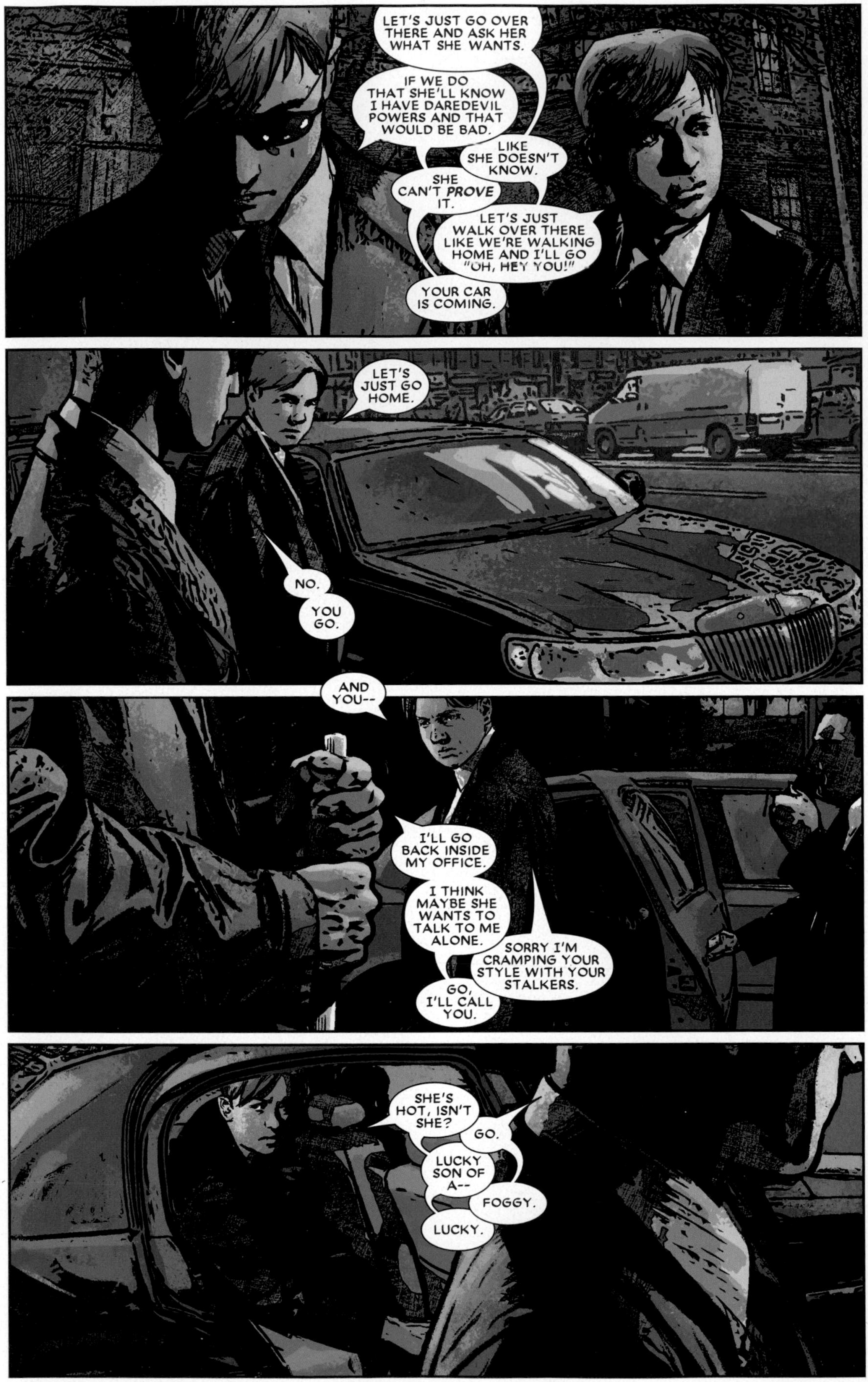
LET'S JUST GO OVER THERE AND ASK HER WHAT SHE WANTS.
IF WE DO THAT SHE'LL KNOW I HAVE DAREDEVIL POWERS AND THAT WOULD BE BAD.
LIKE SHE DOESN'T KNOW.
SHE CAN'T *PROVE* IT.
LET'S JUST WALK OVER THERE LIKE WE'RE WALKING HOME AND I'LL GO "OH, HEY YOU!"
YOUR CAR IS COMING.
LET'S JUST GO HOME.
NO.
YOU GO.
AND YOU--
I'LL GO BACK INSIDE MY OFFICE.
I THINK MAYBE SHE WANTS TO TALK TO ME ALONE.
SORRY I'M CRAMPING YOUR STYLE WITH YOUR STALKERS.
GO, I'LL CALL YOU.
SHE'S HOT, ISN'T SHE?
GO.
LUCKY SON OF A--
FOGGY.
LUCKY.

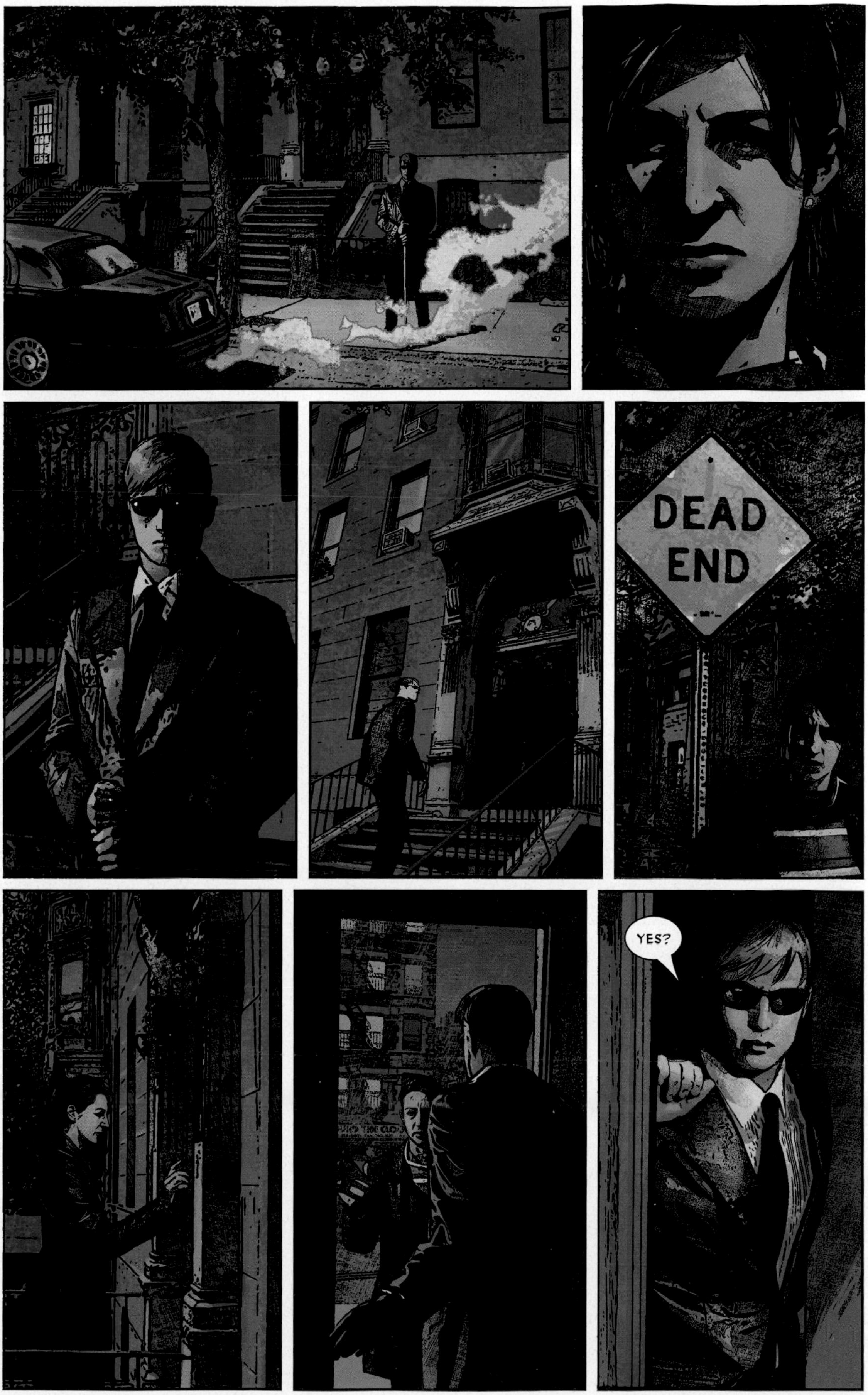
DEAD
END
YES?

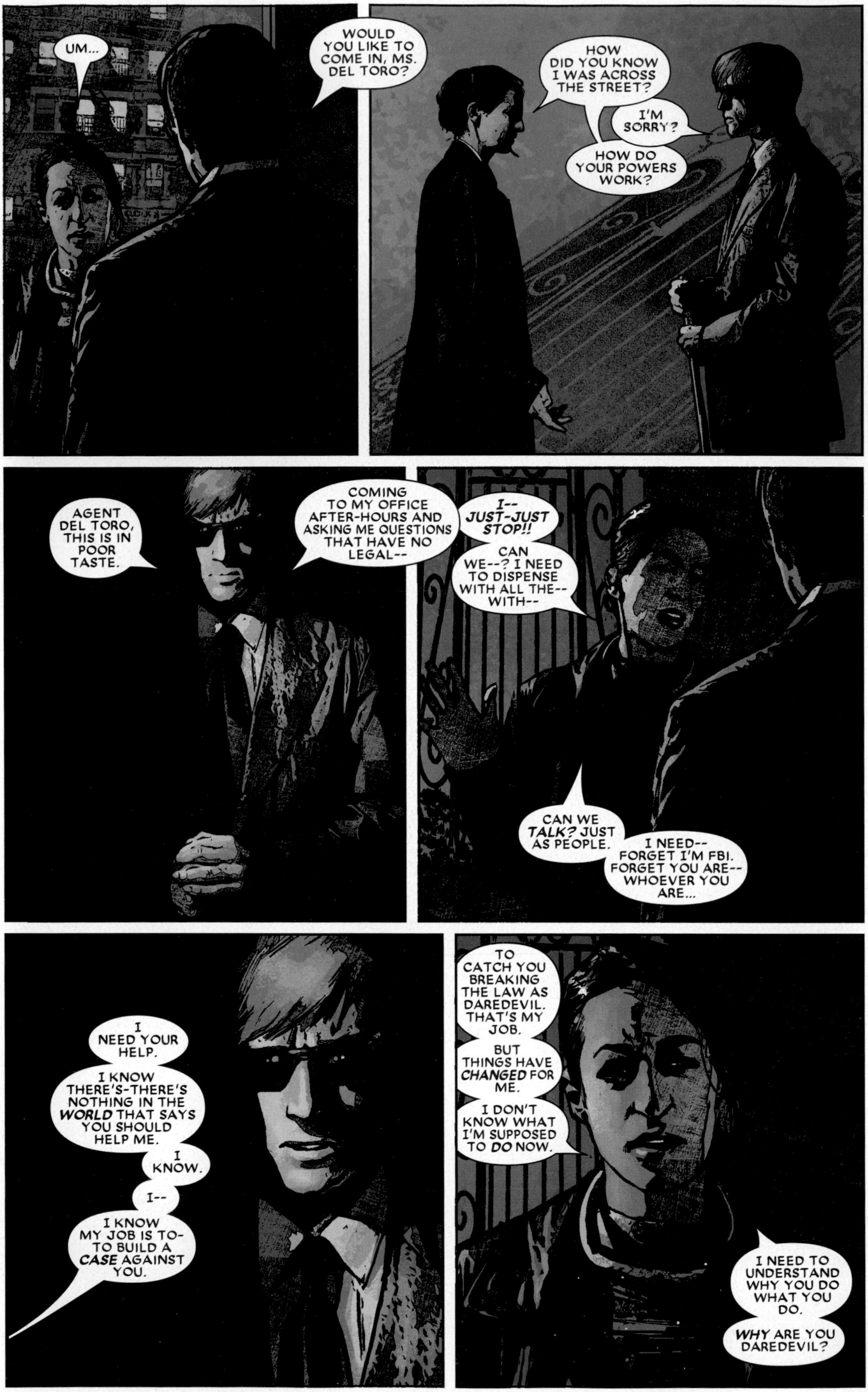
UM...
WOULD YOU LIKE TO COME IN, MS. DEL TORO?
HOW DID YOU KNOW I WAS ACROSS THE STREET?
I'M SORRY?
HOW DO YOUR POWERS WORK?
AGENT DEL TORO, THIS IS IN POOR TASTE.
COMING TO MY OFFICE AFTER-HOURS AND ASKING ME QUESTIONS THAT HAVE NO LEGAL--
I-- JUST-JUST STOP!!
CAN WE--? I NEED TO DISPENSE WITH ALL THE-- WITH--
CAN WE TALK? JUST AS PEOPLE.
I NEED-- FORGET I'M FBI. FORGET YOU ARE-- WHOEVER YOU ARE...
I NEED YOUR HELP.
I KNOW THERE'S-THERE'S NOTHING IN THE WORLD THAT SAYS YOU SHOULD HELP ME.
I KNOW.
I--
I KNOW MY JOB IS TO-TO BUILD A CASE AGAINST YOU.
TO CATCH YOU BREAKING THE LAW AS DAREDEVIL. THAT'S MY JOB.
BUT THINGS HAVE CHANGED FOR ME.
I DON'T KNOW WHAT I'M SUPPOSED TO DO NOW.
I NEED TO UNDERSTAND WHY YOU DO WHAT YOU DO.
WHY ARE YOU DAREDEVIL?

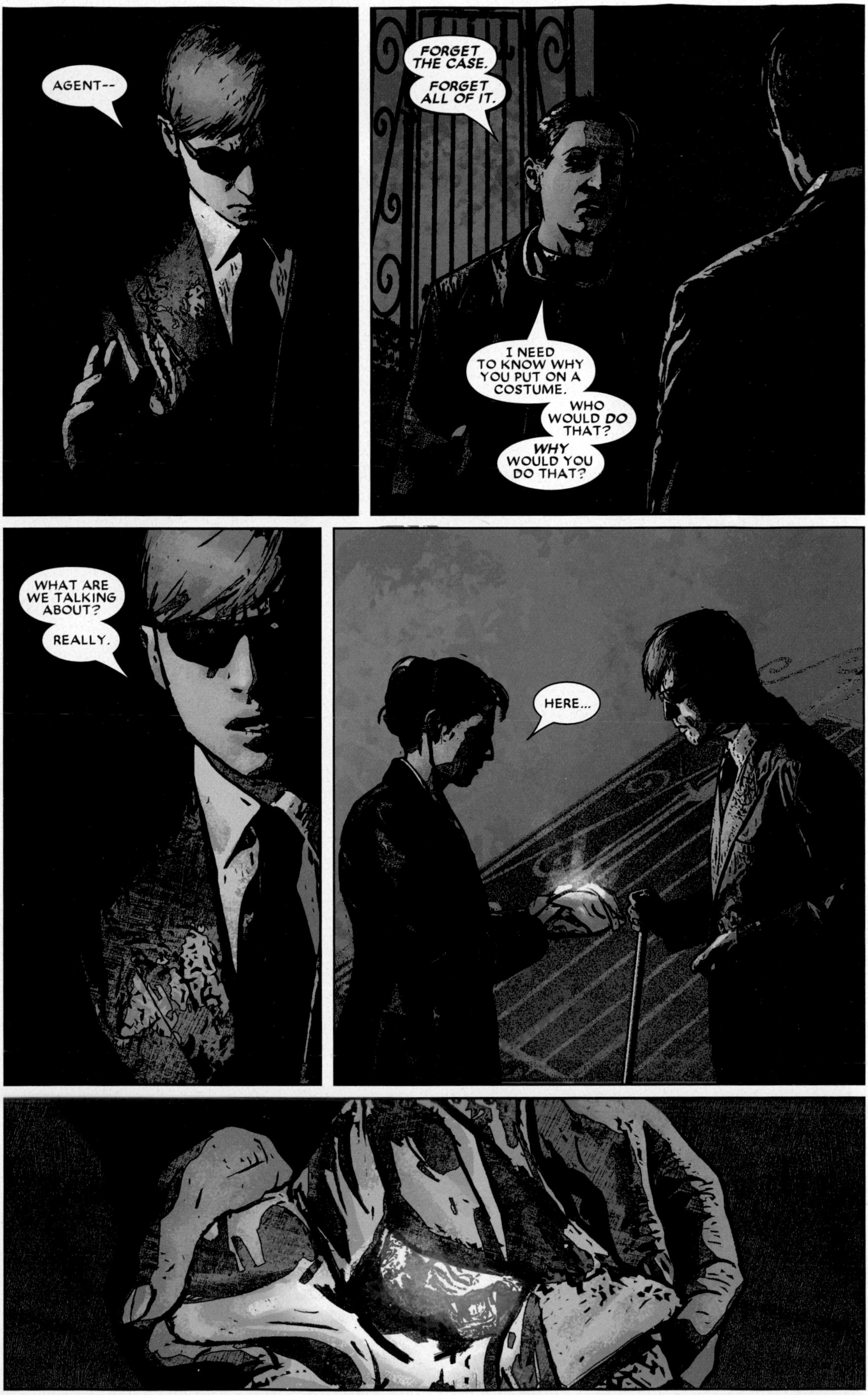
AGENT--
FORGET THE CASE.
FORGET ALL OF IT.
I NEED TO KNOW WHY YOU PUT ON A COSTUME.
WHO WOULD *DO* THAT?
WHY WOULD YOU DO THAT?
WHAT ARE WE TALKING ABOUT?
REALLY.
HERE...

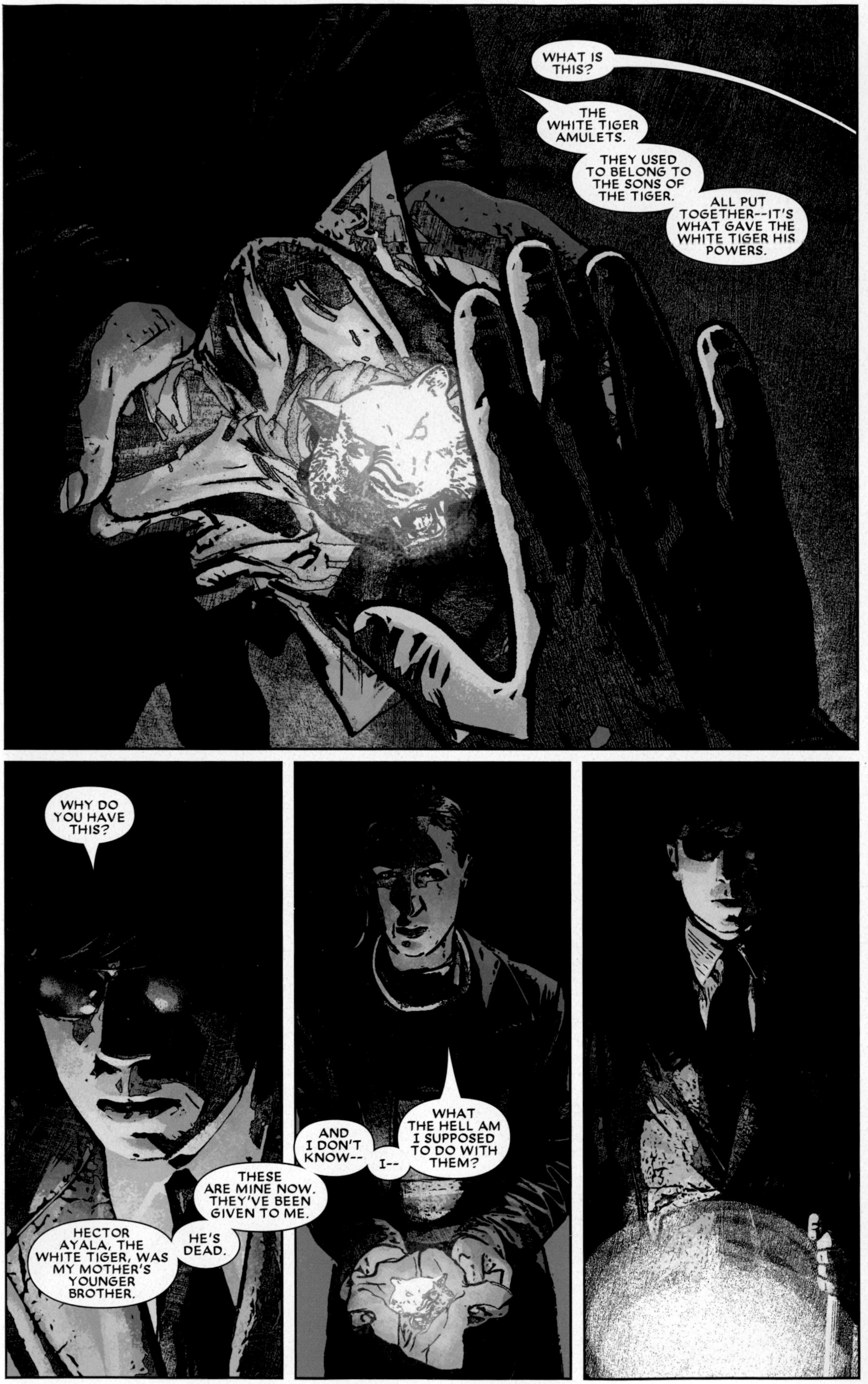
WHAT IS THIS?
THE WHITE TIGER AMULETS.
THEY USED TO BELONG TO THE SONS OF THE TIGER.
ALL PUT TOGETHER--IT'S WHAT GAVE THE WHITE TIGER HIS POWERS.
WHY DO YOU HAVE THIS?
HECTOR AYALA, THE WHITE TIGER, WAS MY MOTHER'S YOUNGER BROTHER.
HE'S DEAD.
THESE ARE MINE NOW. THEY'VE BEEN GIVEN TO ME.
AND I DON'T KNOW--
I--
WHAT THE HELL AM I SUPPOSED TO DO WITH THEM?

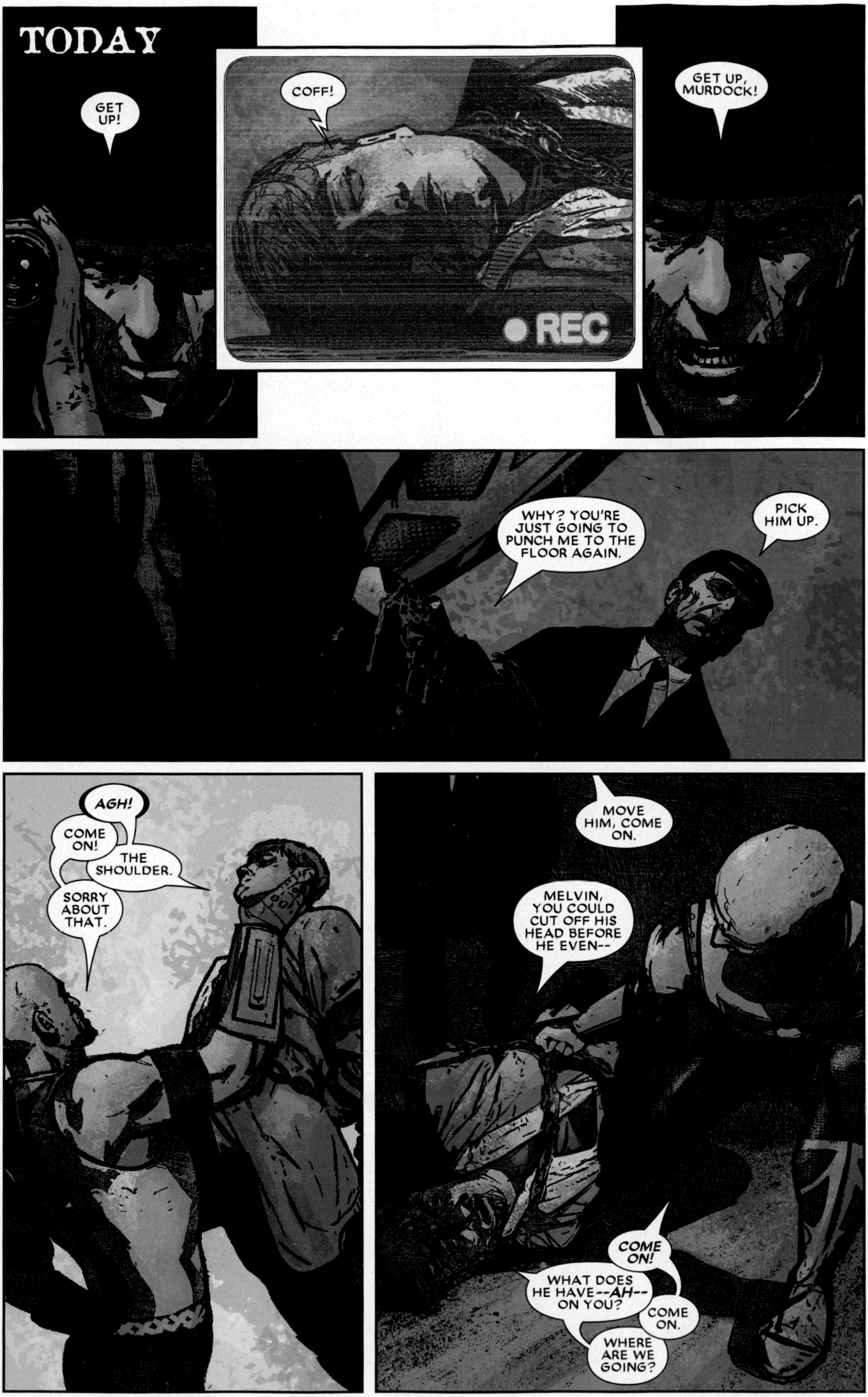
TODAY
GET UP!
COFF!
REC
GET UP, MURDOCK!
WHY? YOU'RE JUST GOING TO PUNCH ME TO THE FLOOR AGAIN.
PICK HIM UP.
AGH!
COME ON!
THE SHOULDER.
SORRY ABOUT THAT.
MOVE HIM, COME ON.
MELVIN, YOU COULD CUT OFF HIS HEAD BEFORE HE EVEN--
COME ON!
WHAT DOES HE HAVE--AH-- ON YOU?
COME ON.
WHERE ARE WE GOING?

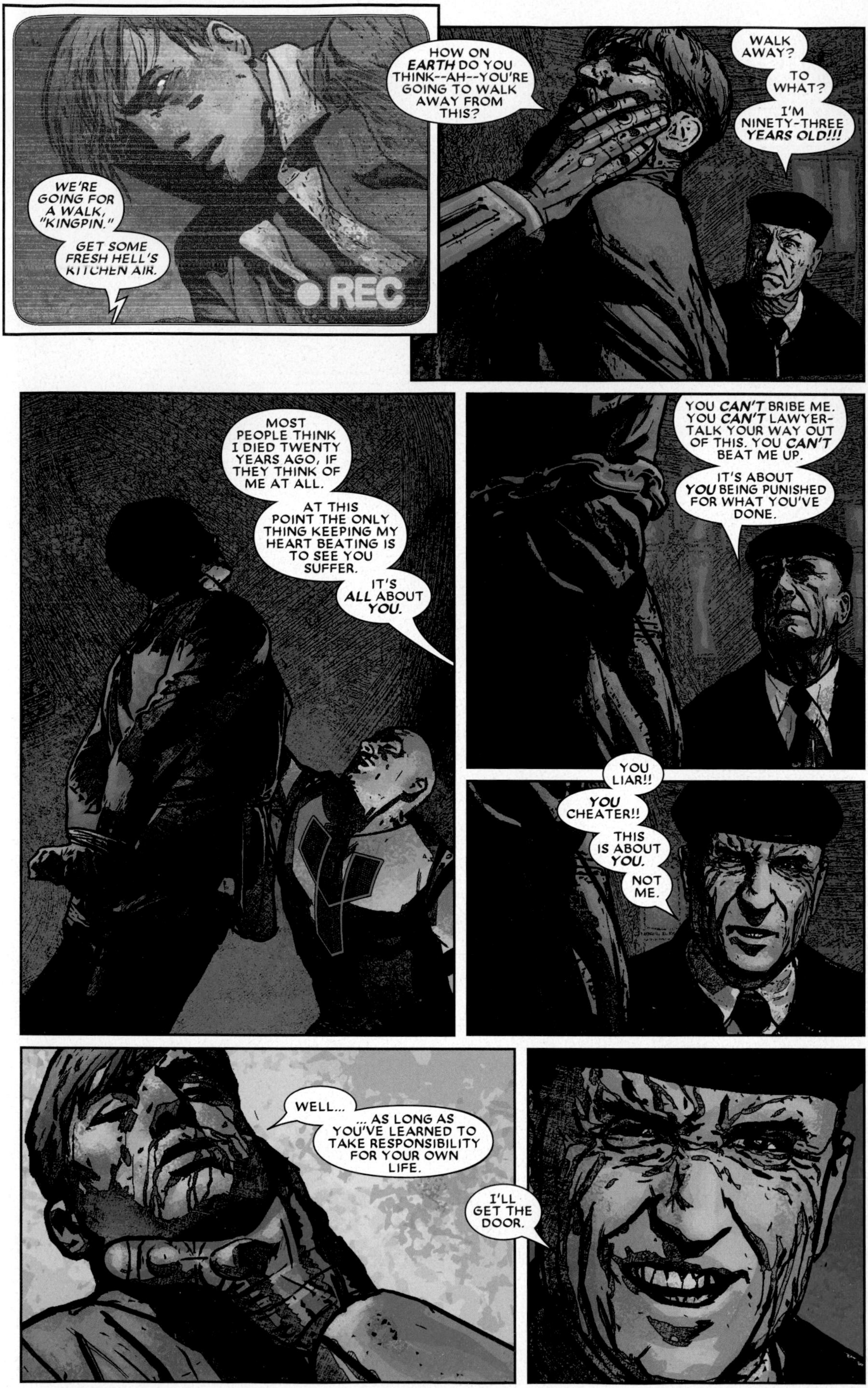
WE'RE GOING FOR A WALK, "KINGPIN."
GET SOME FRESH HELL'S KITCHEN AIR.
REC
HOW ON EARTH DO YOU THINK--AH--YOU'RE GOING TO WALK AWAY FROM THIS?
WALK AWAY?
TO WHAT?
I'M NINETY-THREE YEARS OLD!!!
MOST PEOPLE THINK I DIED TWENTY YEARS AGO, IF THEY THINK OF ME AT ALL.
AT THIS POINT THE ONLY THING KEEPING MY HEART BEATING IS TO SEE YOU SUFFER.
IT'S ALL ABOUT YOU.
YOU CAN'T BRIBE ME. YOU CAN'T LAWYER-TALK YOUR WAY OUT OF THIS. YOU CAN'T BEAT ME UP.
IT'S ABOUT YOU BEING PUNISHED FOR WHAT YOU'VE DONE.
YOU LIAR!!
YOU CHEATER!!
THIS IS ABOUT YOU.
NOT ME.
WELL...
...AS LONG AS YOU'VE LEARNED TO TAKE RESPONSIBILITY FOR YOUR OWN LIFE.
I'LL GET THE DOOR.

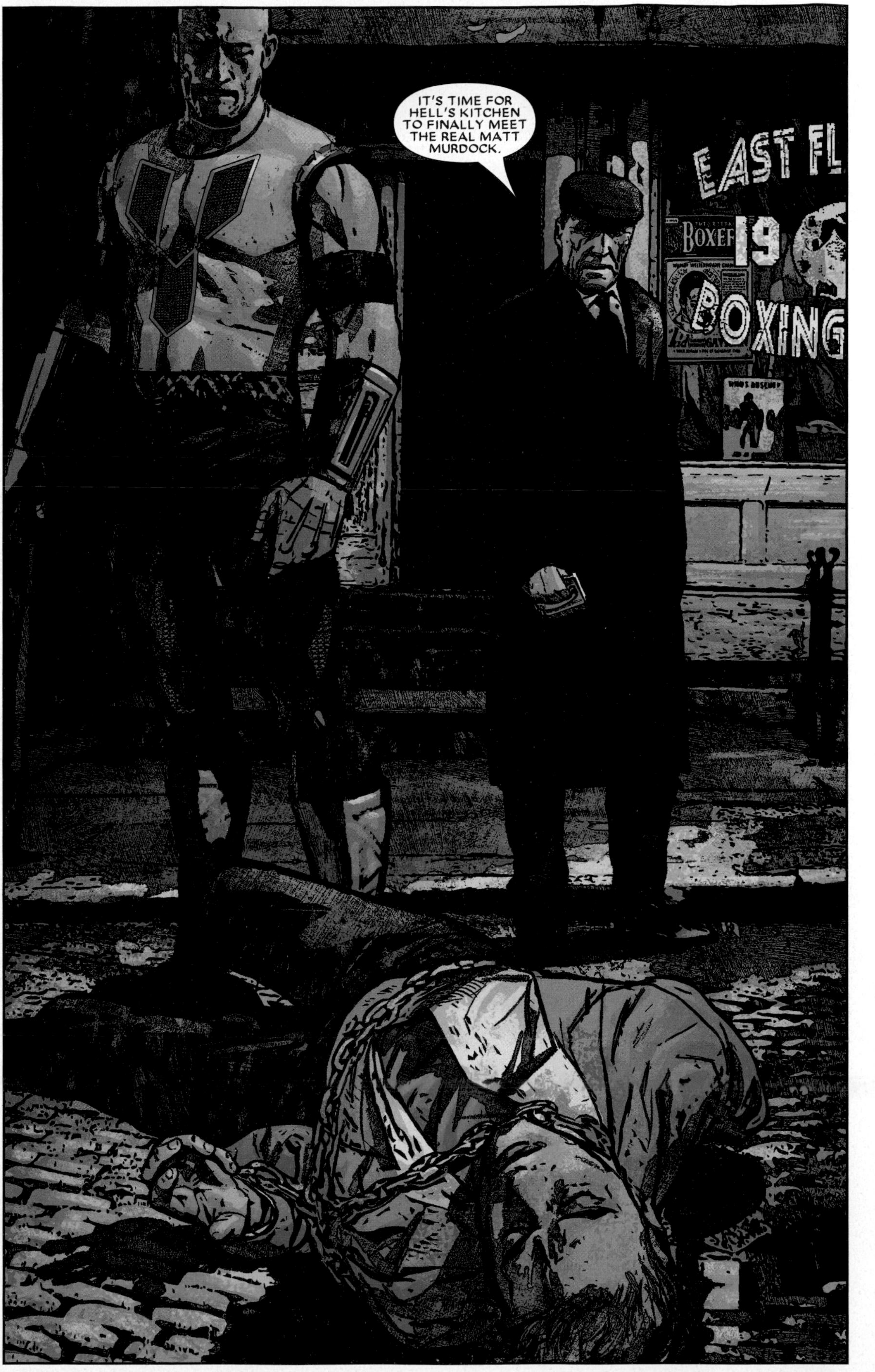
IT'S TIME FOR HELL'S KITCHEN TO FINALLY MEET THE REAL MATT MURDOCK.
EAST FL
BOXER
19
BOXING

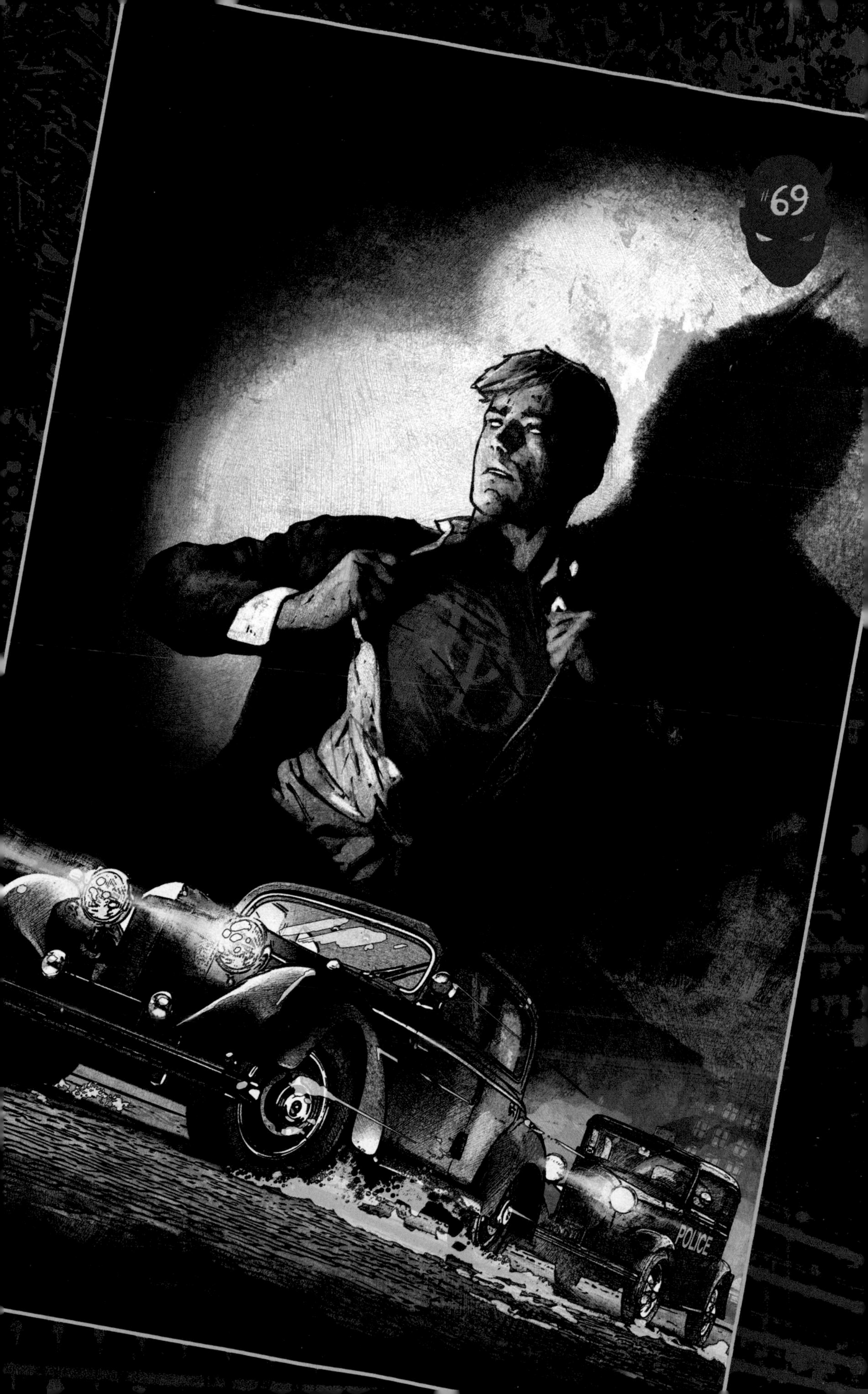
#69
POLICE

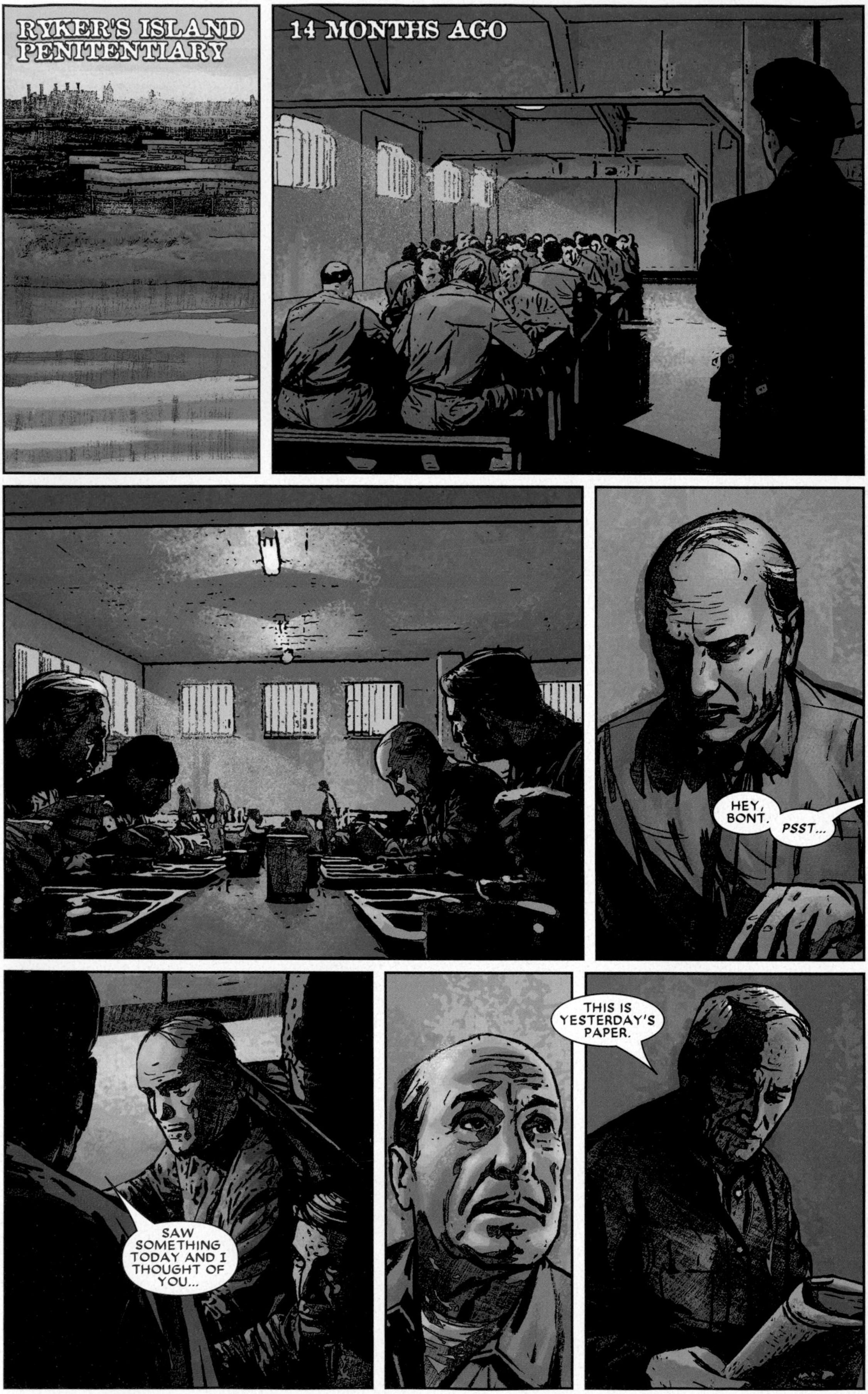
RYKER'S ISLAND PENITENTIARY
14 MONTHS AGO
HEY, BONT.
PSST...
SAW SOMETHING TODAY AND I THOUGHT OF YOU...
THIS IS YESTERDAY'S PAPER.

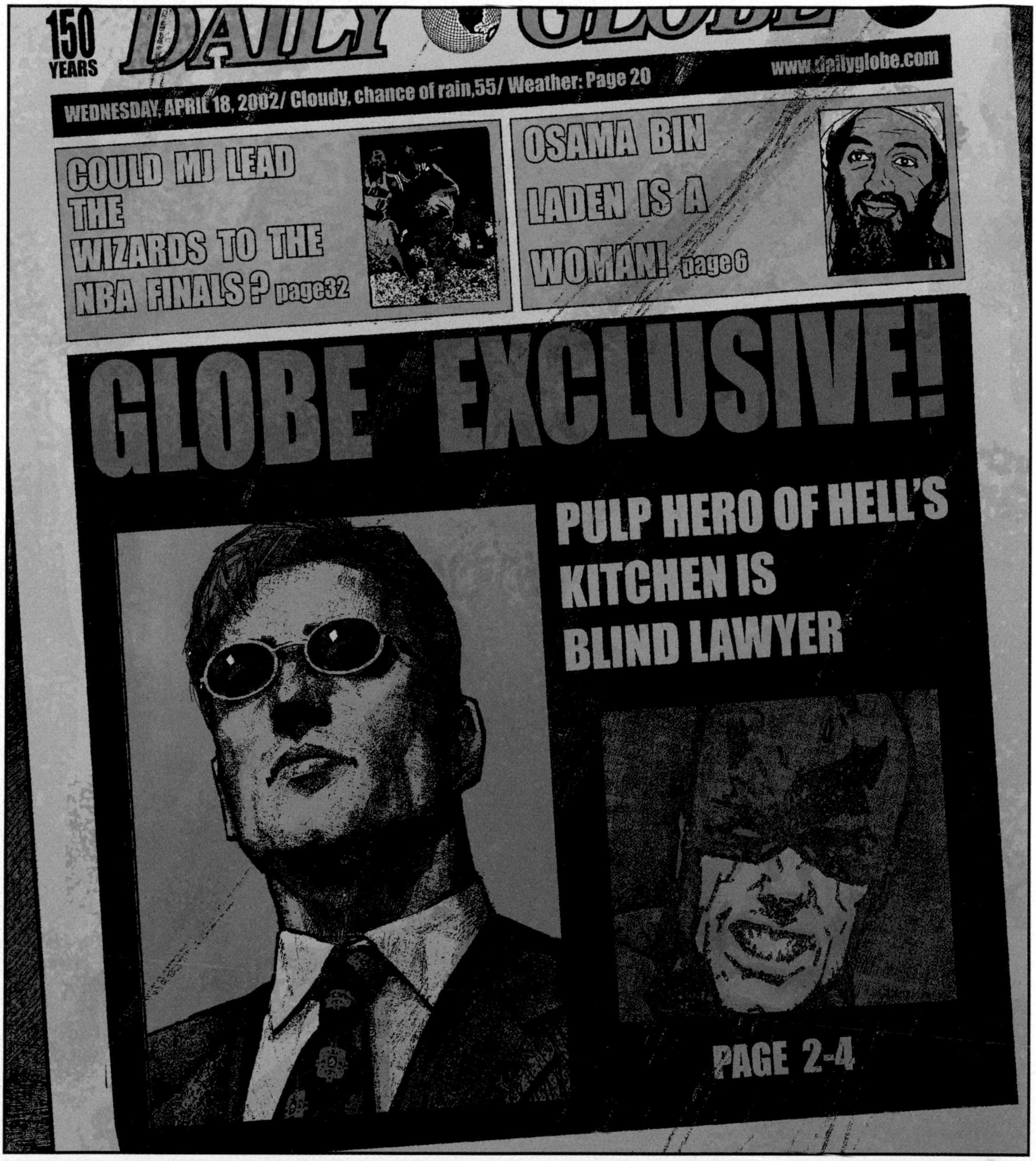
150 YEARS
DAILY GLOBE
www.dailyglobe.com
WEDNESDAY, APRIL 18, 2002/ Cloudy, chance of rain,55/ Weather: Page 20
COULD MJ LEAD THE WIZARDS TO THE NBA FINALS ? page32
OSAMA BIN LADEN IS A WOMAN! page6
GLOBE EXCLUSIVE!
PULP HERO OF HELL'S KITCHEN IS BLIND LAWYER
PAGE 2-4

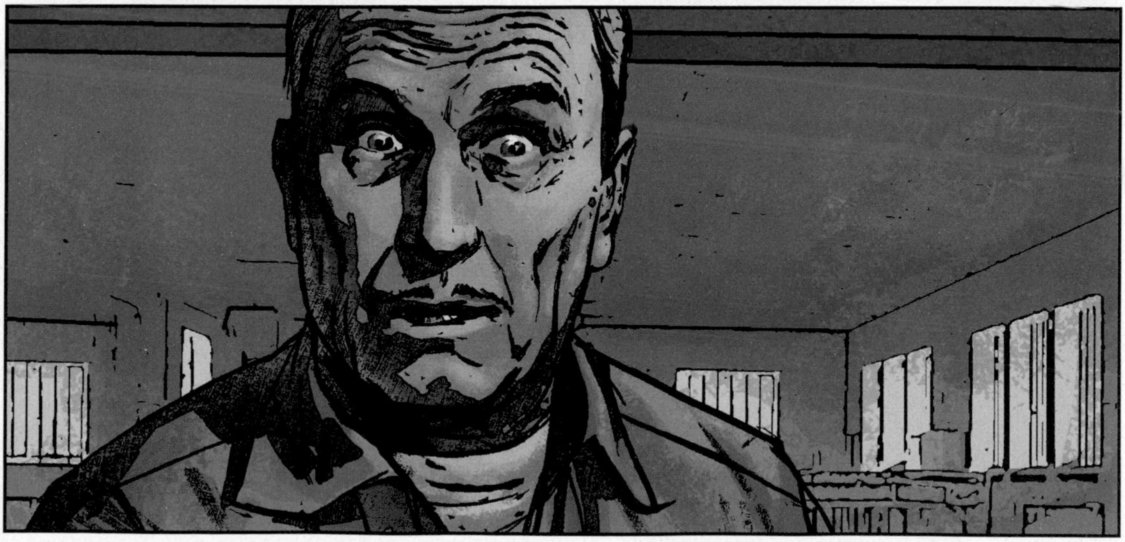

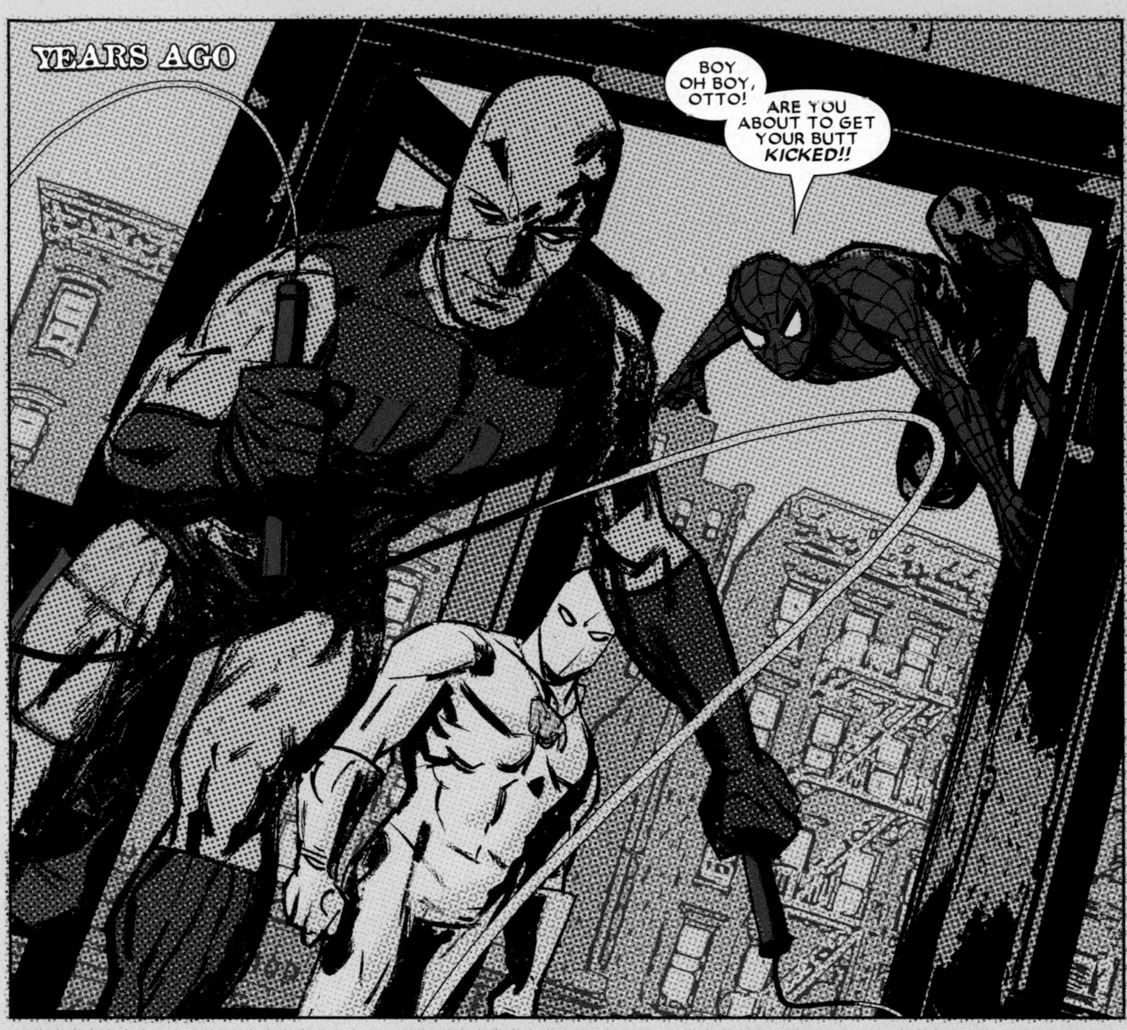
YEARS AGO
BOY OH BOY, OTTO!
ARE YOU ABOUT TO GET YOUR BUTT KICKED!!

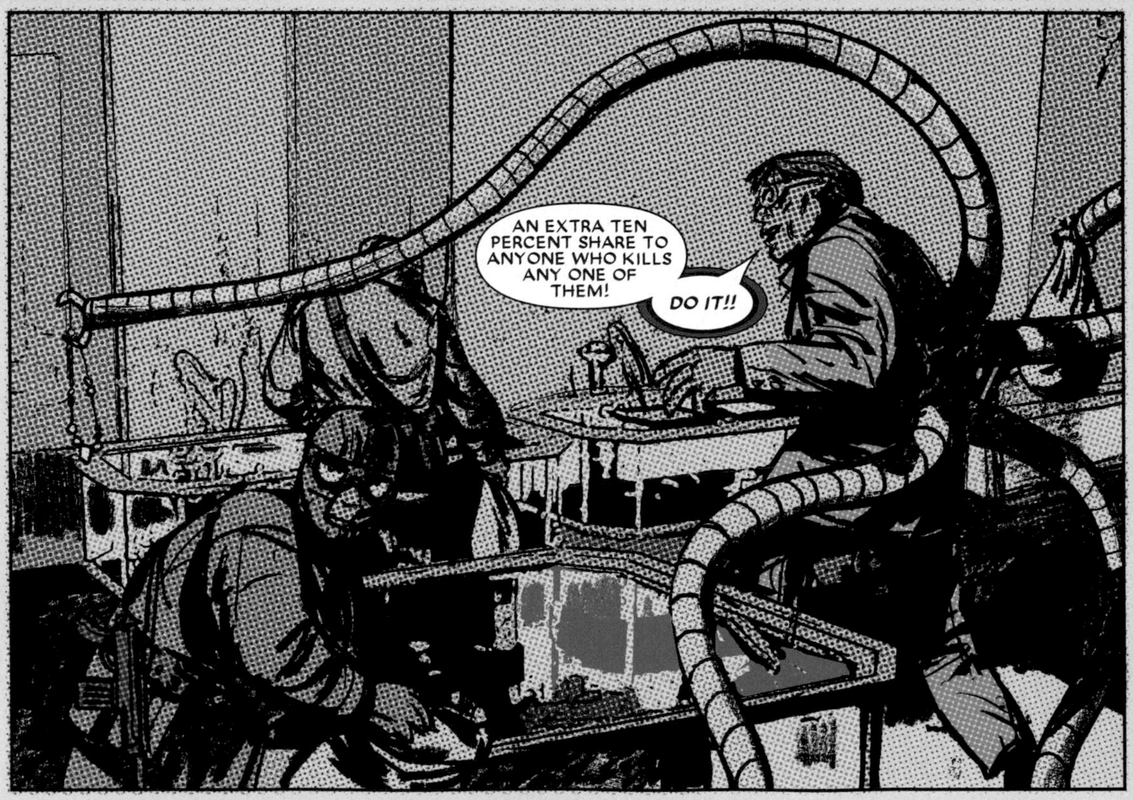
AN EXTRA TEN PERCENT SHARE TO ANYONE WHO KILLS ANY ONE OF THEM!
DO IT!!

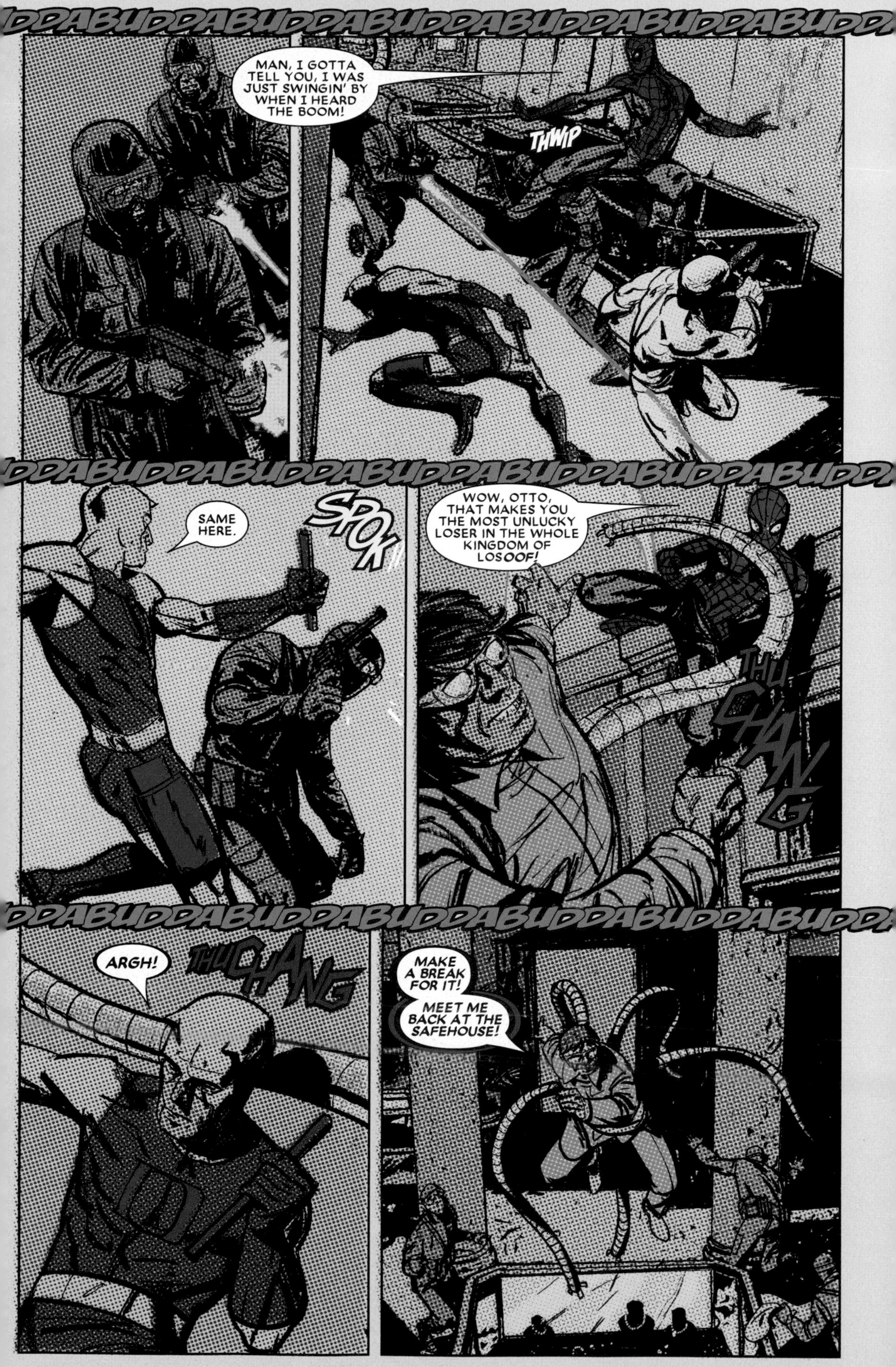
DDABUDDABUDDABUDDABUDDABUDDABUDDABUDD
MAN, I GOTTA TELL YOU, I WAS JUST SWINGIN' BY WHEN I HEARD THE BOOM!
THWIP
DDABUDDABUDDABUDDABUDDABUDDABUDD
SAME HERE.
SPOK
WOW, OTTO, THAT MAKES YOU THE MOST UNLUCKY LOSER IN THE WHOLE KINGDOM OF LOSOOF!
THU CHANG
DDABUDDABUDDABUDDABUDDABUDDABUDD
ARGH!
THU CHANG
MAKE A BREAK FOR IT!
MEET ME BACK AT THE SAFEHOUSE!

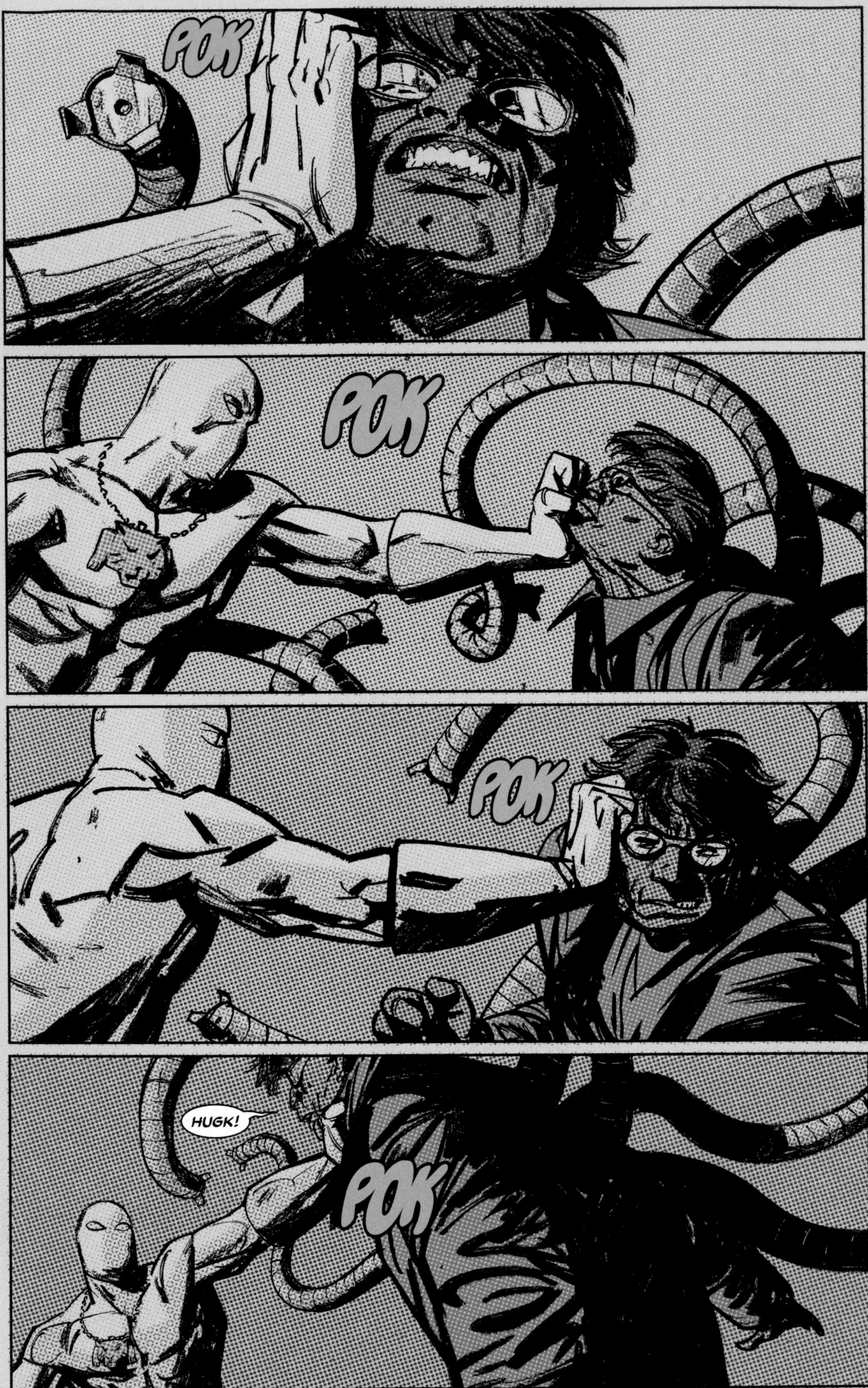
POK
POK
POK
HUGK!
POK

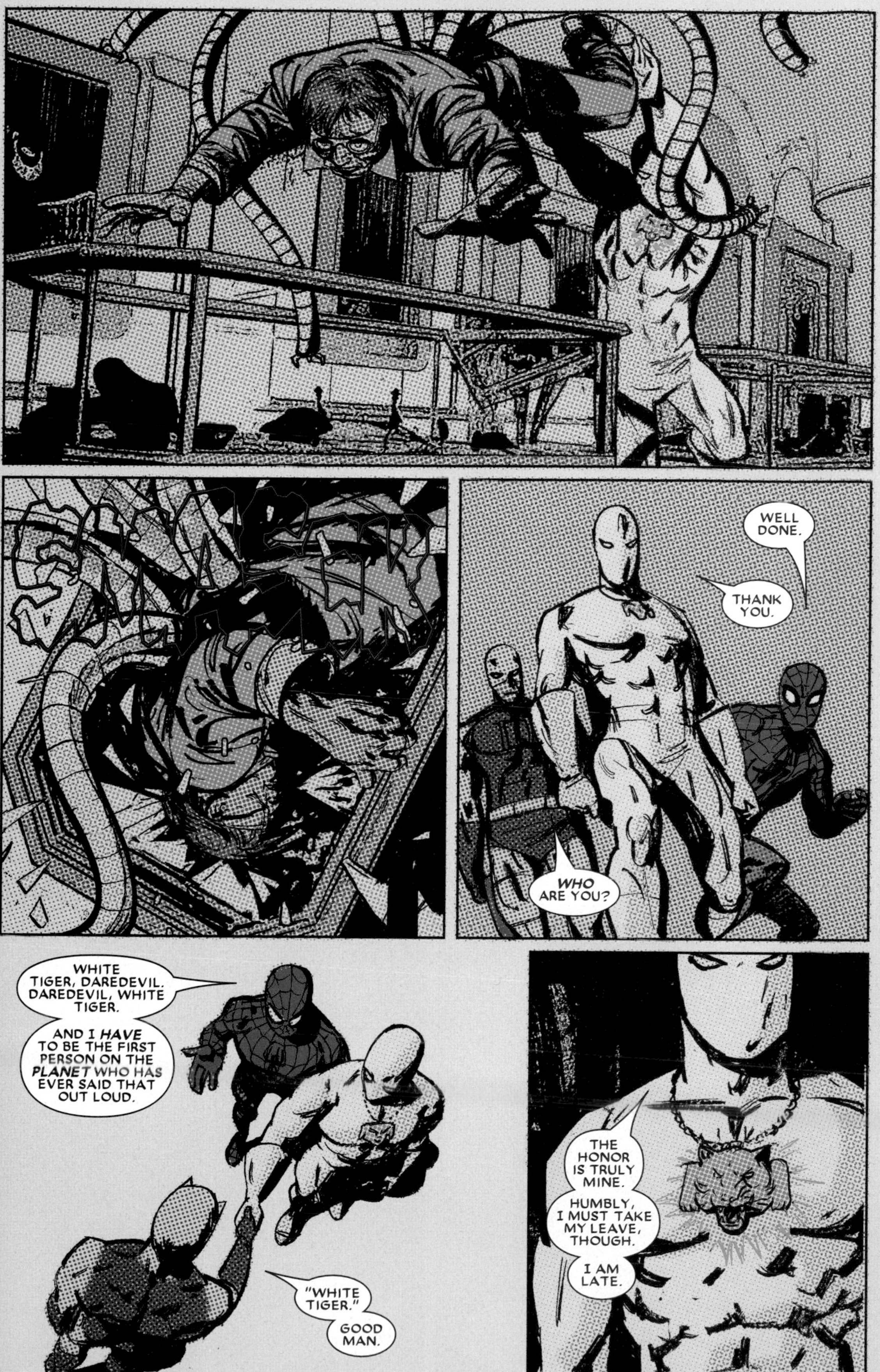
WELL DONE.
THANK YOU.
WHO ARE YOU?
WHITE TIGER, DAREDEVIL. DAREDEVIL, WHITE TIGER.
AND I HAVE TO BE THE FIRST PERSON ON THE PLANET WHO HAS EVER SAID THAT OUT LOUD.
"WHITE TIGER."
GOOD MAN.
THE HONOR IS TRULY MINE.
HUMBLY, I MUST TAKE MY LEAVE, THOUGH.
I AM LATE.

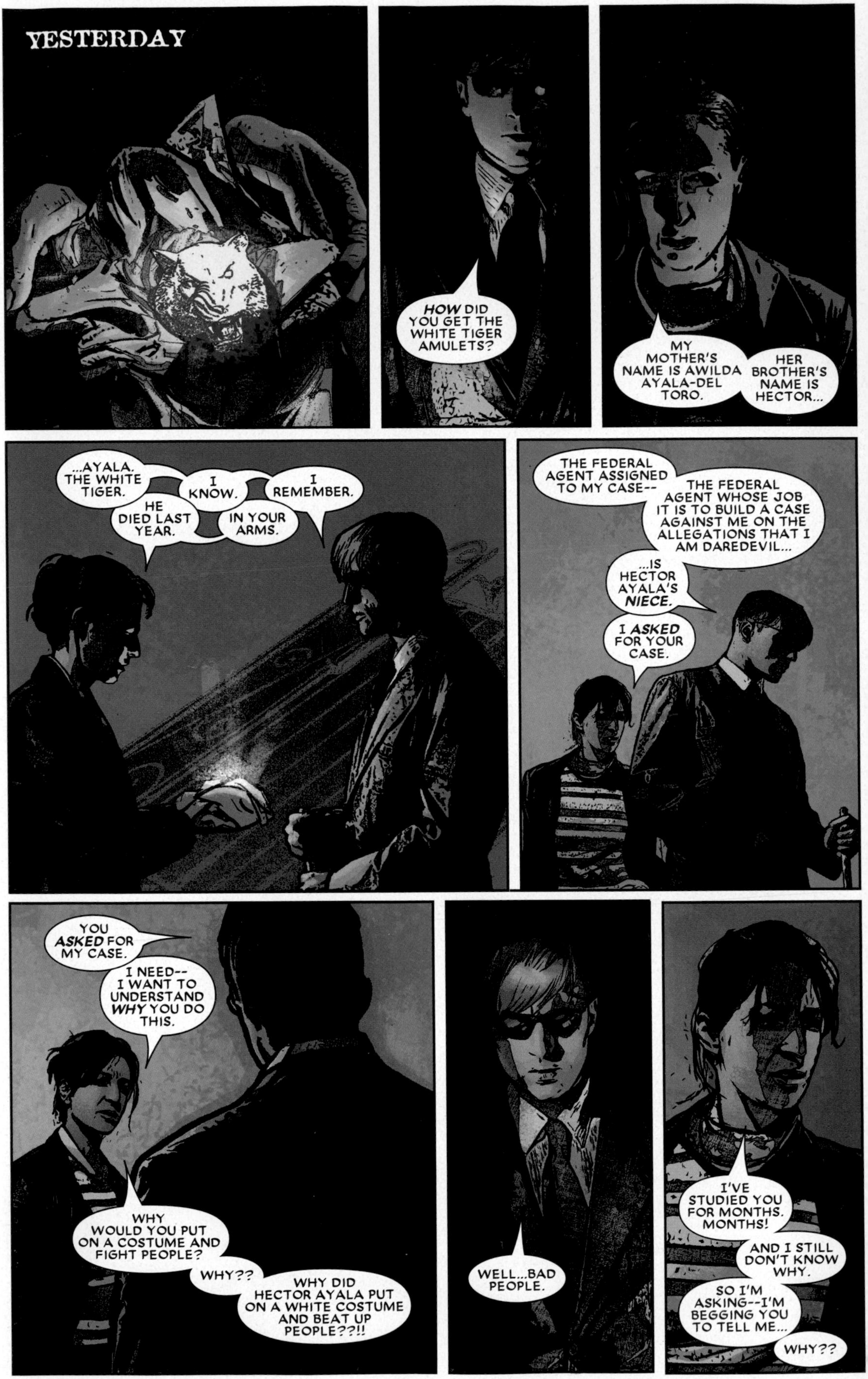
YESTERDAY
HOW DID YOU GET THE WHITE TIGER AMULETS?
MY MOTHER'S NAME IS AWILDA AYALA-DEL TORO.
HER BROTHER'S NAME IS HECTOR...
...AYALA. THE WHITE TIGER.
HE DIED LAST YEAR.
I KNOW.
IN YOUR ARMS.
I REMEMBER.
THE FEDERAL AGENT ASSIGNED TO MY CASE--
THE FEDERAL AGENT WHOSE JOB IT IS TO BUILD A CASE AGAINST ME ON THE ALLEGATIONS THAT I AM DAREDEVIL...
...IS HECTOR AYALA'S NIECE.
I ASKED FOR YOUR CASE.
YOU ASKED FOR MY CASE.
I NEED-- I WANT TO UNDERSTAND WHY YOU DO THIS.
WHY WOULD YOU PUT ON A COSTUME AND FIGHT PEOPLE?
WHY??
WHY DID HECTOR AYALA PUT ON A WHITE COSTUME AND BEAT UP PEOPLE??!!
WELL...BAD PEOPLE.
I'VE STUDIED YOU FOR MONTHS. MONTHS!
AND I STILL DON'T KNOW WHY.
SO I'M ASKING--I'M BEGGING YOU TO TELL ME...
WHY??

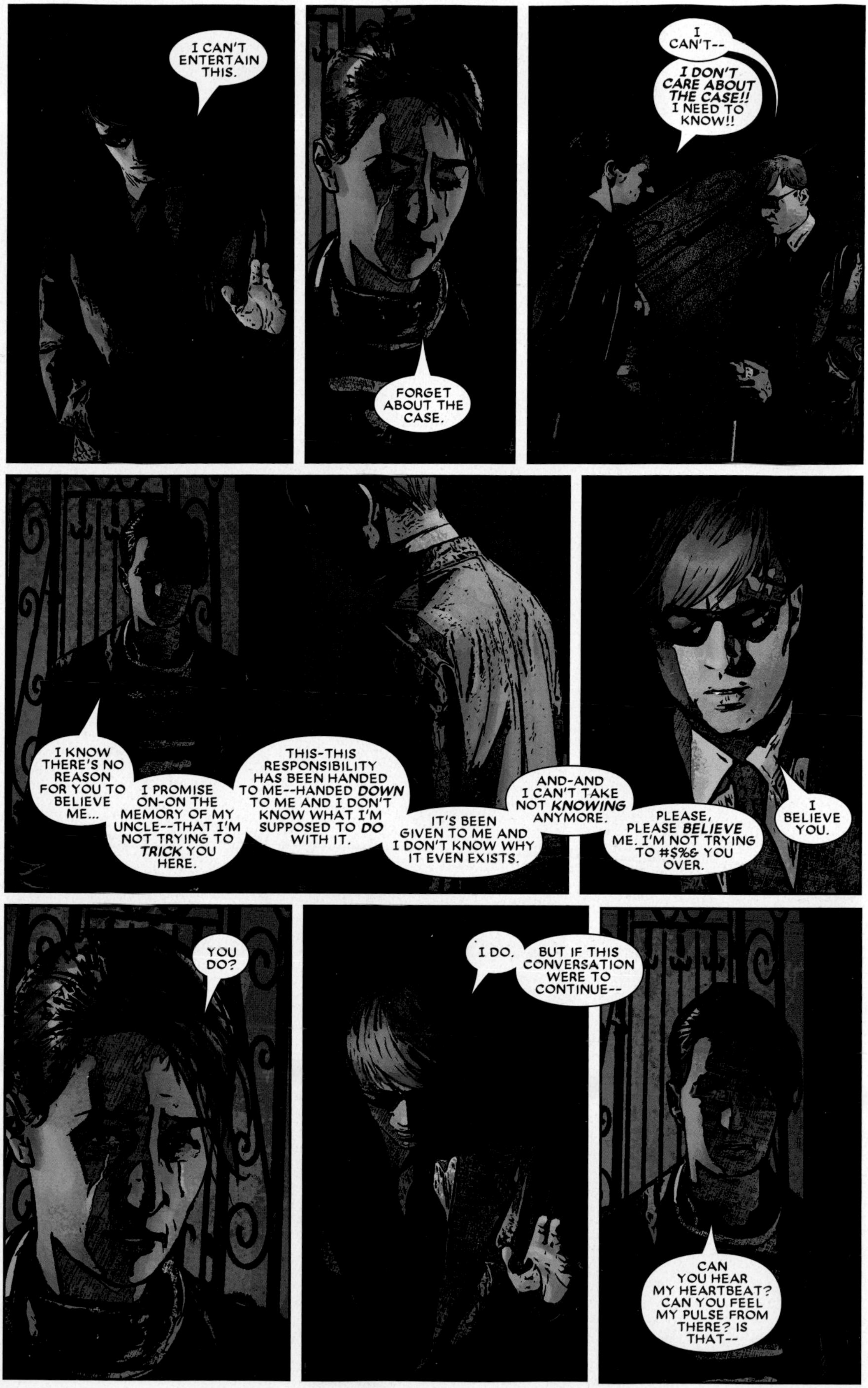
I CAN'T ENTERTAIN THIS.
FORGET ABOUT THE CASE.
I CAN'T--
I DON'T CARE ABOUT THE CASE!! I NEED TO KNOW!!
I KNOW THERE'S NO REASON FOR YOU TO BELIEVE ME...
I PROMISE ON-ON THE MEMORY OF MY UNCLE--THAT I'M NOT TRYING TO TRICK YOU HERE.
THIS-THIS RESPONSIBILITY HAS BEEN HANDED TO ME--HANDED DOWN TO ME AND I DON'T KNOW WHAT I'M SUPPOSED TO DO WITH IT.
IT'S BEEN GIVEN TO ME AND I DON'T KNOW WHY IT EVEN EXISTS.
AND-AND I CAN'T TAKE NOT KNOWING ANYMORE.
PLEASE, PLEASE BELIEVE ME. I'M NOT TRYING TO #$%& YOU OVER.
I BELIEVE YOU.
YOU DO?
I DO.
BUT IF THIS CONVERSATION WERE TO CONTINUE--
CAN YOU HEAR MY HEARTBEAT? CAN YOU FEEL MY PULSE FROM THERE? IS THAT--

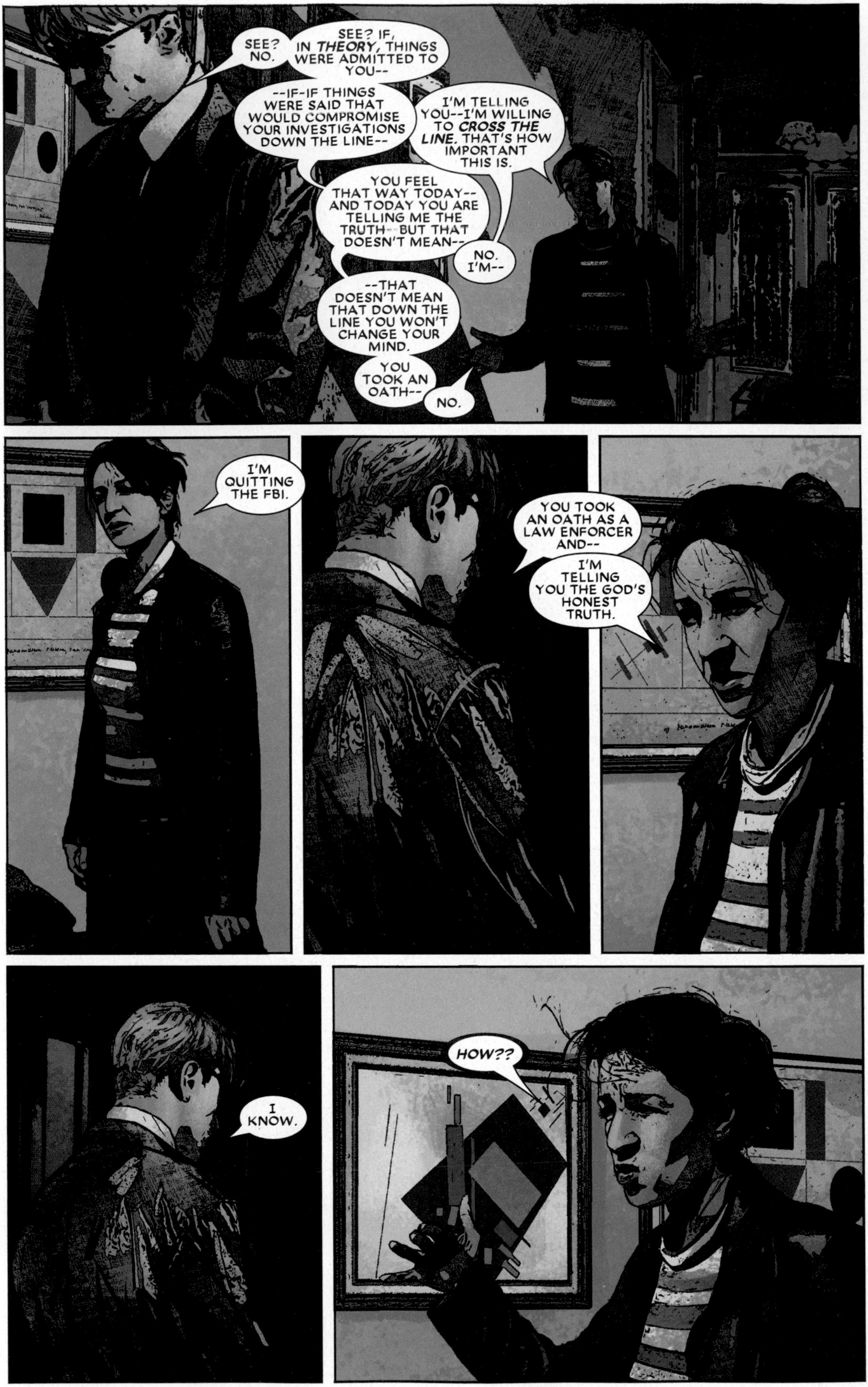
SEE? NO.
SEE? IF, IN THEORY, THINGS WERE ADMITTED TO YOU--
--IF-IF THINGS WERE SAID THAT WOULD COMPROMISE YOUR INVESTIGATIONS DOWN THE LINE--
I'M TELLING YOU--I'M WILLING TO CROSS THE LINE. THAT'S HOW IMPORTANT THIS IS.
YOU FEEL THAT WAY TODAY--AND TODAY YOU ARE TELLING ME THE TRUTH--BUT THAT DOESN'T MEAN--
NO. I'M--
--THAT DOESN'T MEAN THAT DOWN THE LINE YOU WON'T CHANGE YOUR MIND.
YOU TOOK AN OATH--
NO.
I'M QUITTING THE FBI.
YOU TOOK AN OATH AS A LAW ENFORCER AND--
I'M TELLING YOU THE GOD'S HONEST TRUTH.
I KNOW.
HOW??

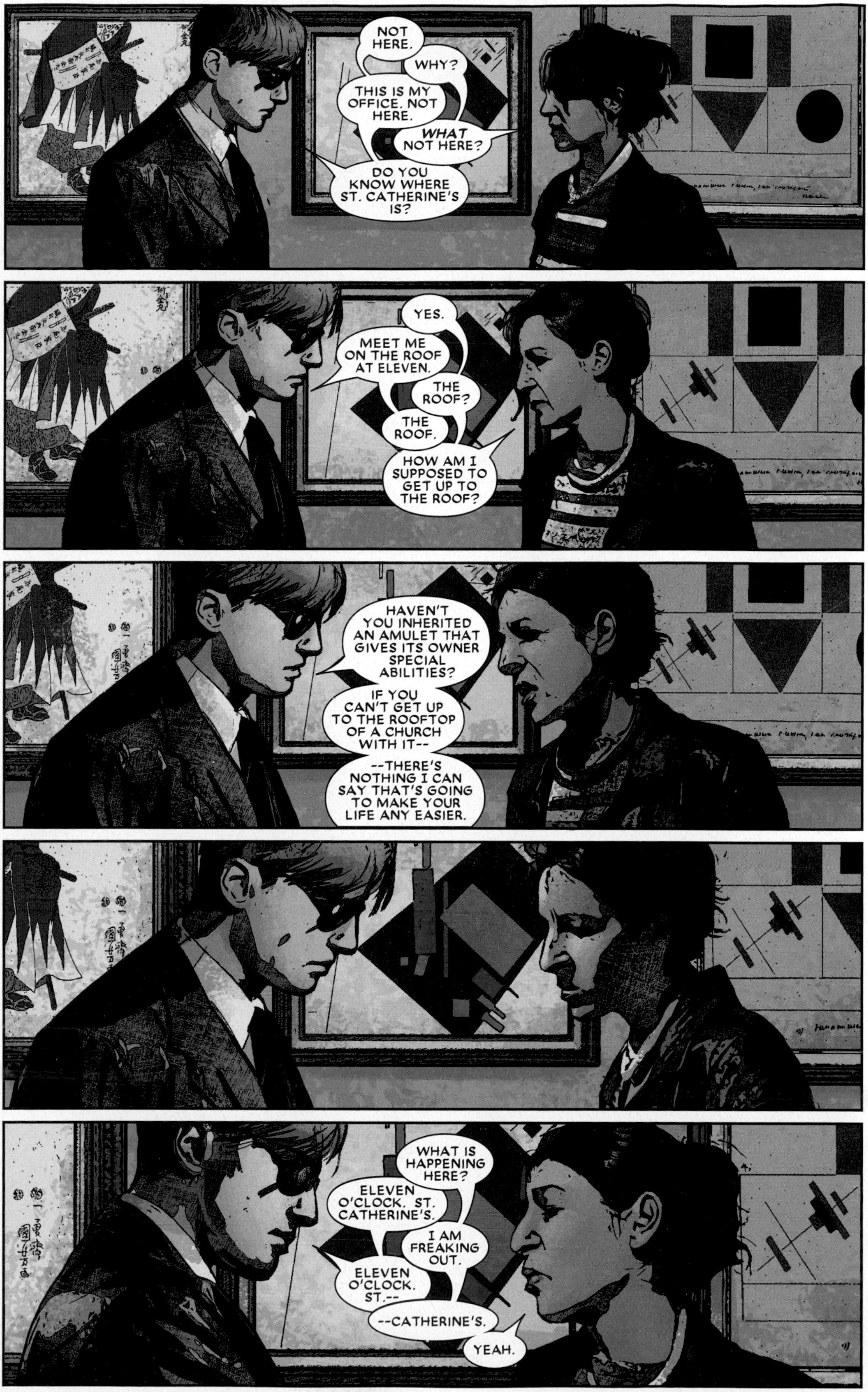
NOT HERE.
WHY?
THIS IS MY OFFICE. NOT HERE.
WHAT NOT HERE?
DO YOU KNOW WHERE ST. CATHERINE'S IS?
YES.
MEET ME ON THE ROOF AT ELEVEN.
THE ROOF?
THE ROOF.
HOW AM I SUPPOSED TO GET UP TO THE ROOF?
HAVEN'T YOU INHERITED AN AMULET THAT GIVES ITS OWNER SPECIAL ABILITIES?
IF YOU CAN'T GET UP TO THE ROOFTOP OF A CHURCH WITH IT--
--THERE'S NOTHING I CAN SAY THAT'S GOING TO MAKE YOUR LIFE ANY EASIER.
WHAT IS HAPPENING HERE?
ELEVEN O'CLOCK. ST. CATHERINE'S.
I AM FREAKING OUT.
ELEVEN O'CLOCK. ST.--
--CATHERINE'S.
YEAH.

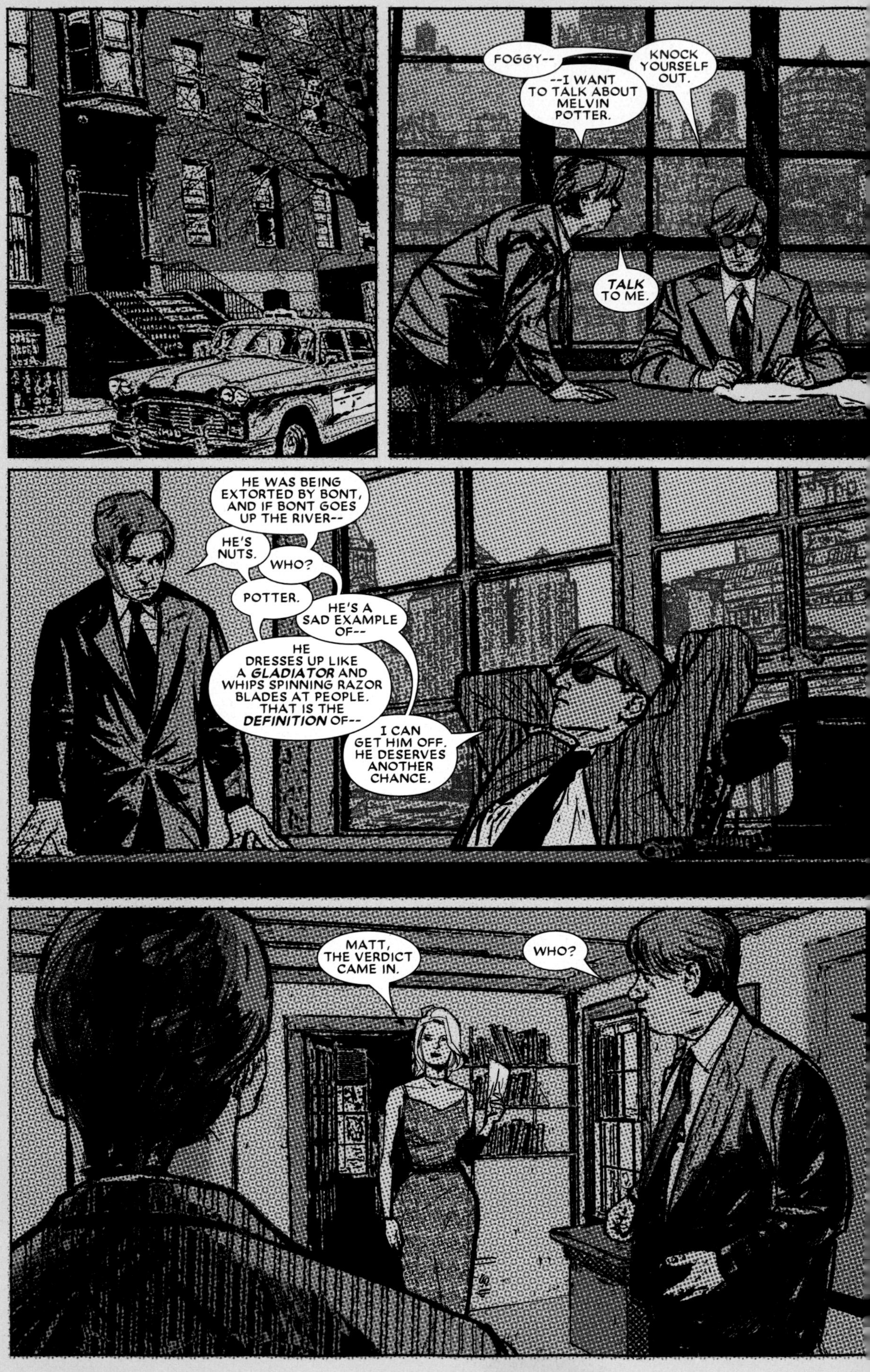
FOGGY--
--I WANT TO TALK ABOUT MELVIN POTTER.
KNOCK YOURSELF OUT.
TALK TO ME.
HE WAS BEING EXTORTED BY BONT, AND IF BONT GOES UP THE RIVER--
HE'S NUTS.
WHO?
POTTER.
HE'S A SAD EXAMPLE OF--
HE DRESSES UP LIKE A *GLADIATOR* AND WHIPS SPINNING RAZOR BLADES AT PEOPLE. THAT IS THE *DEFINITION* OF--
I CAN GET HIM OFF. HE DESERVES ANOTHER CHANCE.
MATT, THE VERDICT CAME IN.
WHO?

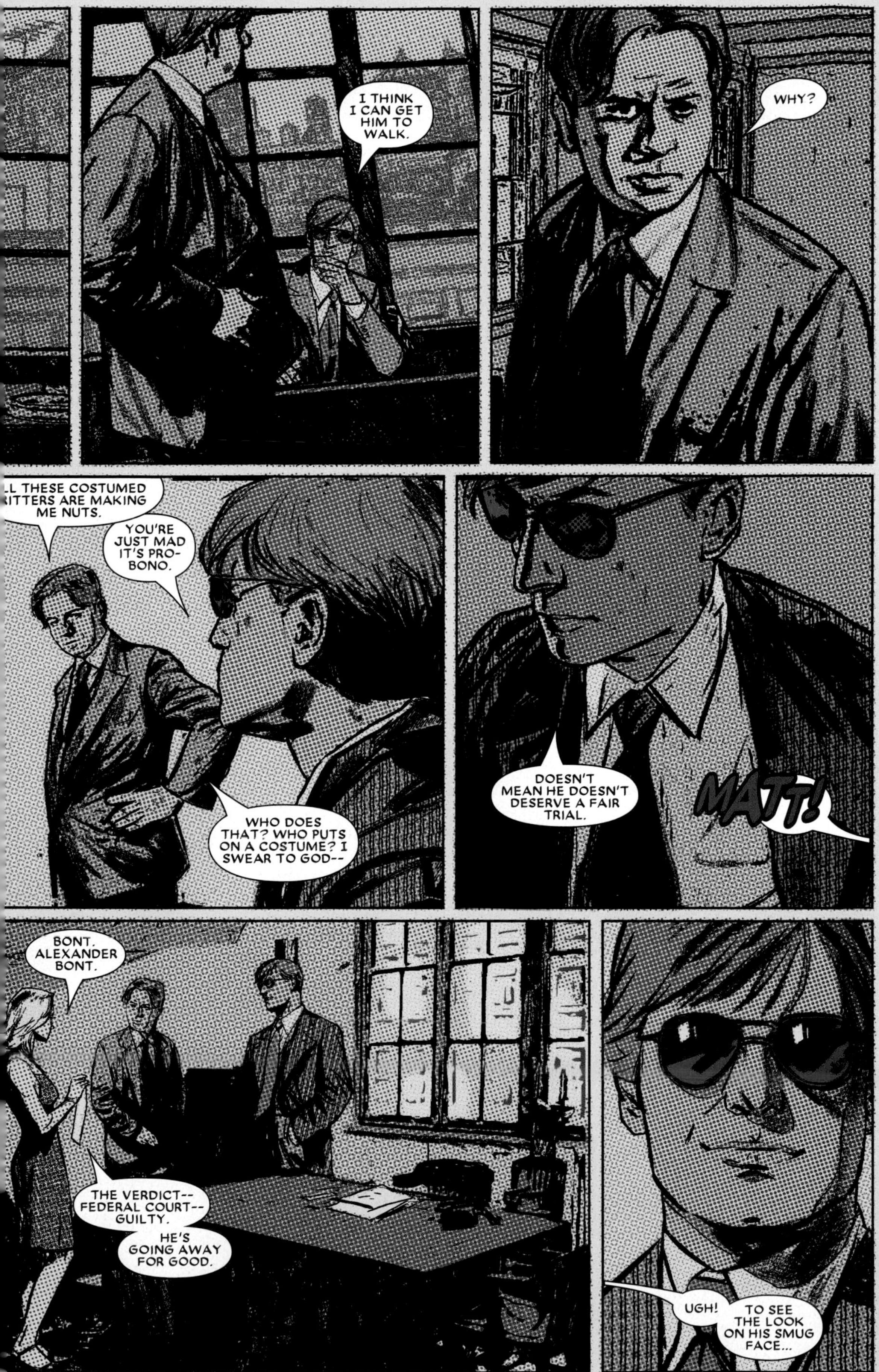

I THINK I CAN GET HIM TO WALK.
WHY?
LL THESE COSTUMED RITTERS ARE MAKING ME NUTS.
YOU'RE JUST MAD IT'S PRO-BONO.
WHO DOES THAT? WHO PUTS ON A COSTUME? I SWEAR TO GOD--
DOESN'T MEAN HE DOESN'T DESERVE A FAIR TRIAL.
MATT!
BONT. ALEXANDER BONT.
THE VERDICT-- FEDERAL COURT-- GUILTY.
HE'S GOING AWAY FOR GOOD.
UGH!
TO SEE THE LOOK ON HIS SMUG FACE...

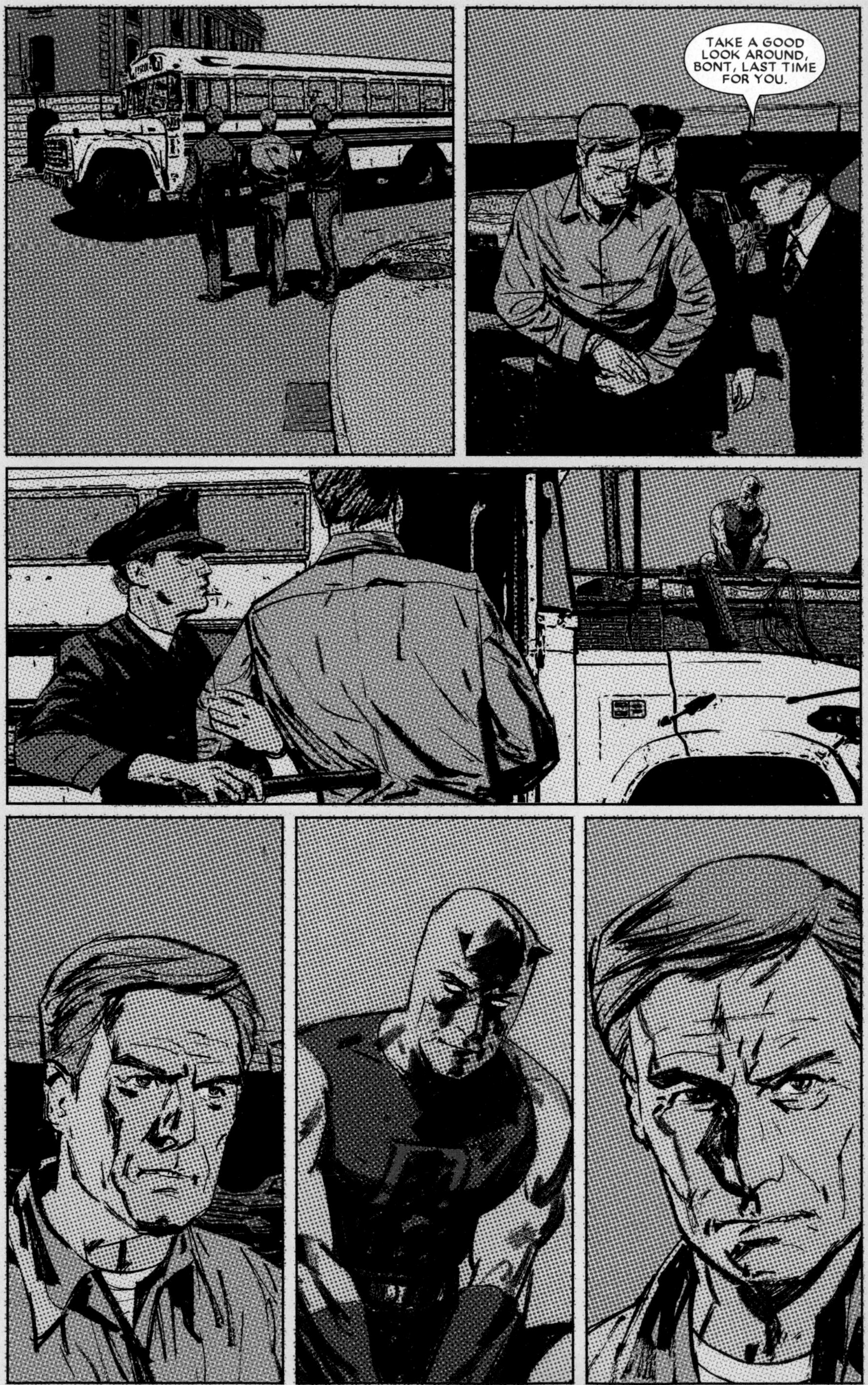
TAKE A GOOD LOOK AROUND, BONT, LAST TIME FOR YOU.

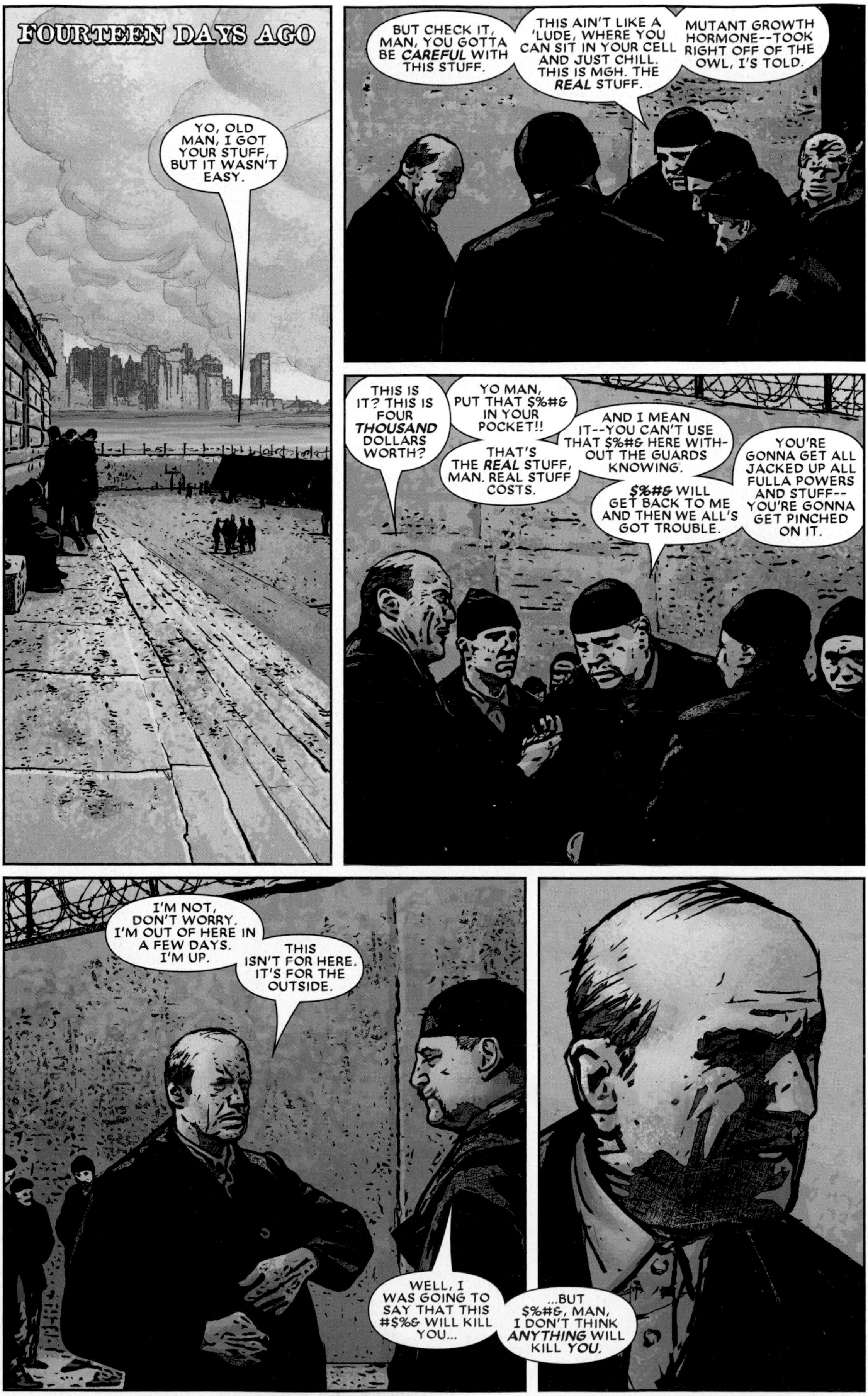
FOURTEEN DAYS AGO
YO, OLD MAN, I GOT YOUR STUFF, BUT IT WASN'T EASY.
BUT CHECK IT, MAN, YOU GOTTA BE CAREFUL WITH THIS STUFF.
THIS AIN'T LIKE A 'LUDE, WHERE YOU CAN SIT IN YOUR CELL AND JUST CHILL. THIS IS MGH. THE REAL STUFF.
MUTANT GROWTH HORMONE--TOOK RIGHT OFF OF THE OWL, I'S TOLD.
THIS IS IT? THIS IS FOUR THOUSAND DOLLARS WORTH?
YO MAN, PUT THAT $%#& IN YOUR POCKET!!
THAT'S THE REAL STUFF, MAN. REAL STUFF COSTS.
AND I MEAN IT--YOU CAN'T USE THAT $%#& HERE WITH-OUT THE GUARDS KNOWING.
$%#& WILL GET BACK TO ME AND THEN WE ALL'S GOT TROUBLE.
YOU'RE GONNA GET ALL JACKED UP ALL FULLA POWERS AND STUFF-- YOU'RE GONNA GET PINCHED ON IT.
I'M NOT, DON'T WORRY. I'M OUT OF HERE IN A FEW DAYS. I'M UP.
THIS ISN'T FOR HERE. IT'S FOR THE OUTSIDE.
WELL, I WAS GOING TO SAY THAT THIS #$%& WILL KILL YOU...
...BUT $%#&, MAN, I DON'T THINK ANYTHING WILL KILL YOU.

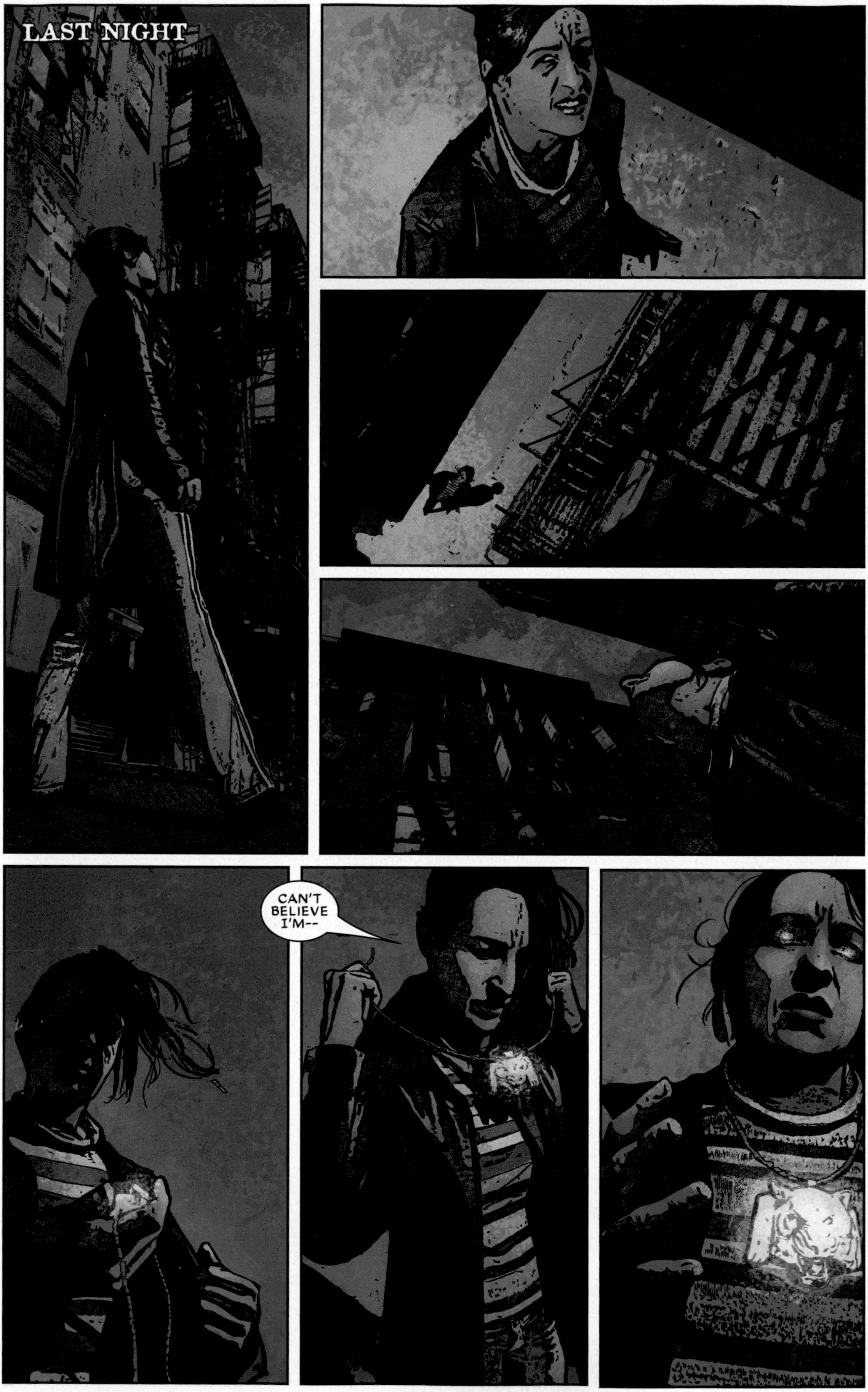
LAST NIGHT
CAN'T BELIEVE I'M--

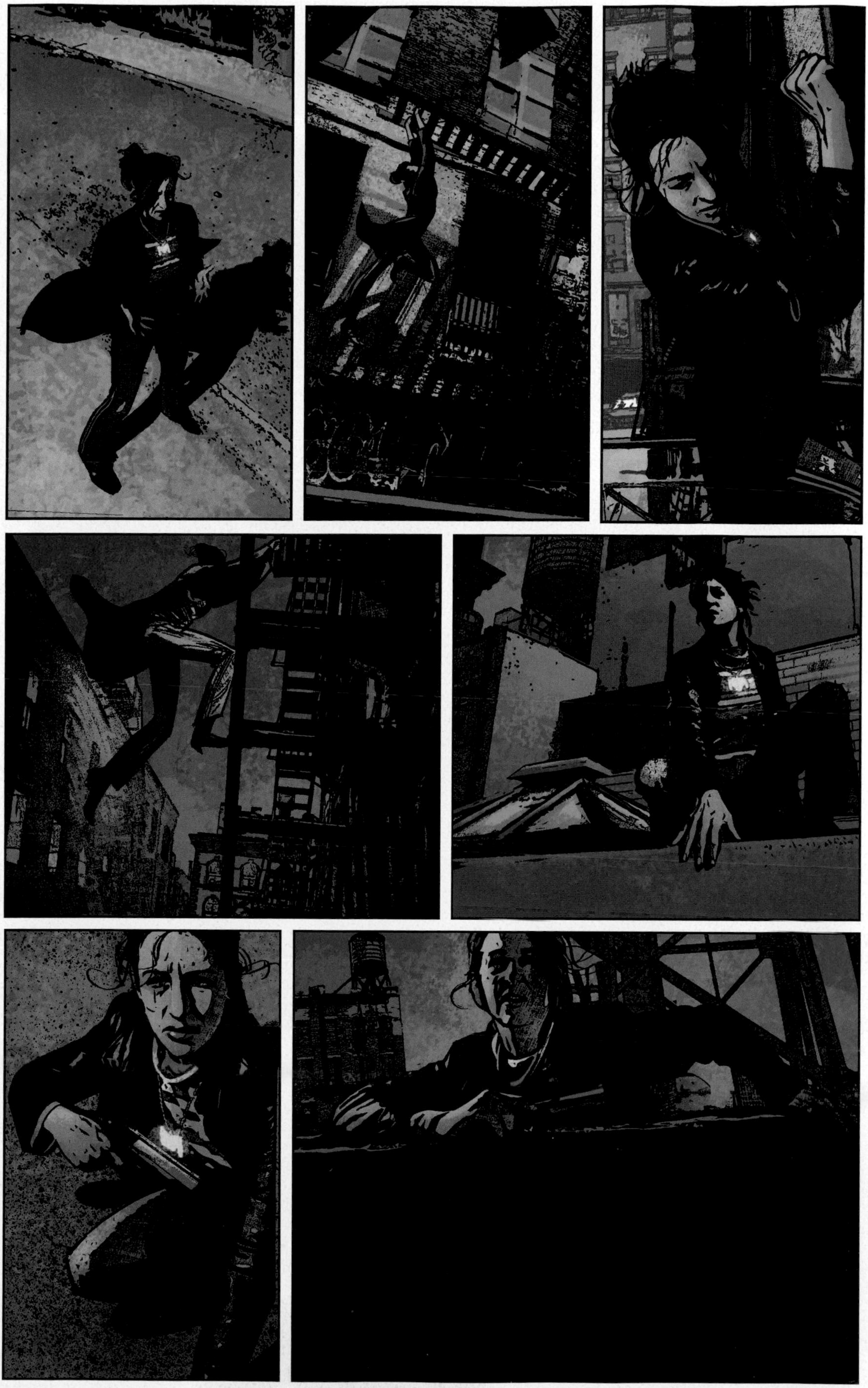

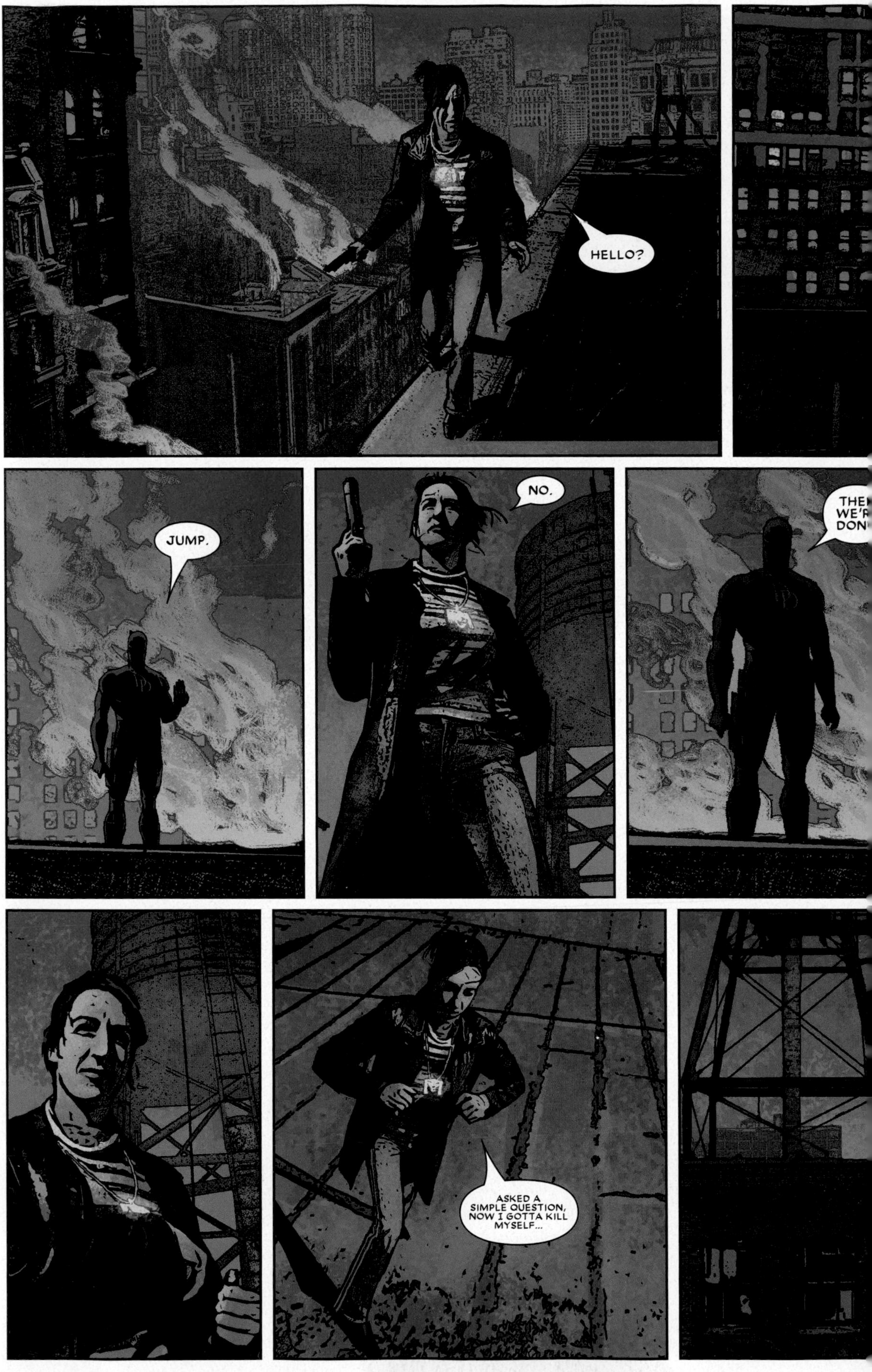
HELLO?
JUMP.
NO.
THE
WE'R
DON
ASKED A SIMPLE QUESTION, NOW I GOTTA KILL MYSELF...

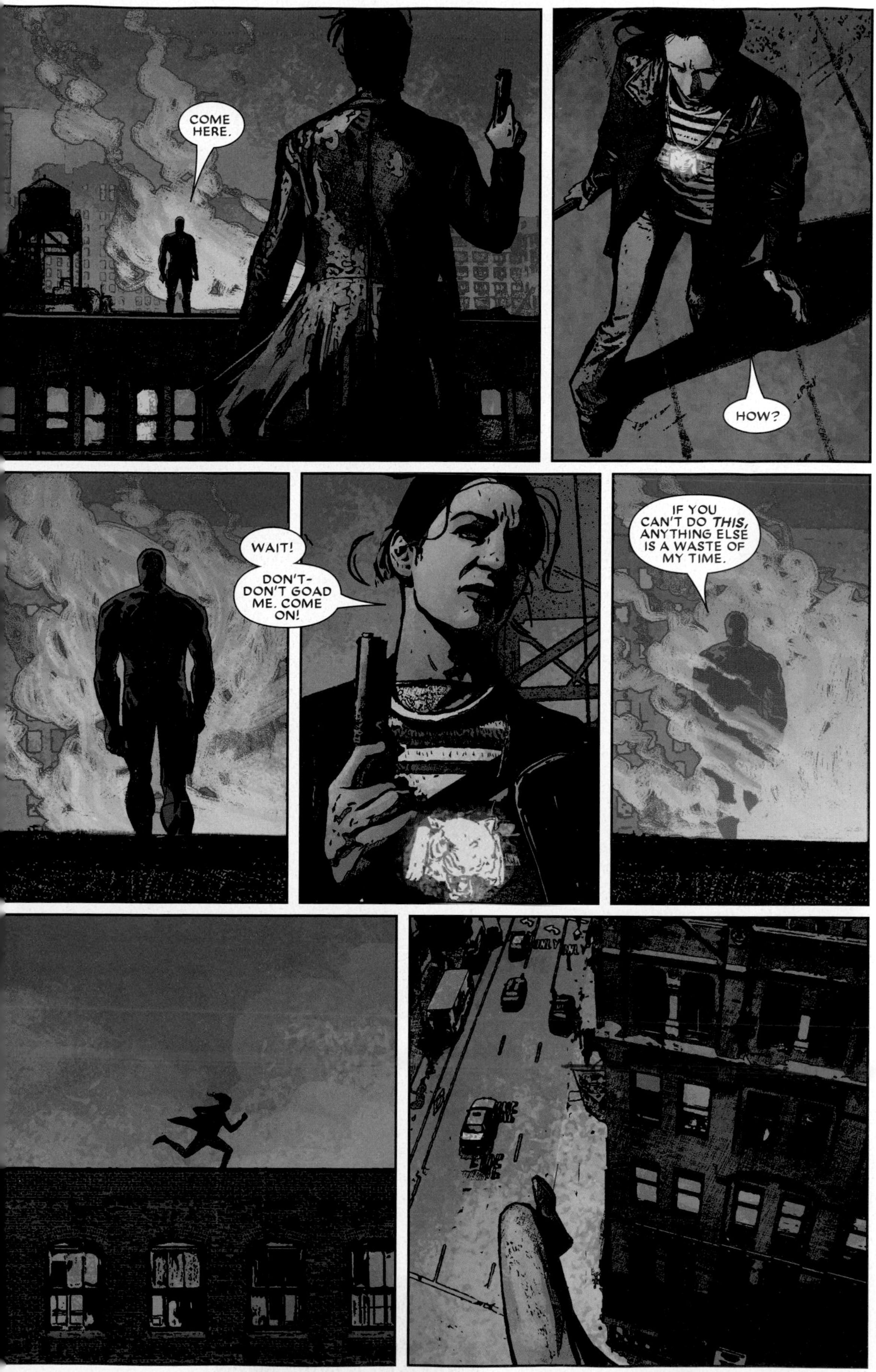
COME HERE.
HOW?
WAIT!
DON'T- DON'T GOAD ME. COME ON!
IF YOU CAN'T DO THIS, ANYTHING ELSE IS A WASTE OF MY TIME.

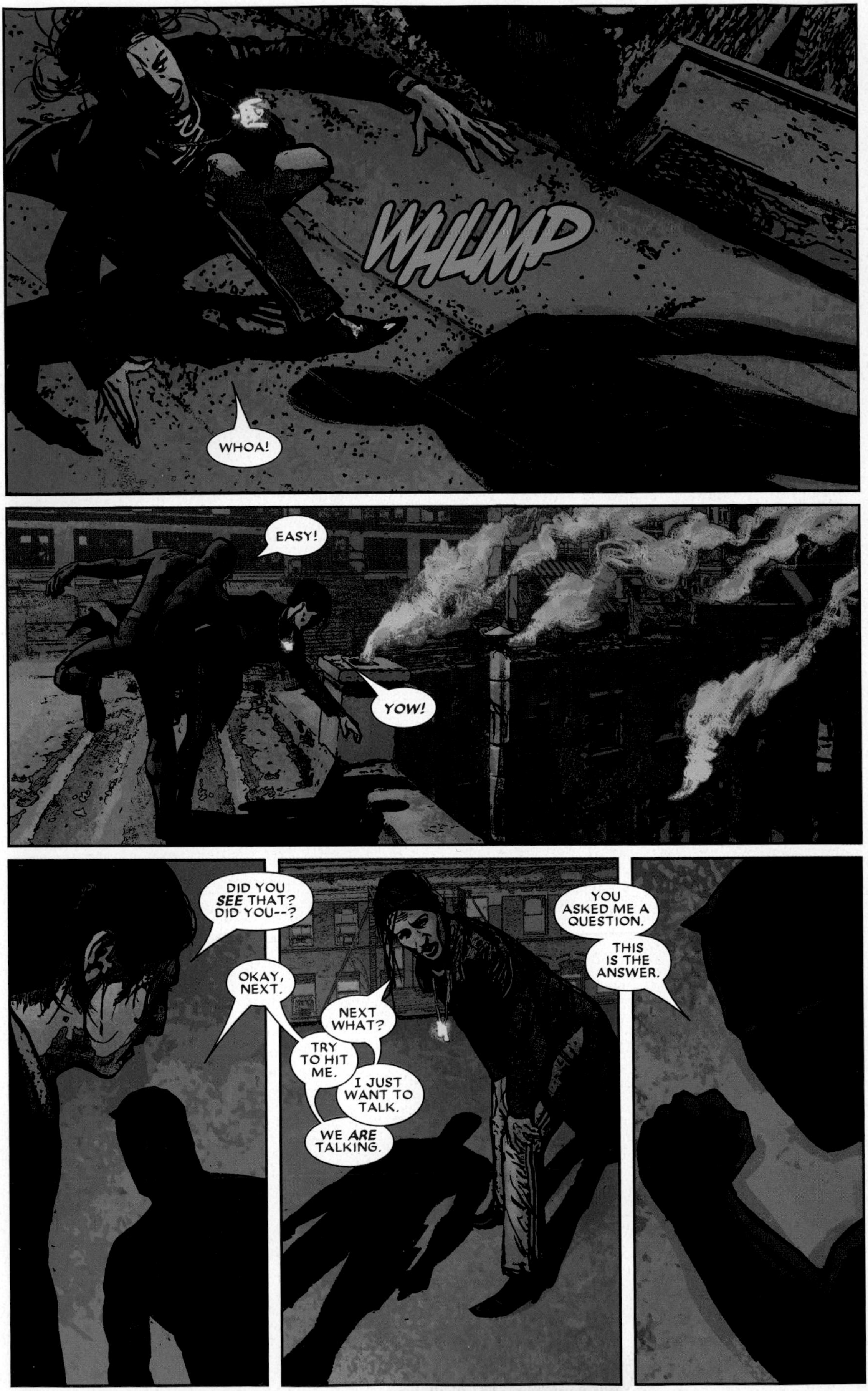

WHLUMP
WHOA!
EASY!
YOW!
DID YOU SEE THAT? DID YOU--?
OKAY, NEXT.
NEXT WHAT?
TRY TO HIT ME.
I JUST WANT TO TALK.
WE ARE TALKING.
YOU ASKED ME A QUESTION.
THIS IS THE ANSWER.

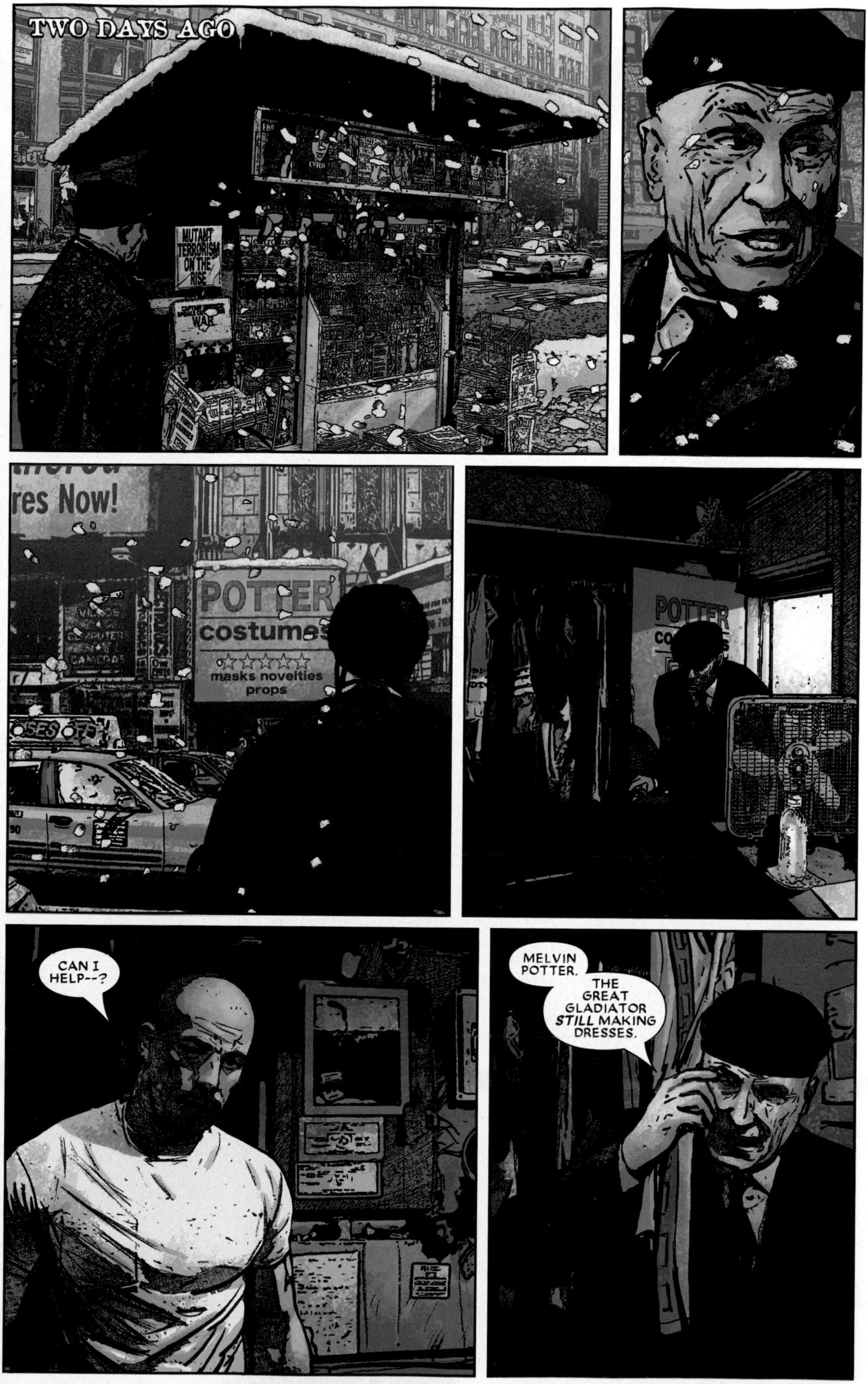
TWO DAYS AGO
MUTANT TERRORISM ON THE RISE
WAR
res Now!
POTTER
costumes
masks novelties
props
CAN I HELP--?
MELVIN POTTER.
THE GREAT GLADIATOR *STILL* MAKING DRESSES.

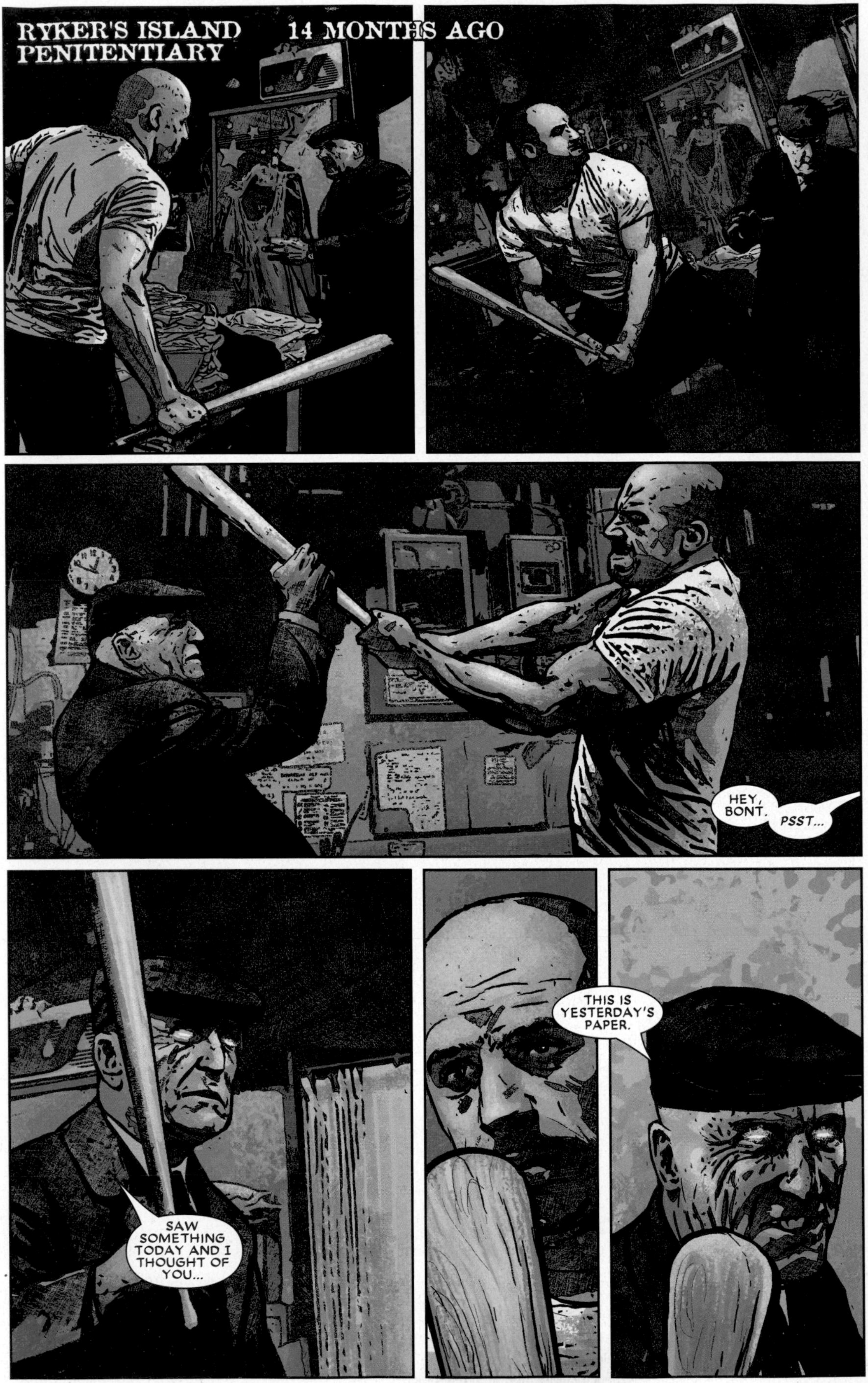
RYKER'S ISLAND PENITENTIARY
14 MONTHS AGO
HEY, BONT.
PSST...
SAW SOMETHING TODAY AND I THOUGHT OF YOU...
THIS IS YESTERDAY'S PAPER.

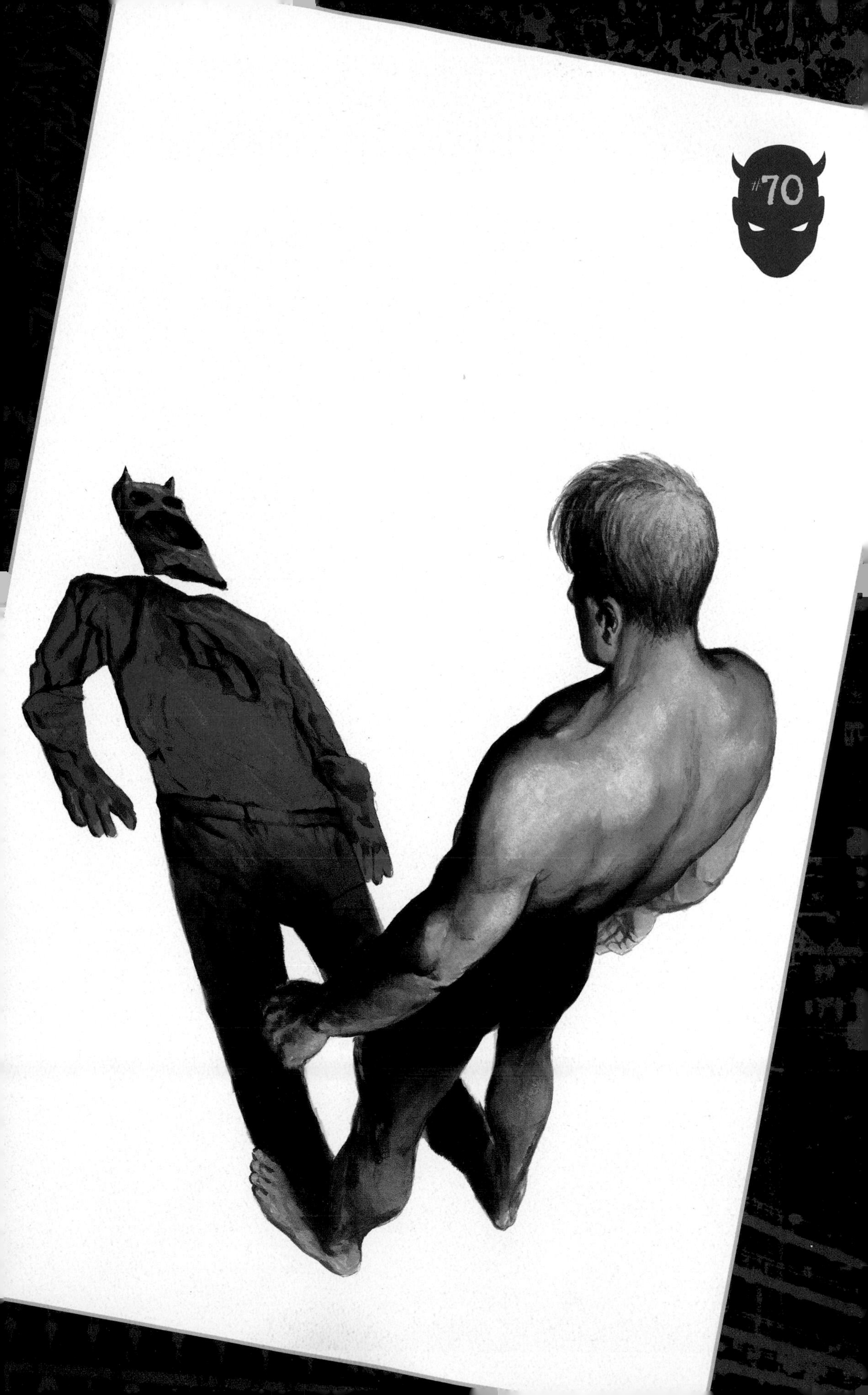
#70

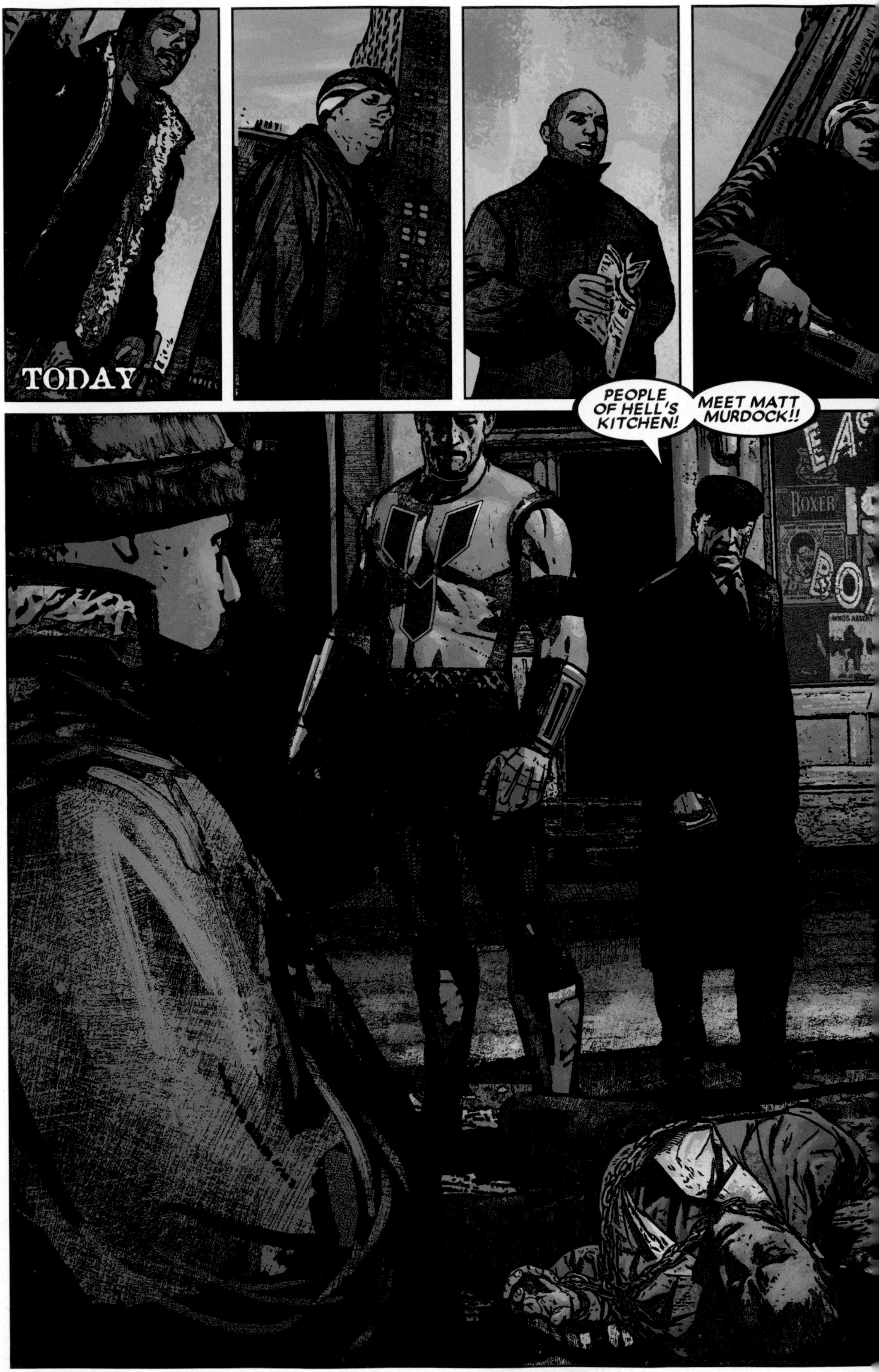
TODAY
PEOPLE OF HELL'S KITCHEN!
MEET MATT MURDOCK!!
BOXER

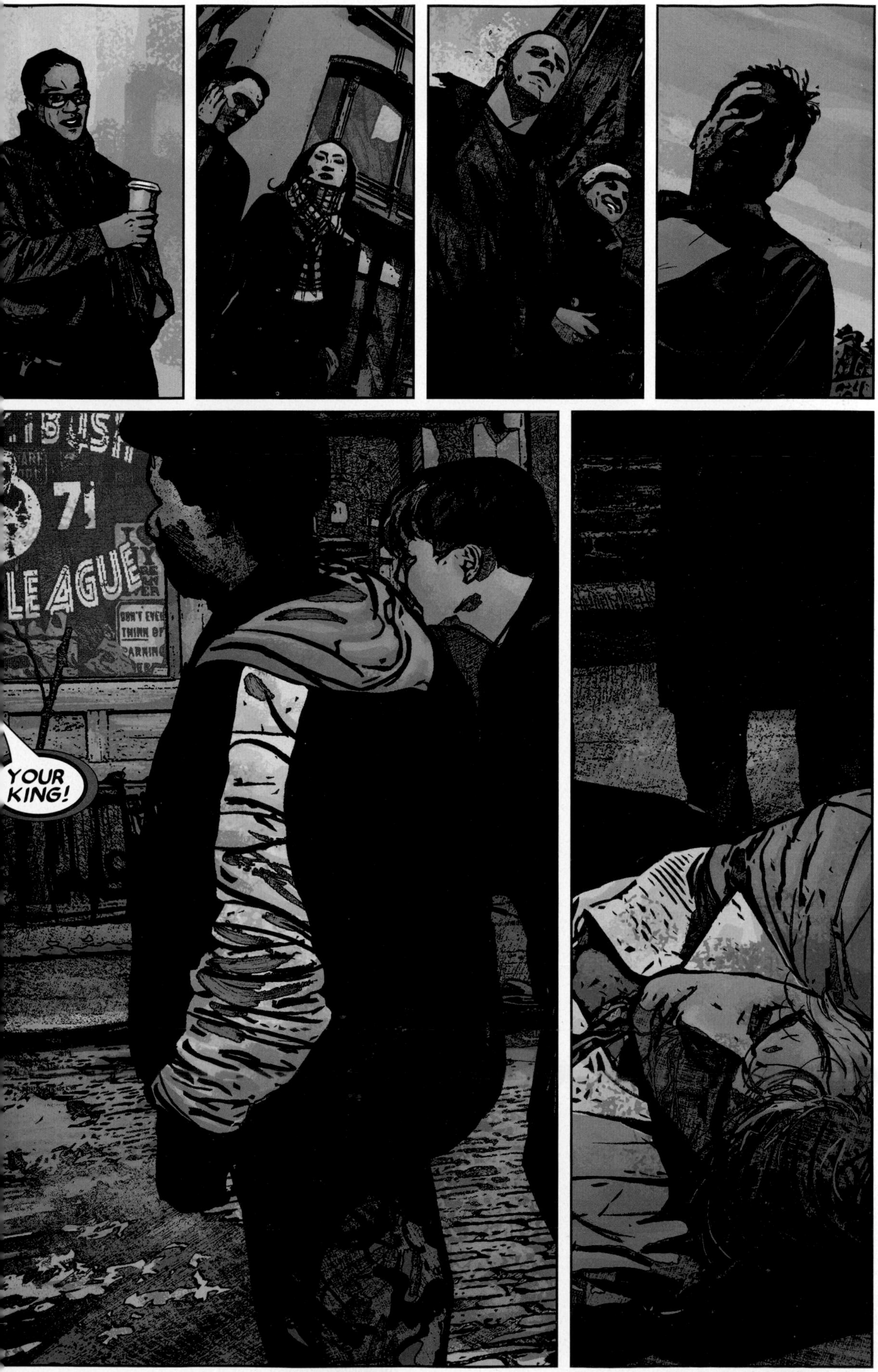
YOUR KING!

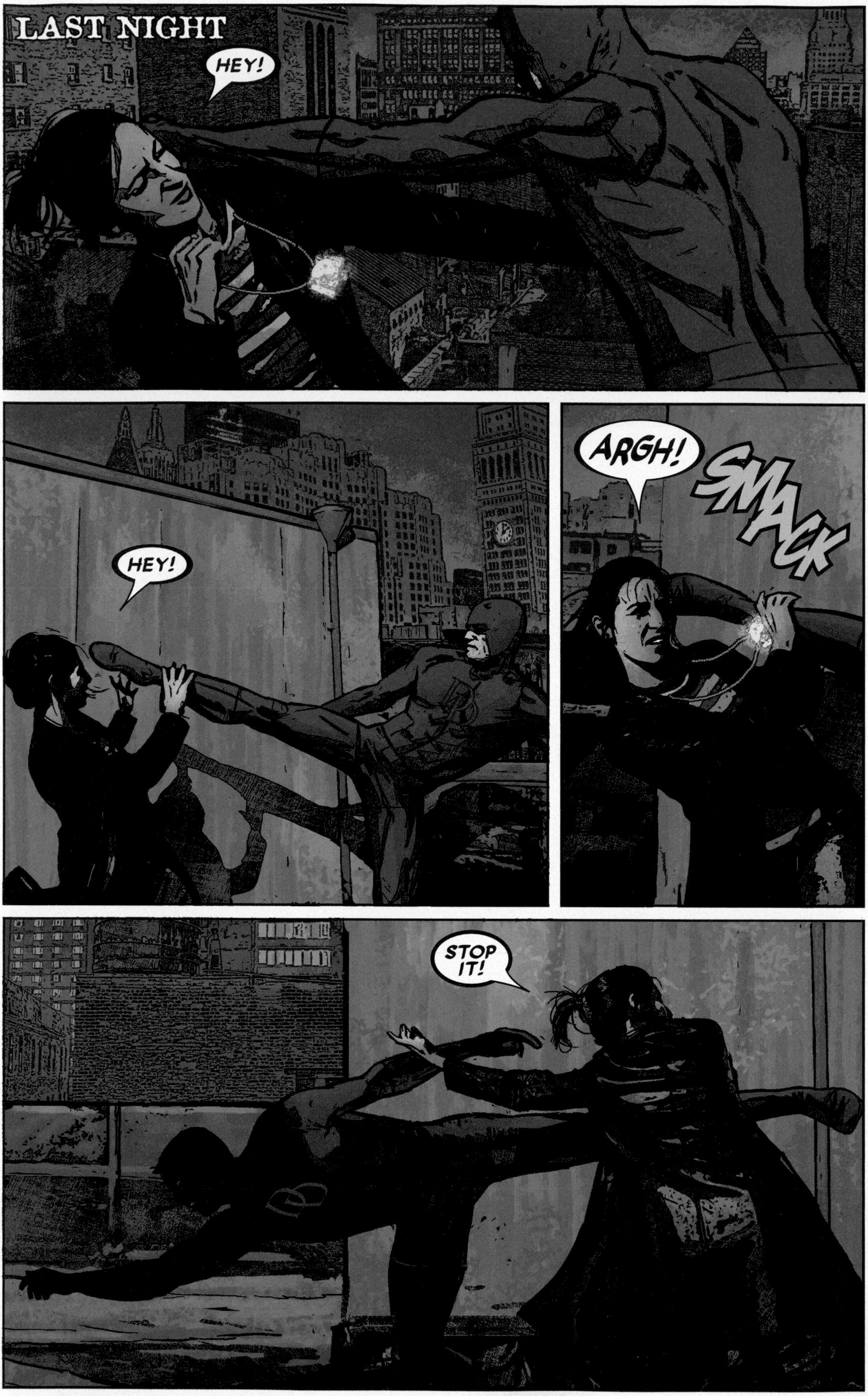
LAST NIGHT
HEY!
HEY!
ARGH!
SMACK
STOP IT!

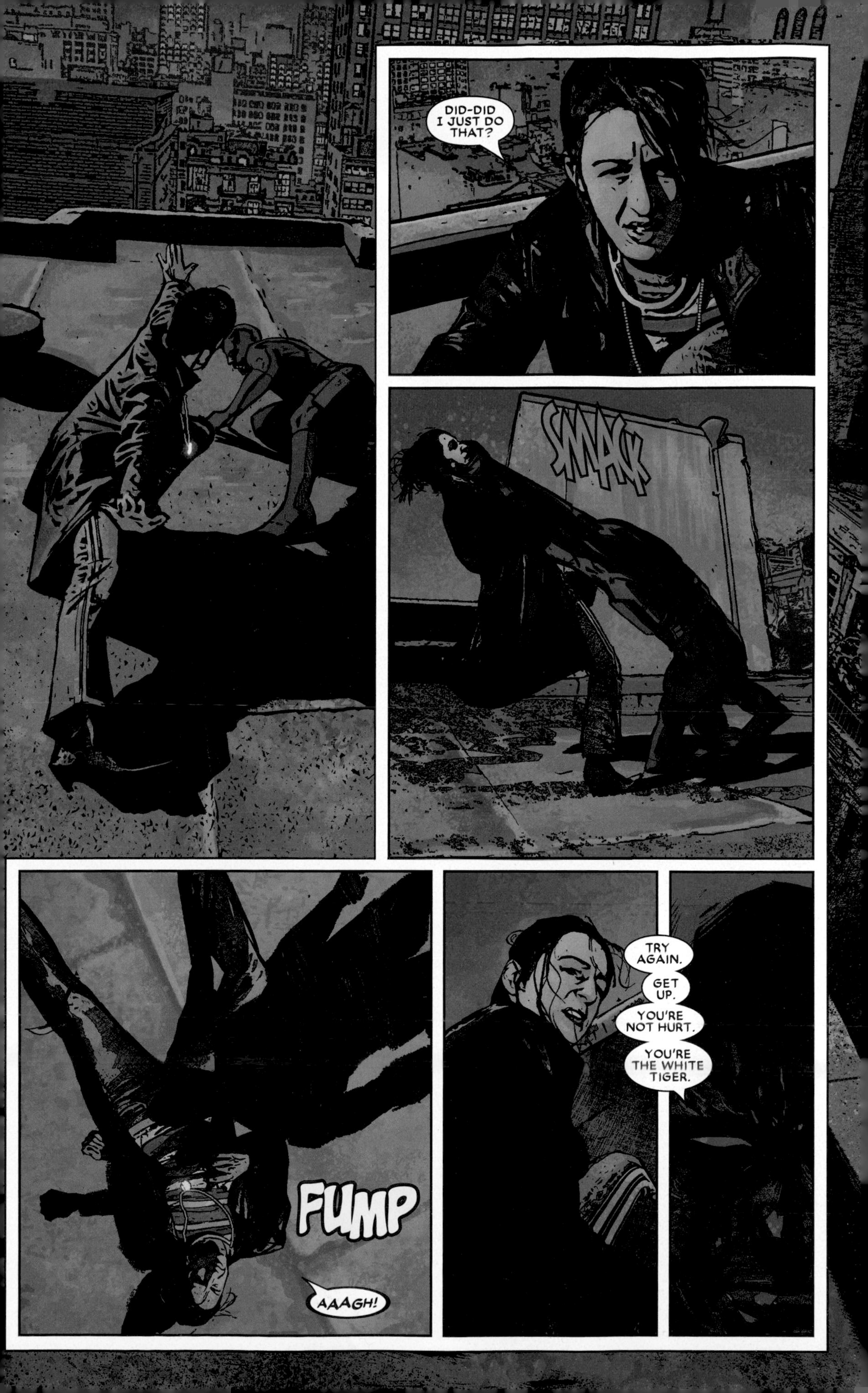
DID-DID I JUST DO THAT?
SMACK
FUMP
AAAGH!
TRY AGAIN.
GET UP.
YOU'RE NOT HURT.
YOU'RE THE WHITE TIGER.

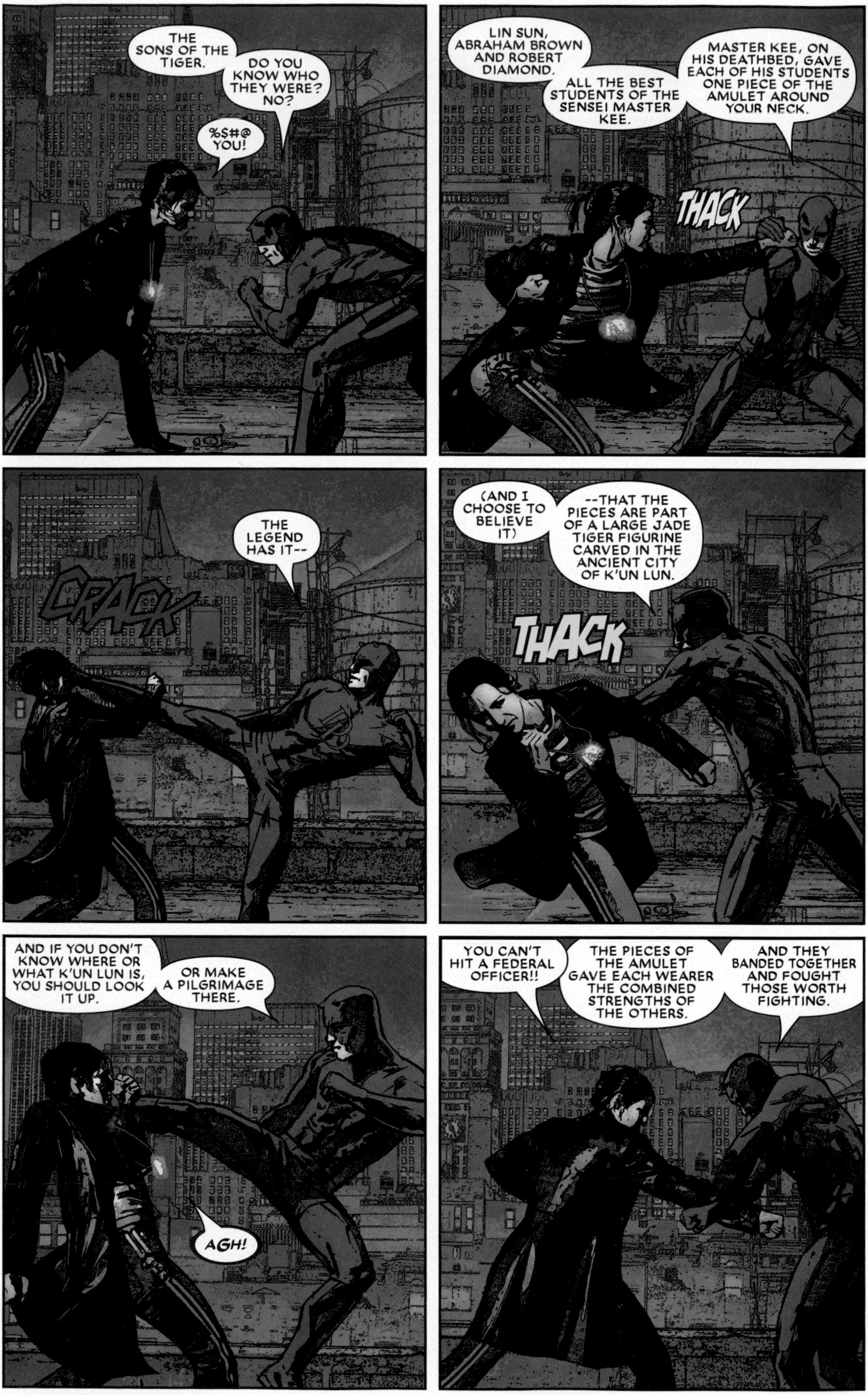
THE SONS OF THE TIGER.
DO YOU KNOW WHO THEY WERE? NO?
%$#@ YOU!
LIN SUN, ABRAHAM BROWN AND ROBERT DIAMOND.
ALL THE BEST STUDENTS OF THE SENSEI MASTER KEE.
MASTER KEE, ON HIS DEATHBED, GAVE EACH OF HIS STUDENTS ONE PIECE OF THE AMULET AROUND YOUR NECK.
THACK
THE LEGEND HAS IT--
CRACK
(AND I CHOOSE TO BELIEVE IT)
--THAT THE PIECES ARE PART OF A LARGE JADE TIGER FIGURINE CARVED IN THE ANCIENT CITY OF K'UN LUN.
THACK
AND IF YOU DON'T KNOW WHERE OR WHAT K'UN LUN IS, YOU SHOULD LOOK IT UP.
OR MAKE A PILGRIMAGE THERE.
AGH!
YOU CAN'T HIT A FEDERAL OFFICER!!
THE PIECES OF THE AMULET GAVE EACH WEARER THE COMBINED STRENGTHS OF THE OTHERS.
AND THEY BANDED TOGETHER AND FOUGHT THOSE WORTH FIGHTING.

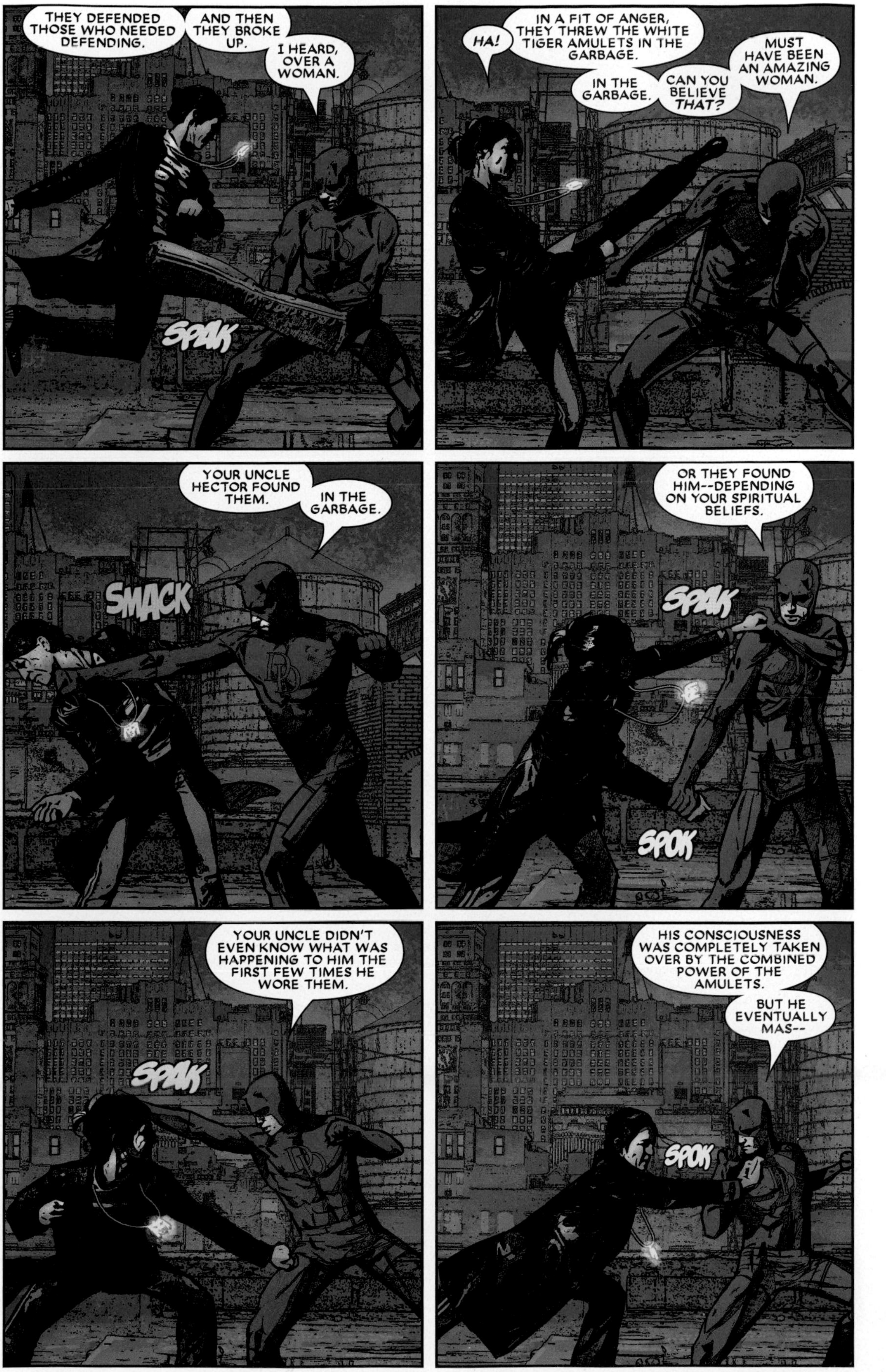
THEY DEFENDED THOSE WHO NEEDED DEFENDING.
AND THEN THEY BROKE UP.
I HEARD, OVER A WOMAN.
SPAK
HA!
IN A FIT OF ANGER, THEY THREW THE WHITE TIGER AMULETS IN THE GARBAGE.
IN THE GARBAGE.
CAN YOU BELIEVE THAT?
MUST HAVE BEEN AN AMAZING WOMAN.
YOUR UNCLE HECTOR FOUND THEM.
IN THE GARBAGE.
SMACK
OR THEY FOUND HIM--DEPENDING ON YOUR SPIRITUAL BELIEFS.
SPAK
SPOK
YOUR UNCLE DIDN'T EVEN KNOW WHAT WAS HAPPENING TO HIM THE FIRST FEW TIMES HE WORE THEM.
SPAK
HIS CONSCIOUSNESS WAS COMPLETELY TAKEN OVER BY THE COMBINED POWER OF THE AMULETS.
BUT HE EVENTUALLY MAS--
SPOK

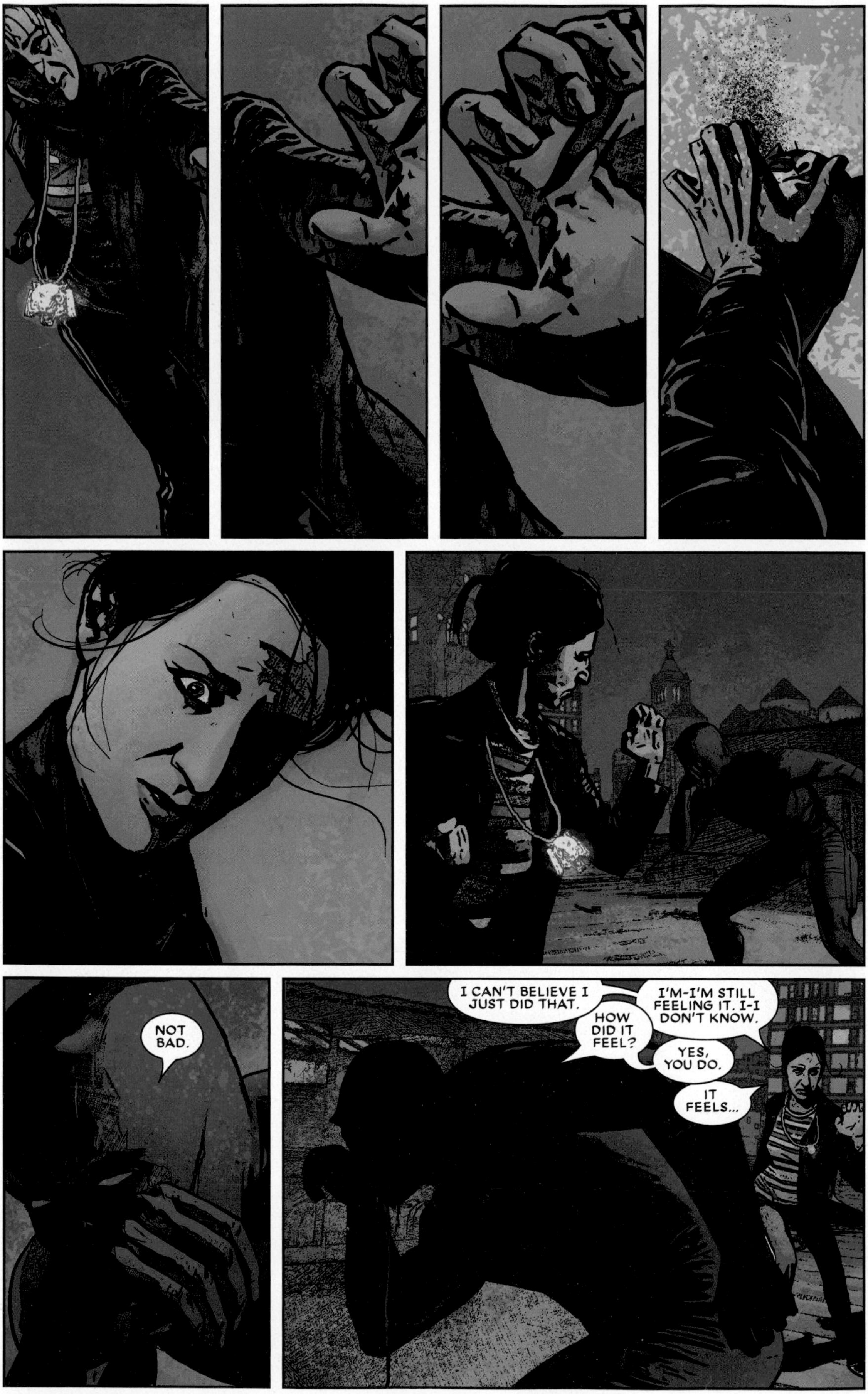
NOT BAD.
I CAN'T BELIEVE I JUST DID THAT.
HOW DID IT FEEL?
I'M-I'M STILL FEELING IT. I-I DON'T KNOW.
YES, YOU DO.
IT FEELS...

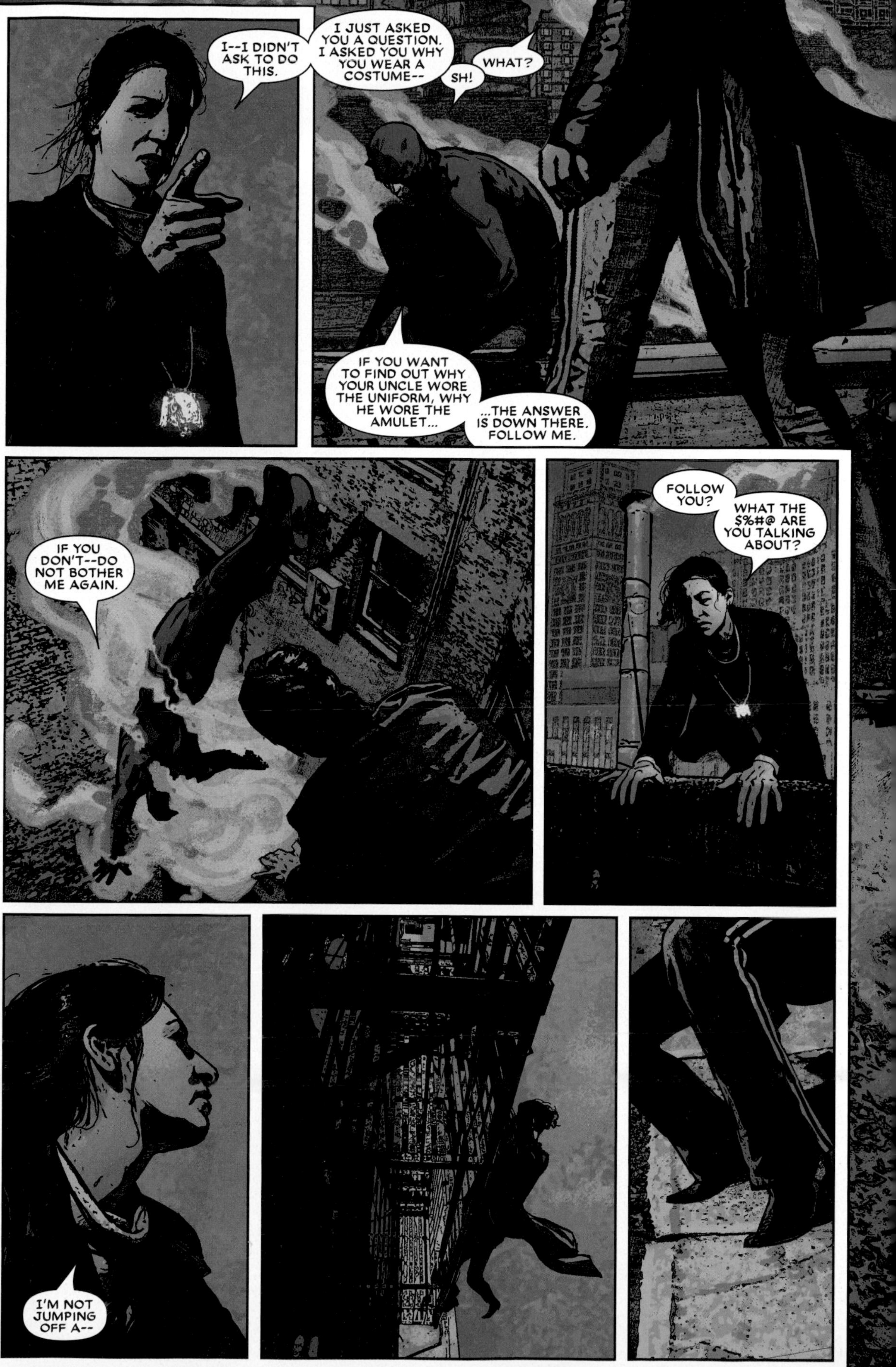
I--I DIDN'T ASK TO DO THIS.
I JUST ASKED YOU A QUESTION. I ASKED YOU WHY YOU WEAR A COSTUME--
WHAT?
SH!
IF YOU WANT TO FIND OUT WHY YOUR UNCLE WORE THE UNIFORM, WHY HE WORE THE AMULET...
...THE ANSWER IS DOWN THERE. FOLLOW ME.
IF YOU DON'T--DO NOT BOTHER ME AGAIN.
FOLLOW YOU?
WHAT THE $%#@ ARE YOU TALKING ABOUT?
I'M NOT JUMPING OFF A--

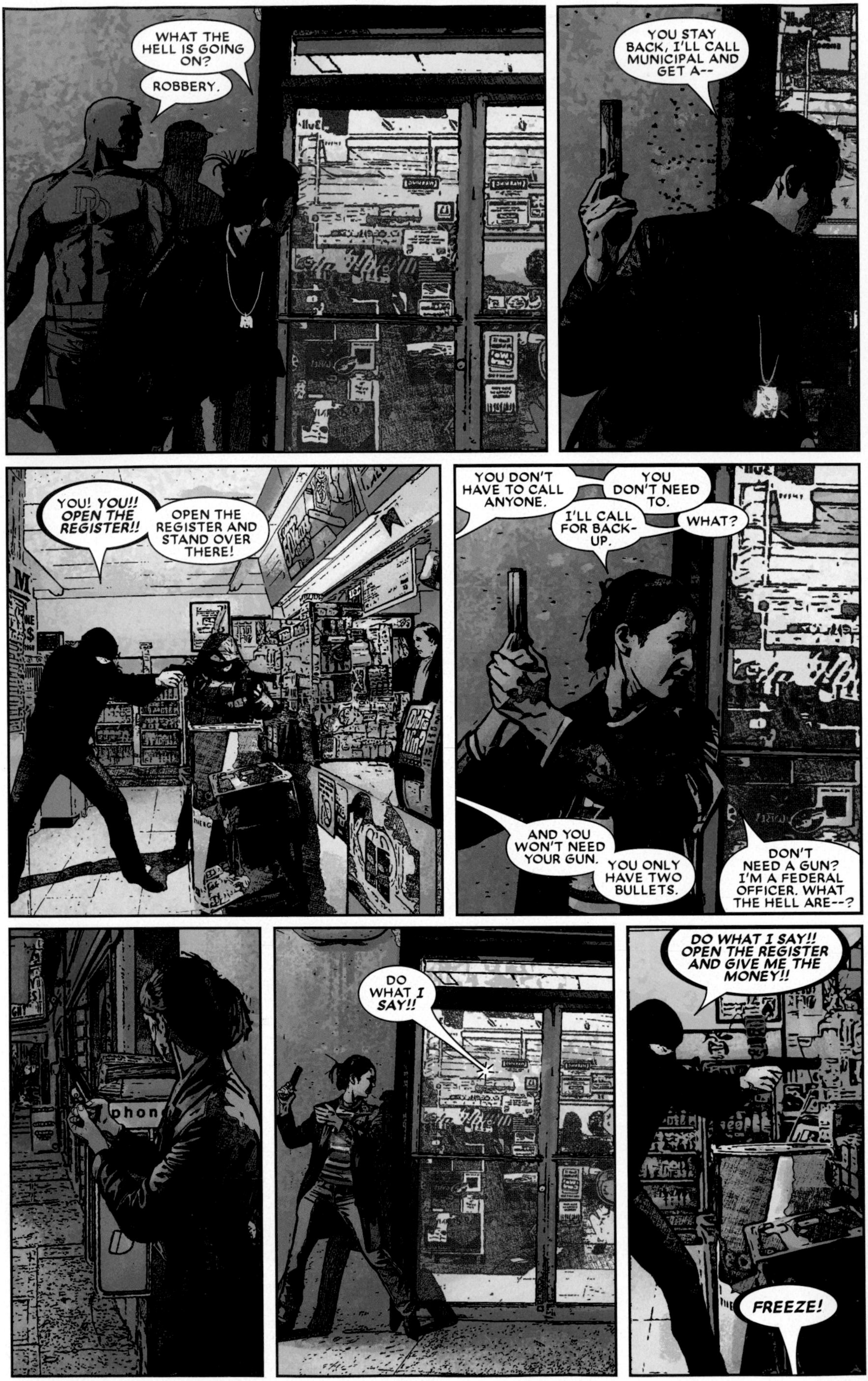
WHAT THE HELL IS GOING ON?
ROBBERY.
YOU STAY BACK, I'LL CALL MUNICIPAL AND GET A--
YOU! YOU!! OPEN THE REGISTER!!
OPEN THE REGISTER AND STAND OVER THERE!
YOU DON'T HAVE TO CALL ANYONE.
YOU DON'T NEED TO.
I'LL CALL FOR BACK-UP.
WHAT?
AND YOU WON'T NEED YOUR GUN.
YOU ONLY HAVE TWO BULLETS.
DON'T NEED A GUN? I'M A FEDERAL OFFICER. WHAT THE HELL ARE--?
DO WHAT I SAY!!
DO WHAT I SAY!! OPEN THE REGISTER AND GIVE ME THE MONEY!!
FREEZE!

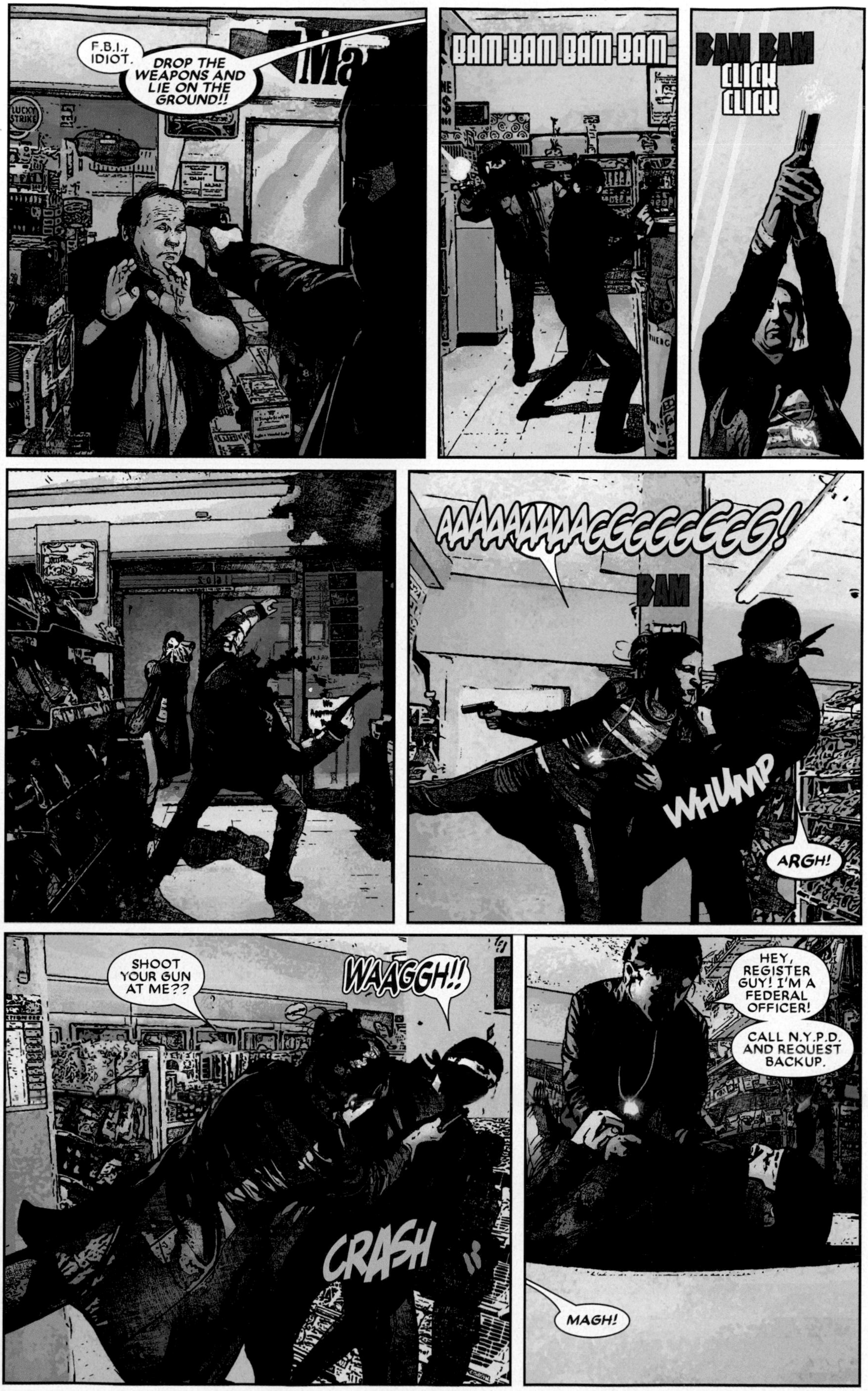
F.B.I., IDIOT.
DROP THE WEAPONS AND LIE ON THE GROUND!!
BAM BAM BAM BAM
BAM BAM
CLICK CLICK
AAAAAAAAGGGGGGG!
BAM
WHUMP
ARGH!
SHOOT YOUR GUN AT ME??
WAAGGH!!
CRASH
HEY, REGISTER GUY! I'M A FEDERAL OFFICER!
CALL N.Y.P.D. AND REQUEST BACKUP.
MAGH!

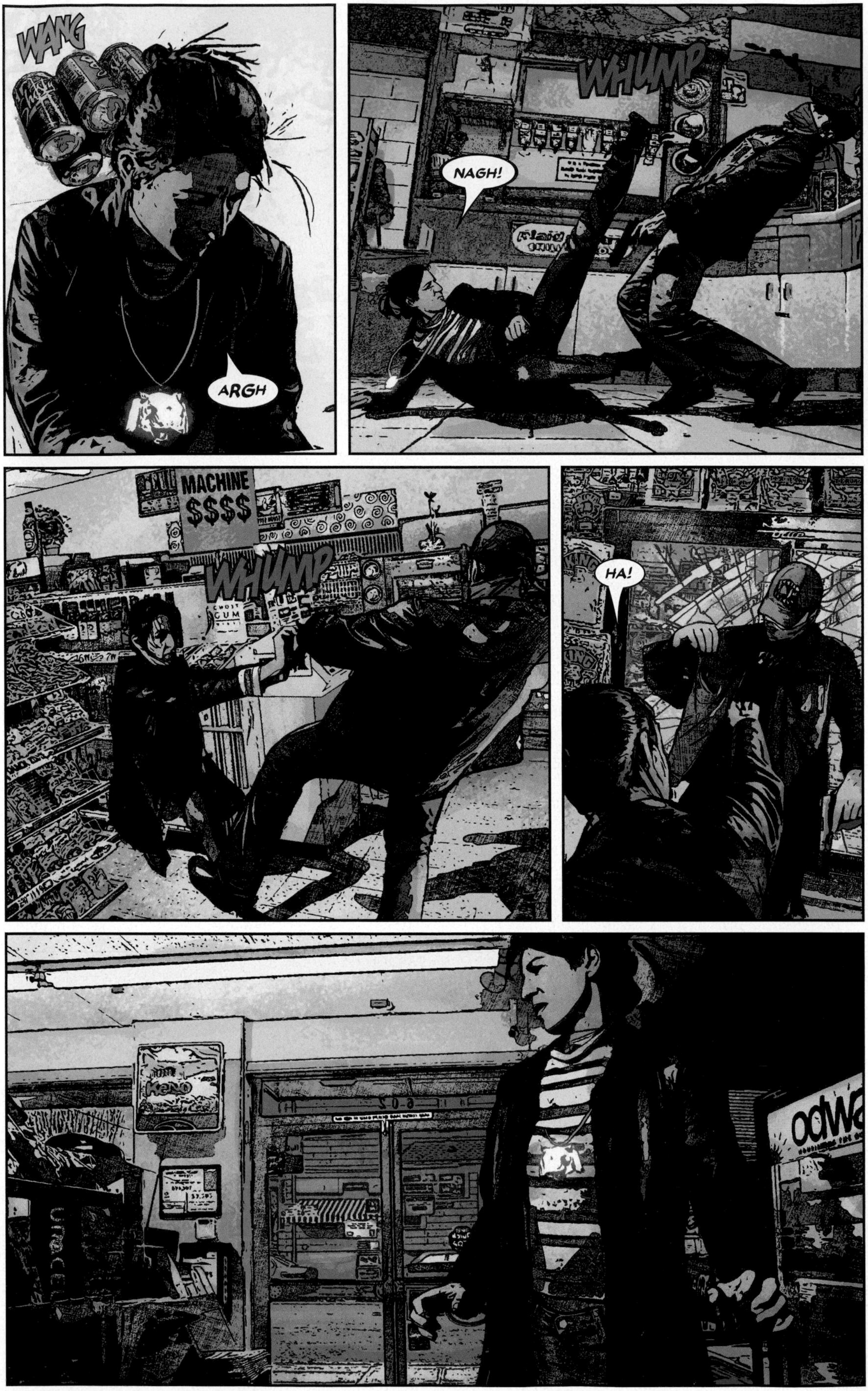
WANG
ARGH
WHUMP
NAGH!
MACHINE
$$$$
WHUMP
GHOST
GUM
HA!

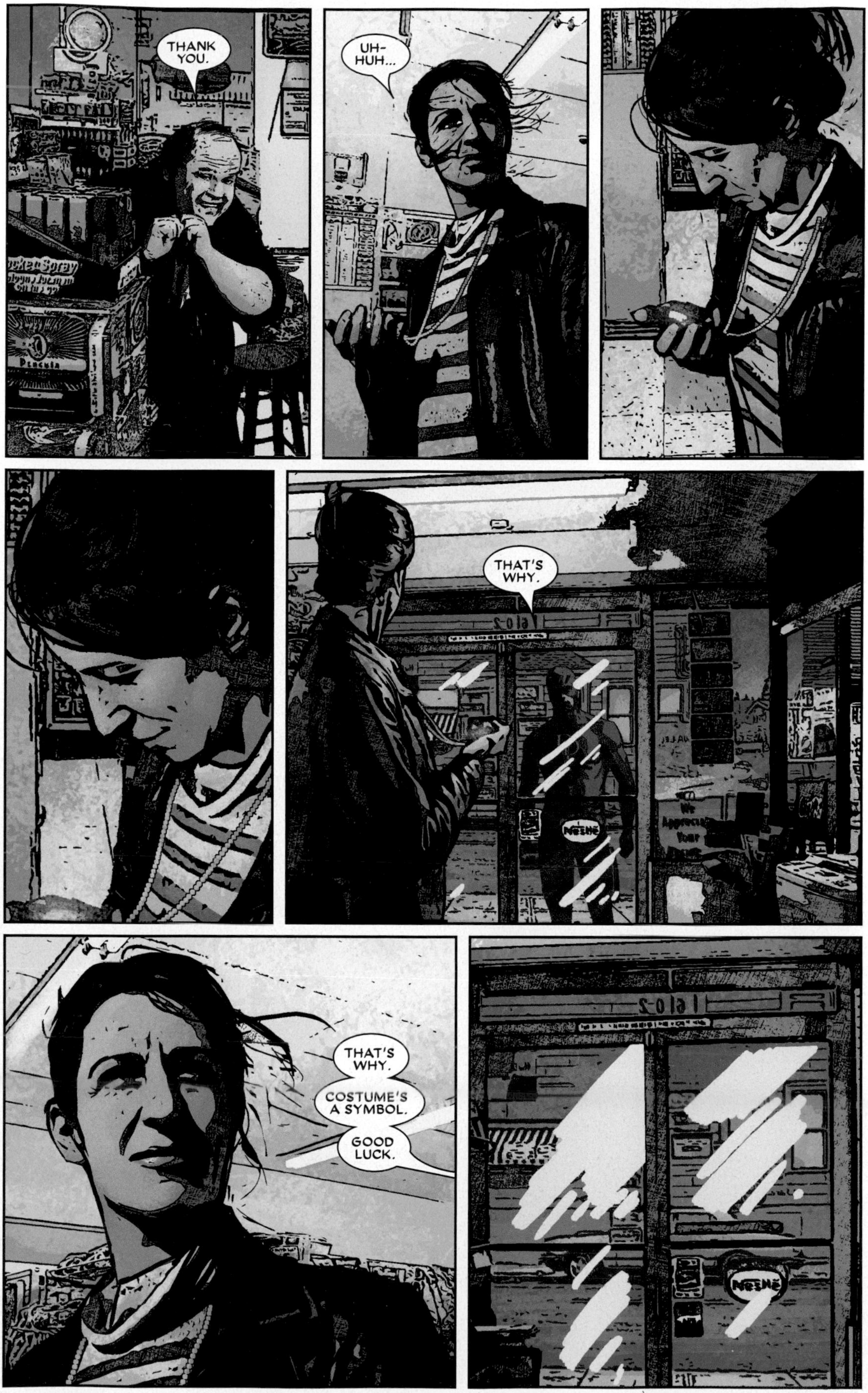
THANK YOU.
UH-HUH...
THAT'S WHY.
THAT'S WHY.
COSTUME'S A SYMBOL.
GOOD LUCK.

MELVIN POTTER? ARE YOU WEARING YOUR GLADIATOR COSTUME?

MELVIN?

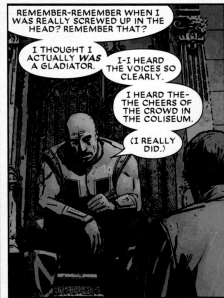

REMEMBER-REMEMBER WHEN I WAS REALLY SCREWED UP IN THE HEAD? REMEMBER THAT?

I THOUGHT I ACTUALLY WAS A GLADIATOR.

I-I HEARD THE VOICES SO CLEARLY.

I HEARD THE- THE CHEERS OF THE CROWD IN THE COLISEUM.

(I REALLY DID.)

BUT YOU'RE OKAY NOW...

...RIGHT?

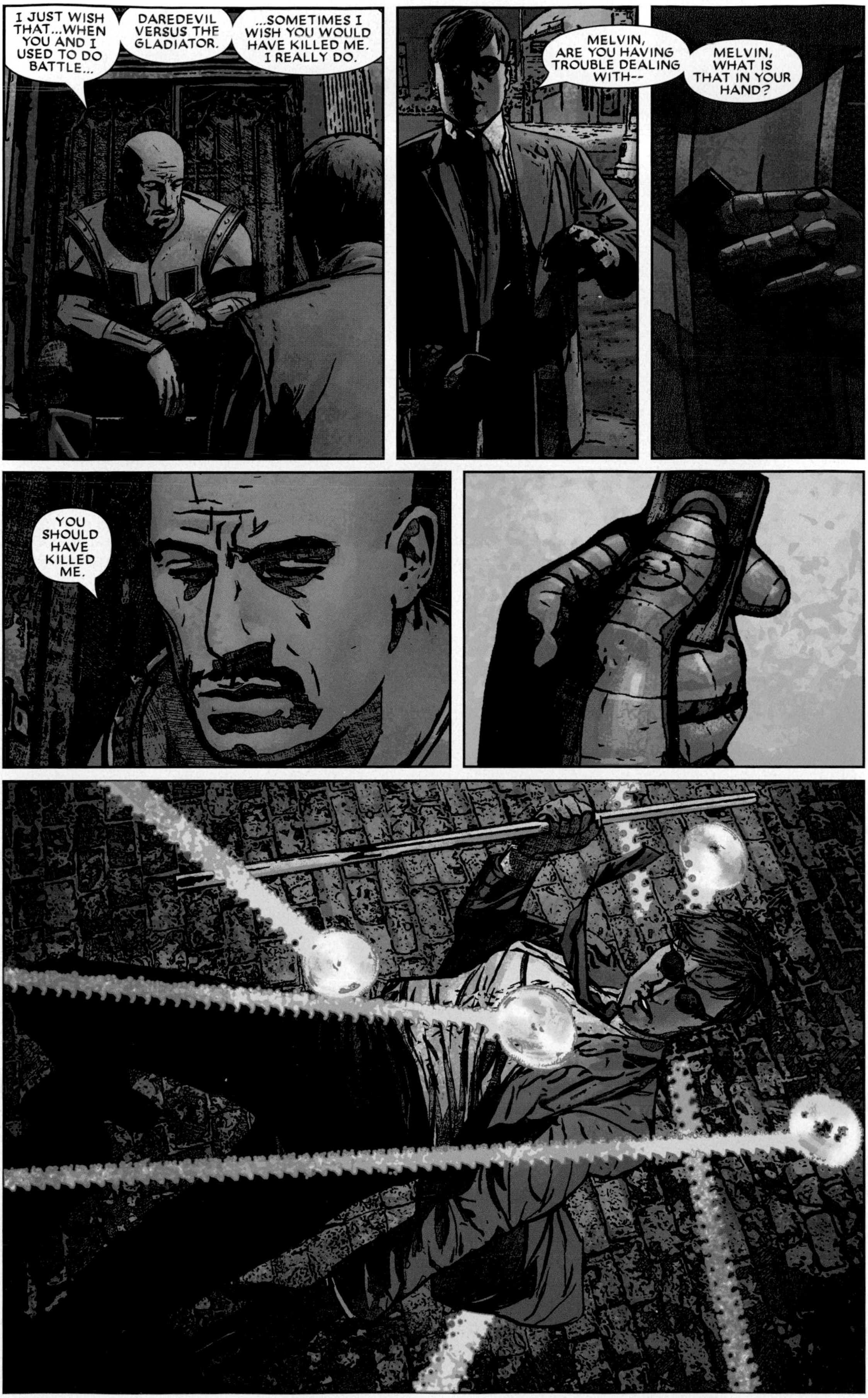
I JUST WISH THAT...WHEN YOU AND I USED TO DO BATTLE...
DAREDEVIL VERSUS THE GLADIATOR.
...SOMETIMES I WISH YOU WOULD HAVE KILLED ME. I REALLY DO.
MELVIN, ARE YOU HAVING TROUBLE DEALING WITH--
MELVIN, WHAT IS THAT IN YOUR HAND?
YOU SHOULD HAVE KILLED ME.

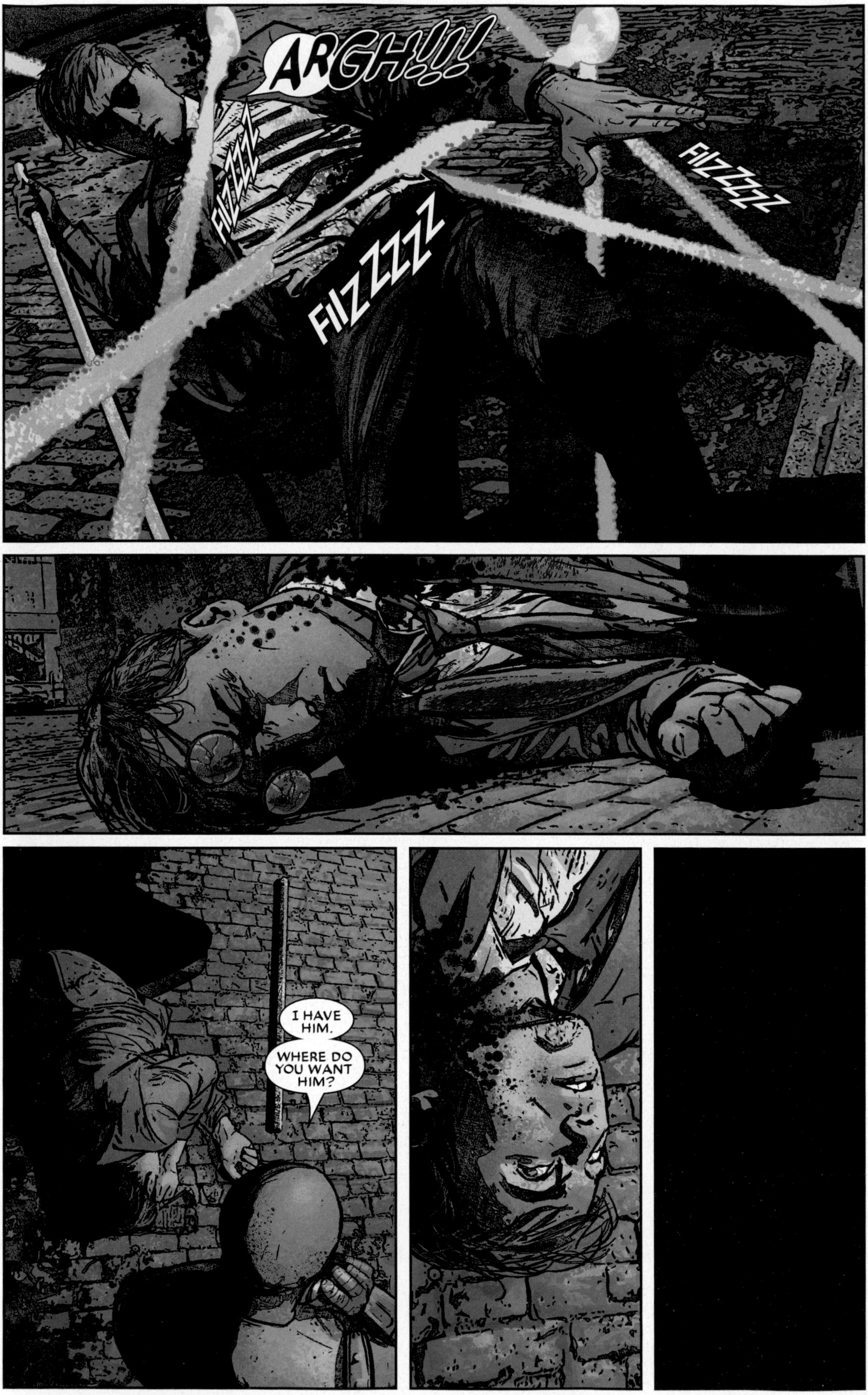
ARGH!!!
FIIZZZZZ
FIIZZZZZ
FIIZZZZZ
I HAVE HIM.
WHERE DO YOU WANT HIM?

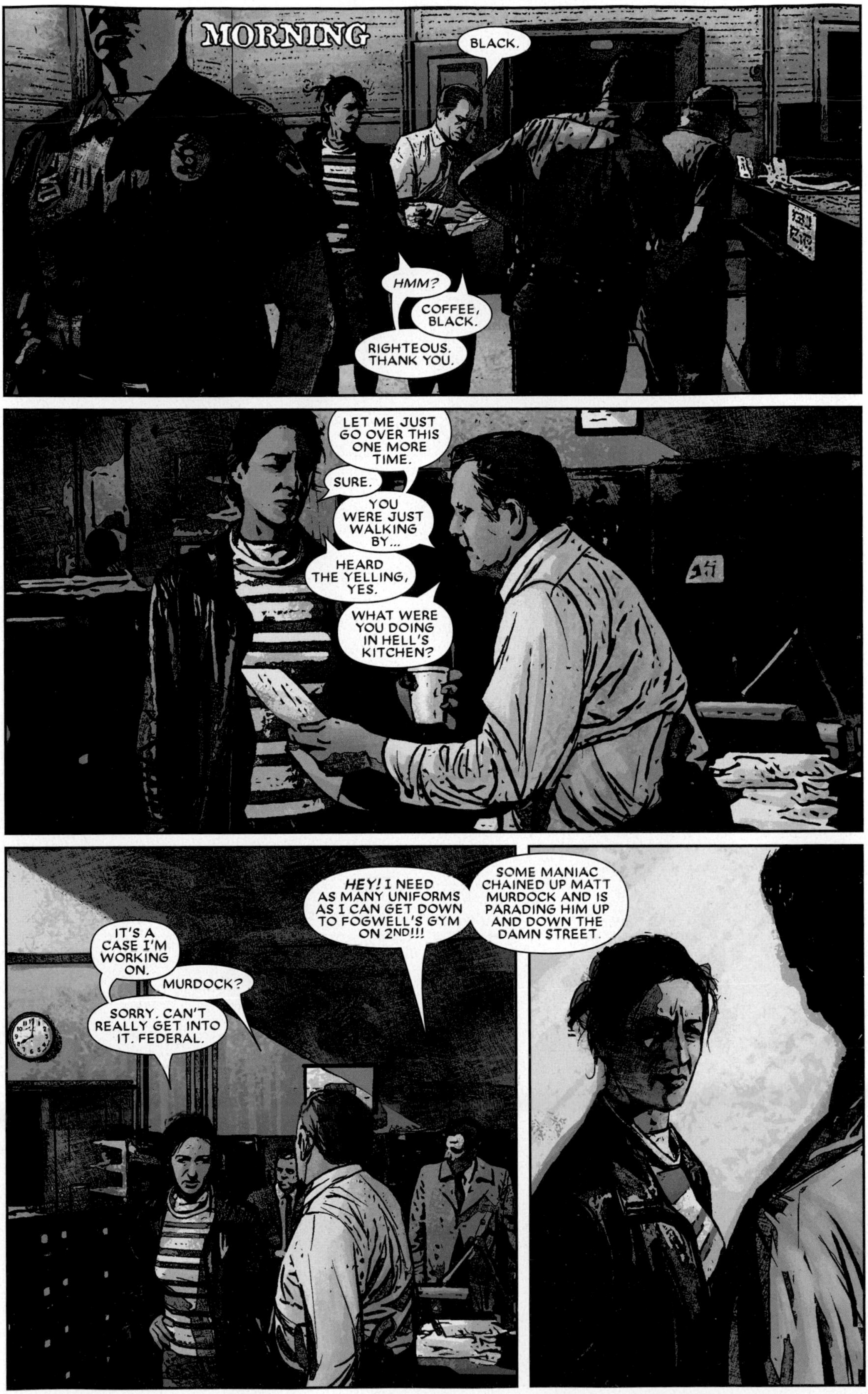
MORNING
BLACK.
HMM?
COFFEE, BLACK.
RIGHTEOUS. THANK YOU.
LET ME JUST GO OVER THIS ONE MORE TIME.
SURE.
YOU WERE JUST WALKING BY...
HEARD THE YELLING, YES.
WHAT WERE YOU DOING IN HELL'S KITCHEN?
IT'S A CASE I'M WORKING ON.
MURDOCK?
SORRY. CAN'T REALLY GET INTO IT. FEDERAL.
HEY! I NEED AS MANY UNIFORMS AS I CAN GET DOWN TO FOGWELL'S GYM ON 2ND!!!
SOME MANIAC CHAINED UP MATT MURDOCK AND IS PARADING HIM UP AND DOWN THE DAMN STREET.

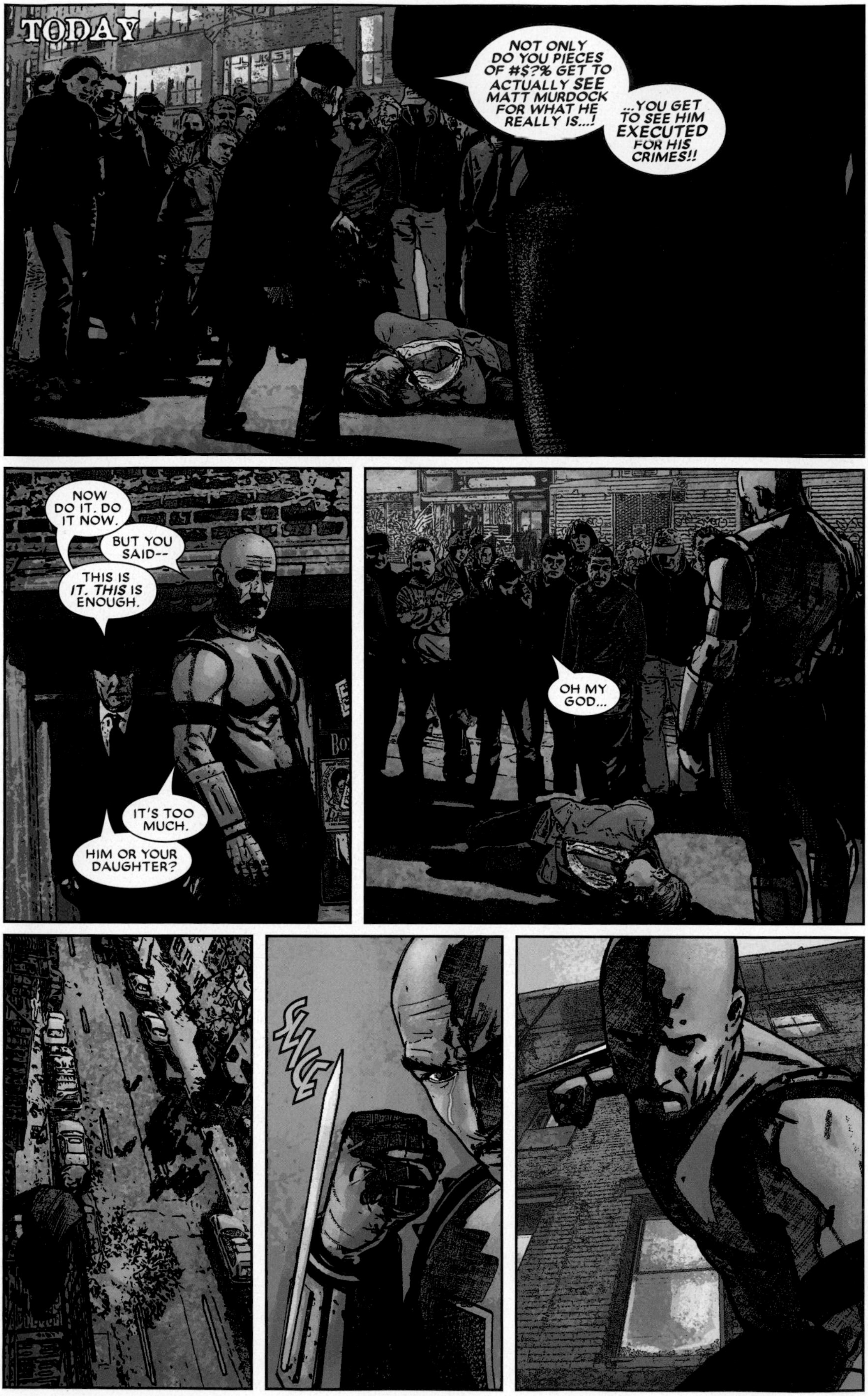
TODAY
NOT ONLY DO YOU PIECES OF #$?% GET TO ACTUALLY SEE MATT MURDOCK FOR WHAT HE REALLY IS...!
...YOU GET TO SEE HIM EXECUTED FOR HIS CRIMES!!
NOW DO IT. DO IT NOW.
BUT YOU SAID--
THIS IS IT. THIS IS ENOUGH.
IT'S TOO MUCH.
HIM OR YOUR DAUGHTER?
OH MY GOD...

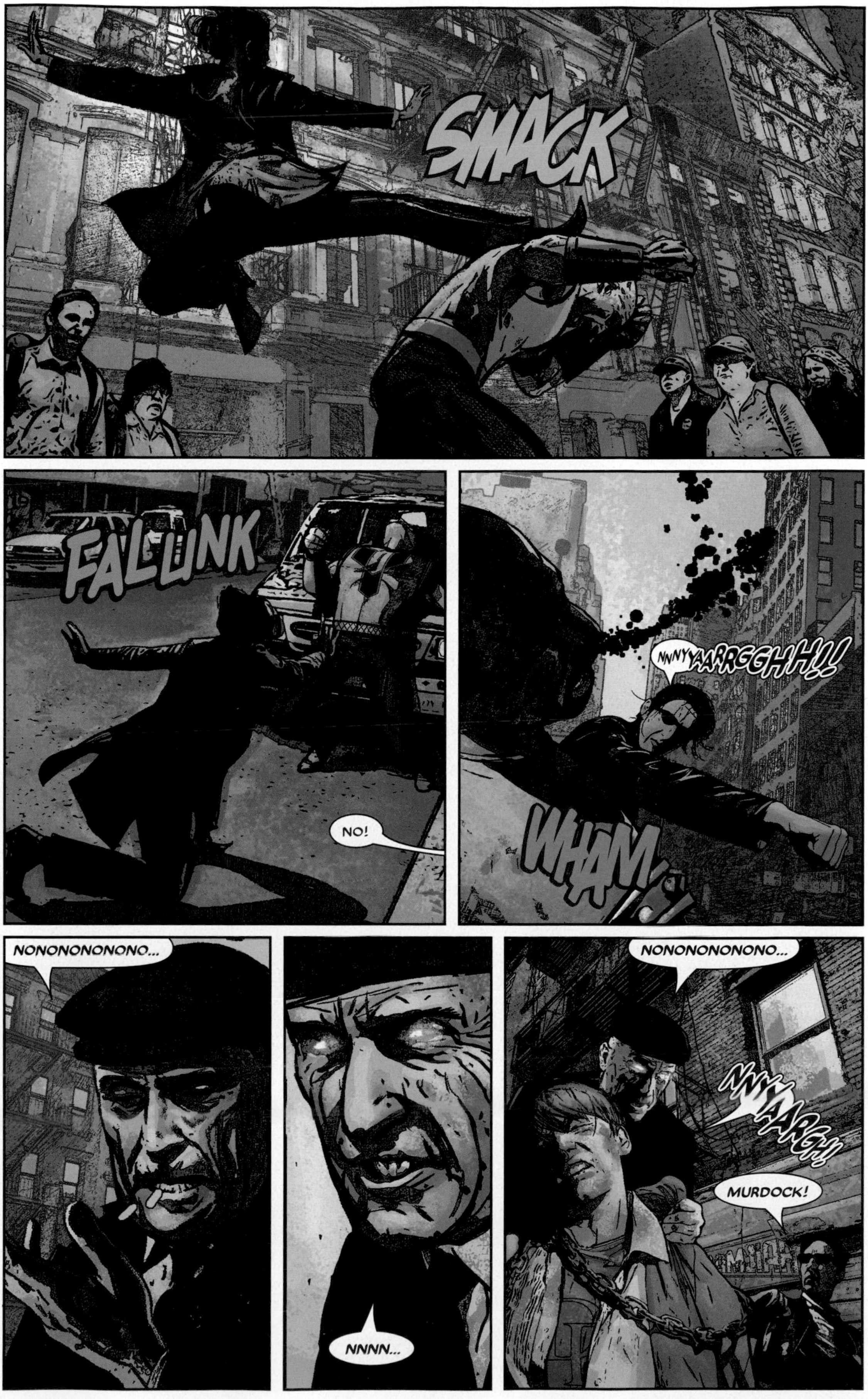
SMACK
FALUNK
NO!
NNNYYAARRGGHH!!
WHAM
NONONONONONO...
NNNN...
NONONONONONO...
NNYAARGH!
MURDOCK!

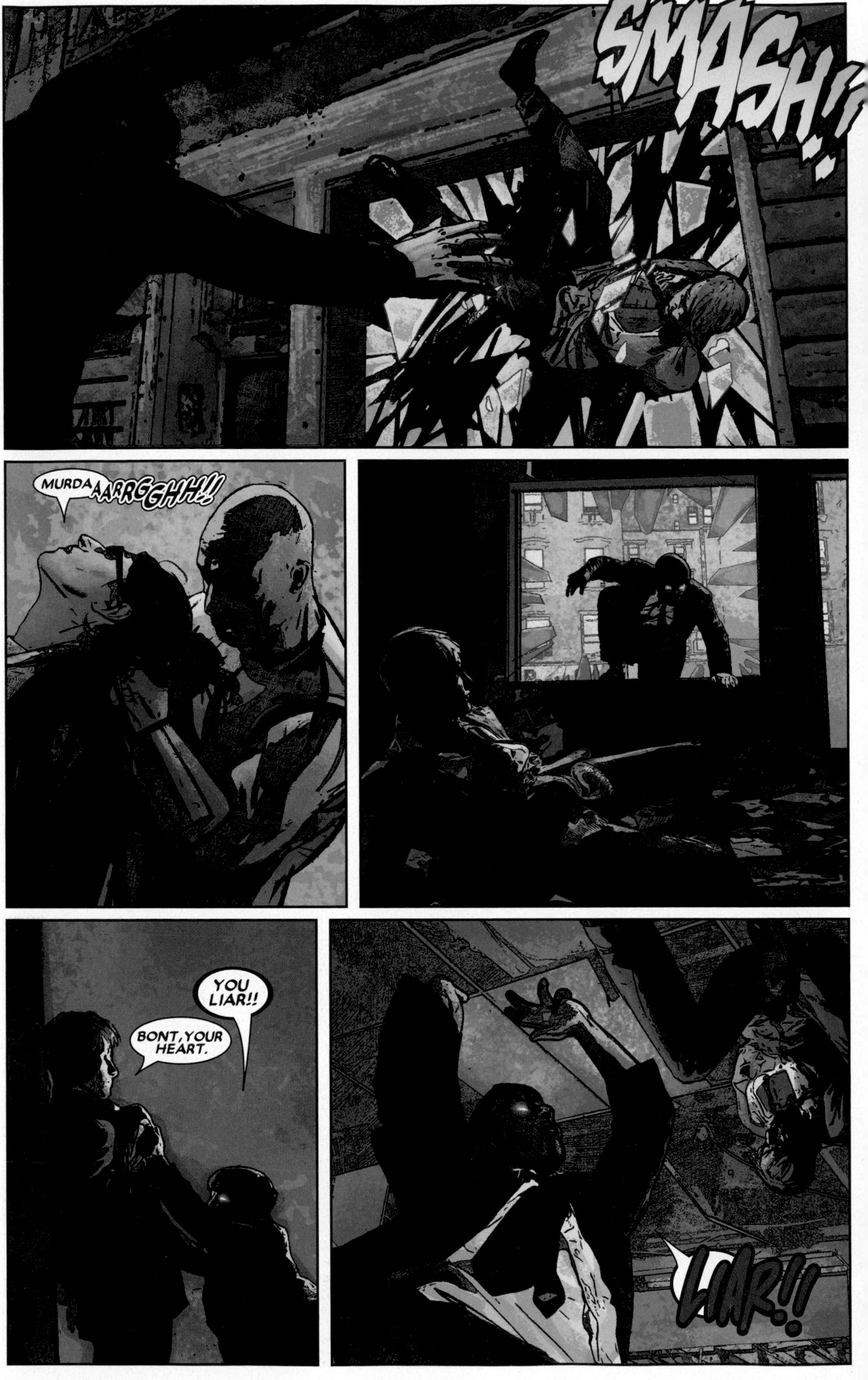
SMASH!!
MURDA AARRGGHH!!
YOU LIAR!!
BONT, YOUR HEART.
LIAR!!

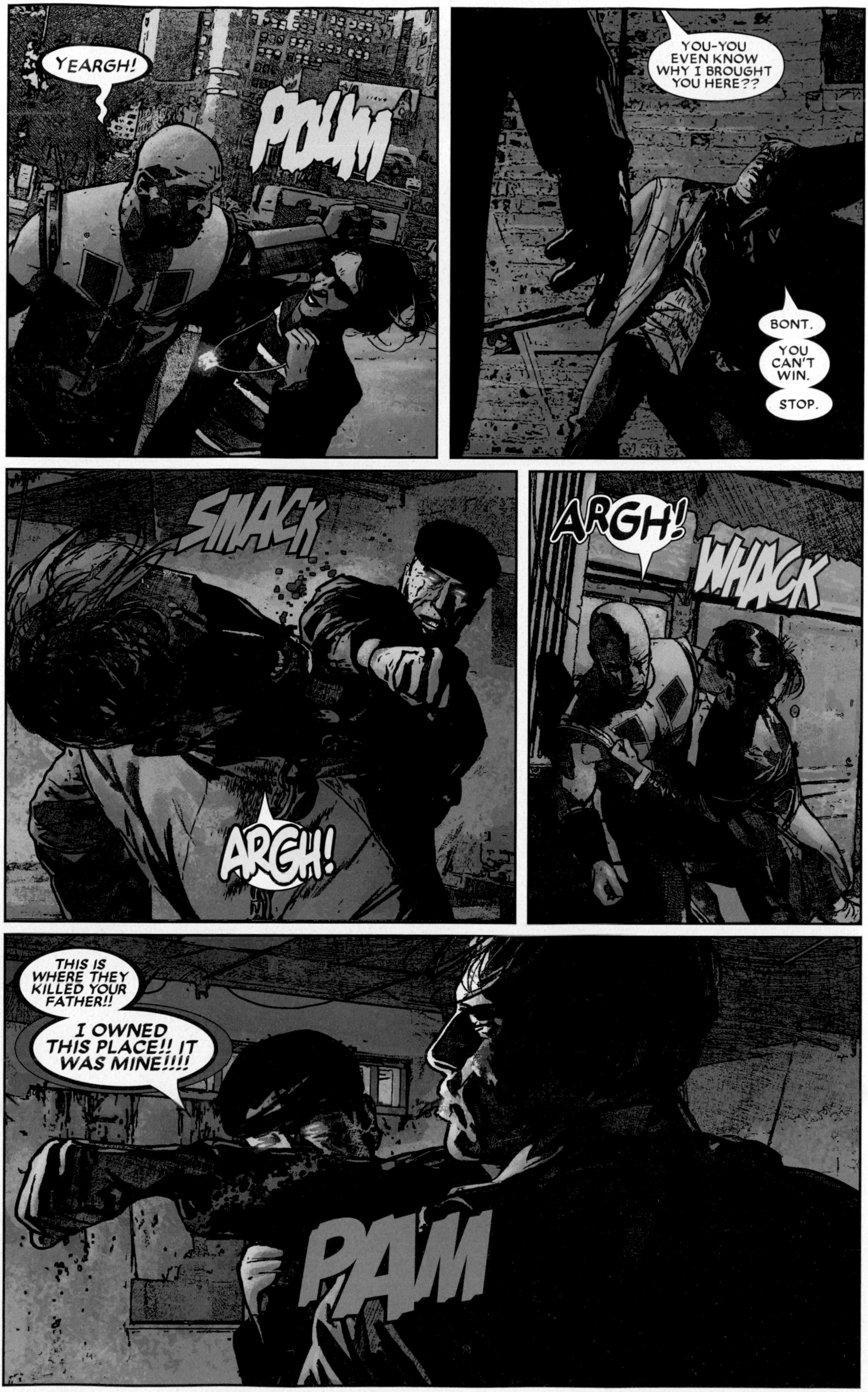
YEARGH!
POUM
YOU-YOU EVEN KNOW WHY I BROUGHT YOU HERE??
BONT.
YOU CAN'T WIN.
STOP.
SMACK
ARGH!
ARGH!
WHACK
THIS IS WHERE THEY KILLED YOUR FATHER!!
I OWNED THIS PLACE!! IT WAS MINE!!!!
PAM

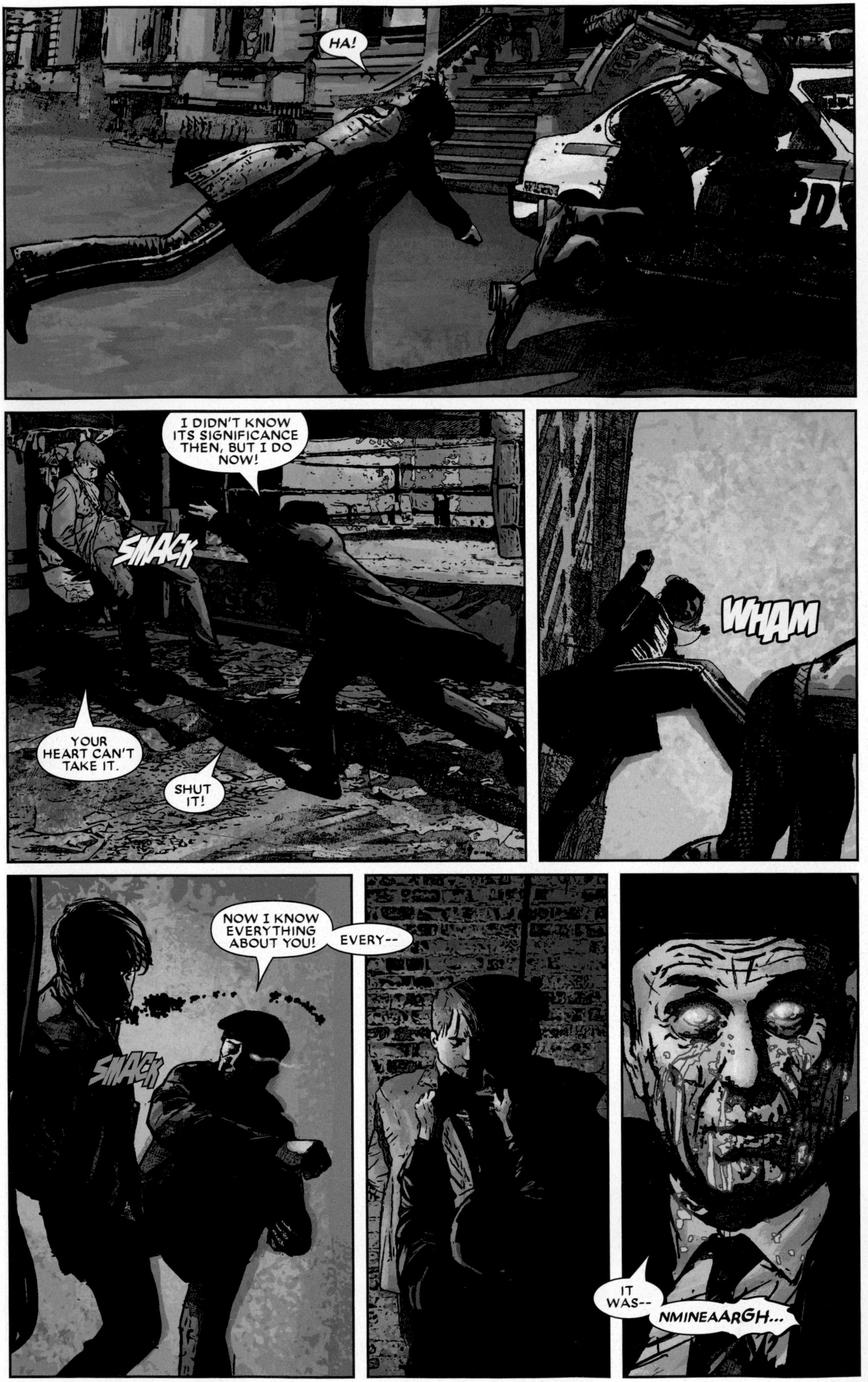
HA!
I DIDN'T KNOW ITS SIGNIFICANCE THEN, BUT I DO NOW!
SMACK
YOUR HEART CAN'T TAKE IT.
SHUT IT!
WHAM
NOW I KNOW EVERYTHING ABOUT YOU!
EVERY--
SMACK
IT WAS--
NMINEAARGH...

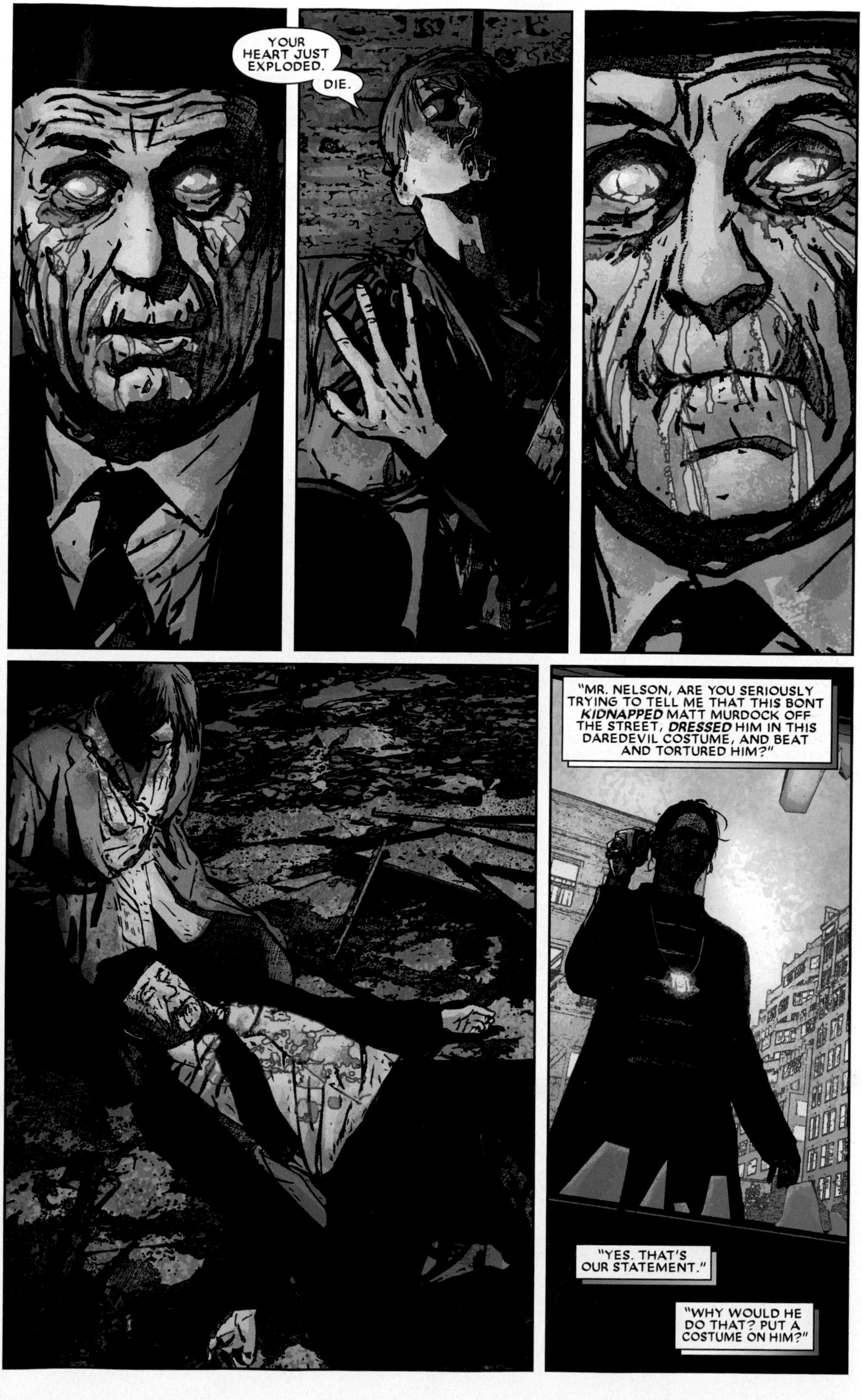
YOUR HEART JUST EXPLODED.
DIE.
"MR. NELSON, ARE YOU SERIOUSLY TRYING TO TELL ME THAT THIS BONT KIDNAPPED MATT MURDOCK OFF THE STREET, DRESSED HIM IN THIS DAREDEVIL COSTUME, AND BEAT AND TORTURED HIM?"
"YES. THAT'S OUR STATEMENT."
"WHY WOULD HE DO THAT? PUT A COSTUME ON HIM?"

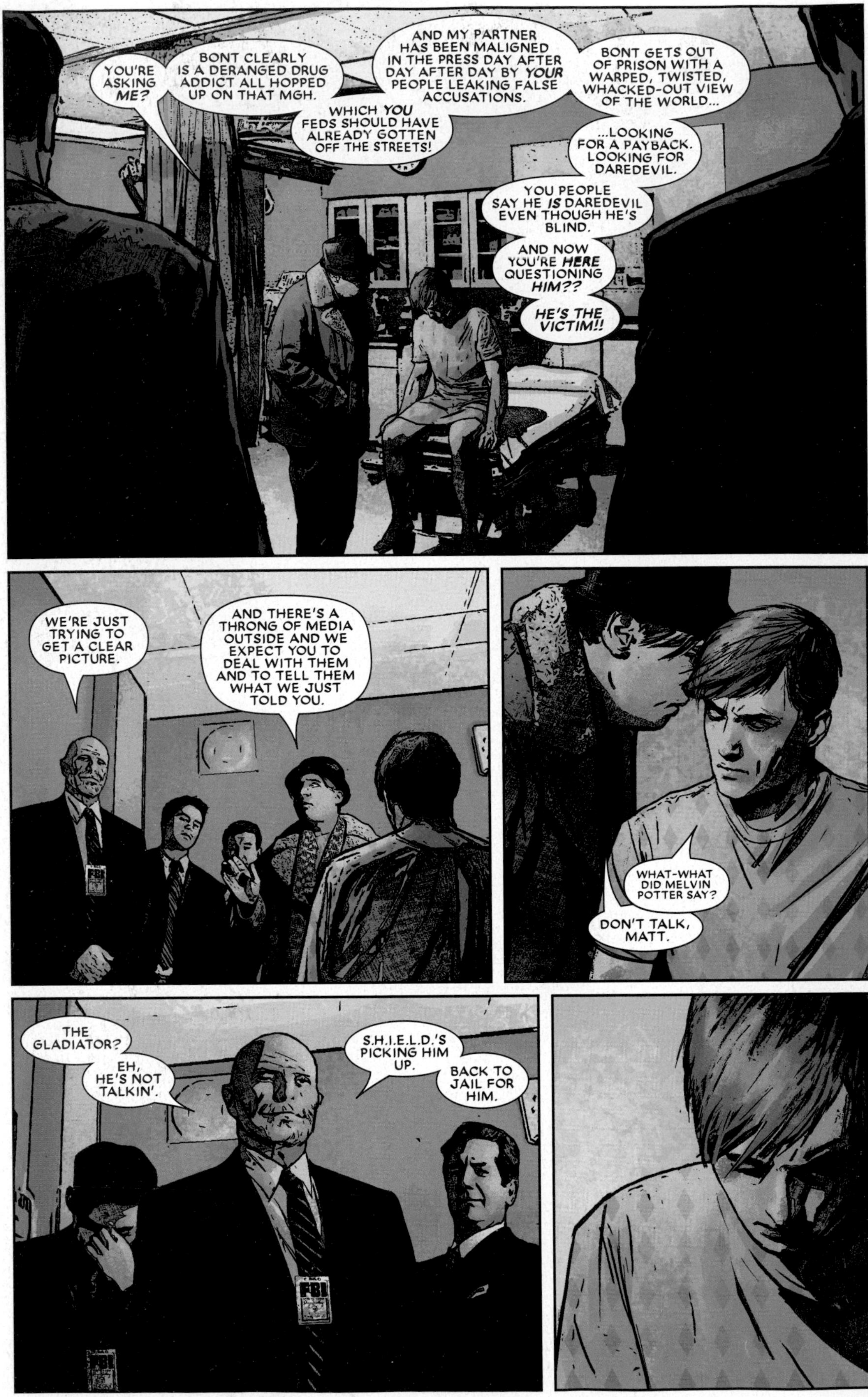
YOU'RE ASKING ME?
BONT CLEARLY IS A DERANGED DRUG ADDICT ALL HOPPED UP ON THAT MGH.
WHICH YOU FEDS SHOULD HAVE ALREADY GOTTEN OFF THE STREETS!
AND MY PARTNER HAS BEEN MALIGNED IN THE PRESS DAY AFTER DAY AFTER DAY BY YOUR PEOPLE LEAKING FALSE ACCUSATIONS.
BONT GETS OUT OF PRISON WITH A WARPED, TWISTED, WHACKED-OUT VIEW OF THE WORLD...
...LOOKING FOR A PAYBACK. LOOKING FOR DAREDEVIL.
YOU PEOPLE SAY HE IS DAREDEVIL EVEN THOUGH HE'S BLIND.
AND NOW YOU'RE HERE QUESTIONING HIM??
HE'S THE VICTIM!!
WE'RE JUST TRYING TO GET A CLEAR PICTURE.
AND THERE'S A THRONG OF MEDIA OUTSIDE AND WE EXPECT YOU TO DEAL WITH THEM AND TO TELL THEM WHAT WE JUST TOLD YOU.
WHAT-WHAT DID MELVIN POTTER SAY?
DON'T TALK, MATT.
THE GLADIATOR?
EH, HE'S NOT TALKIN'.
S.H.I.E.L.D.'S PICKING HIM UP.
BACK TO JAIL FOR HIM.

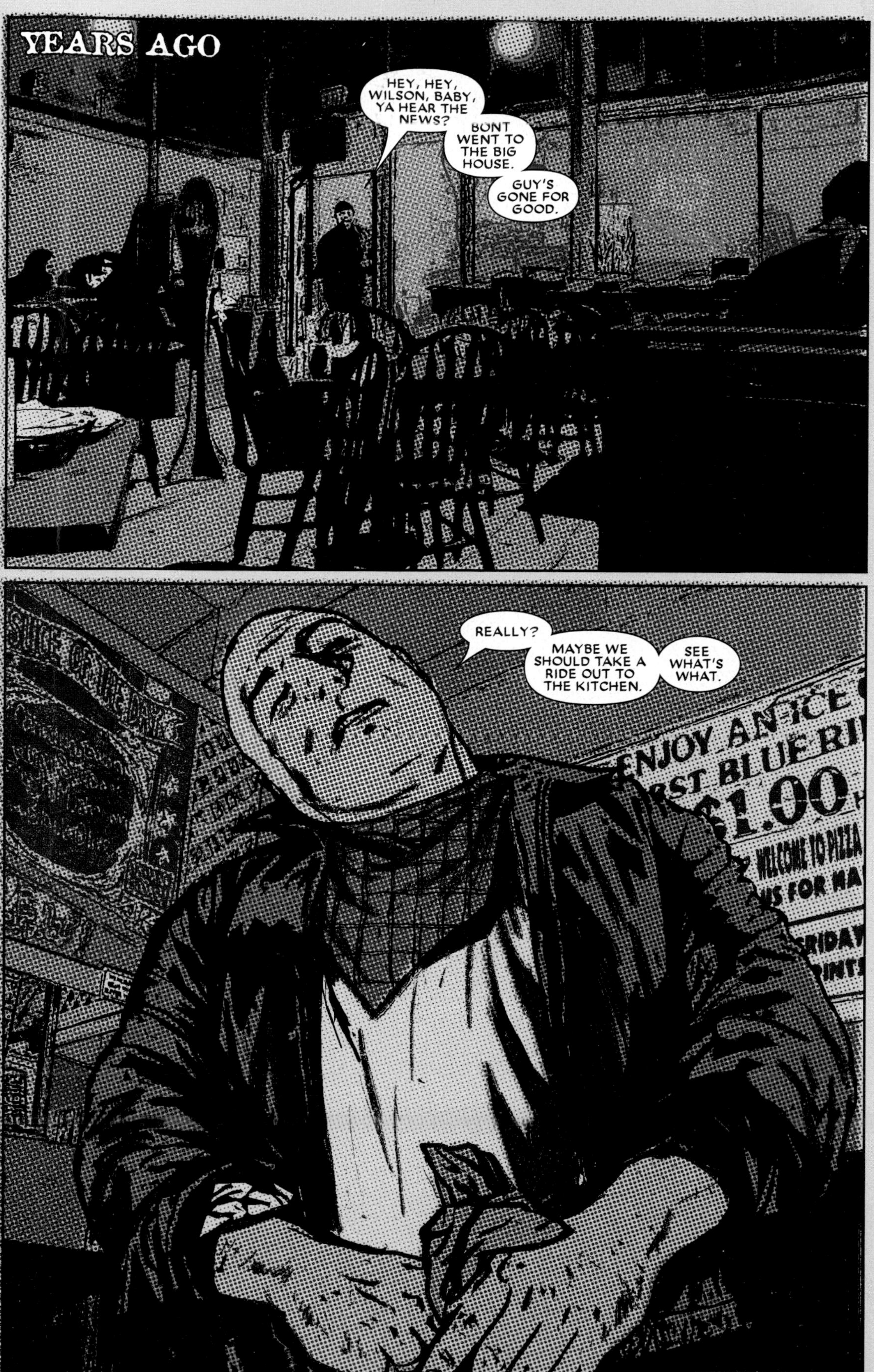
YEARS AGO
HEY, HEY, WILSON, BABY, YA HEAR THE NEWS?
BONT WENT TO THE BIG HOUSE.
GUY'S GONE FOR GOOD.
REALLY?
MAYBE WE SHOULD TAKE A RIDE OUT TO THE KITCHEN.
SEE WHAT'S WHAT.
THE END

Next: DECALOGUE

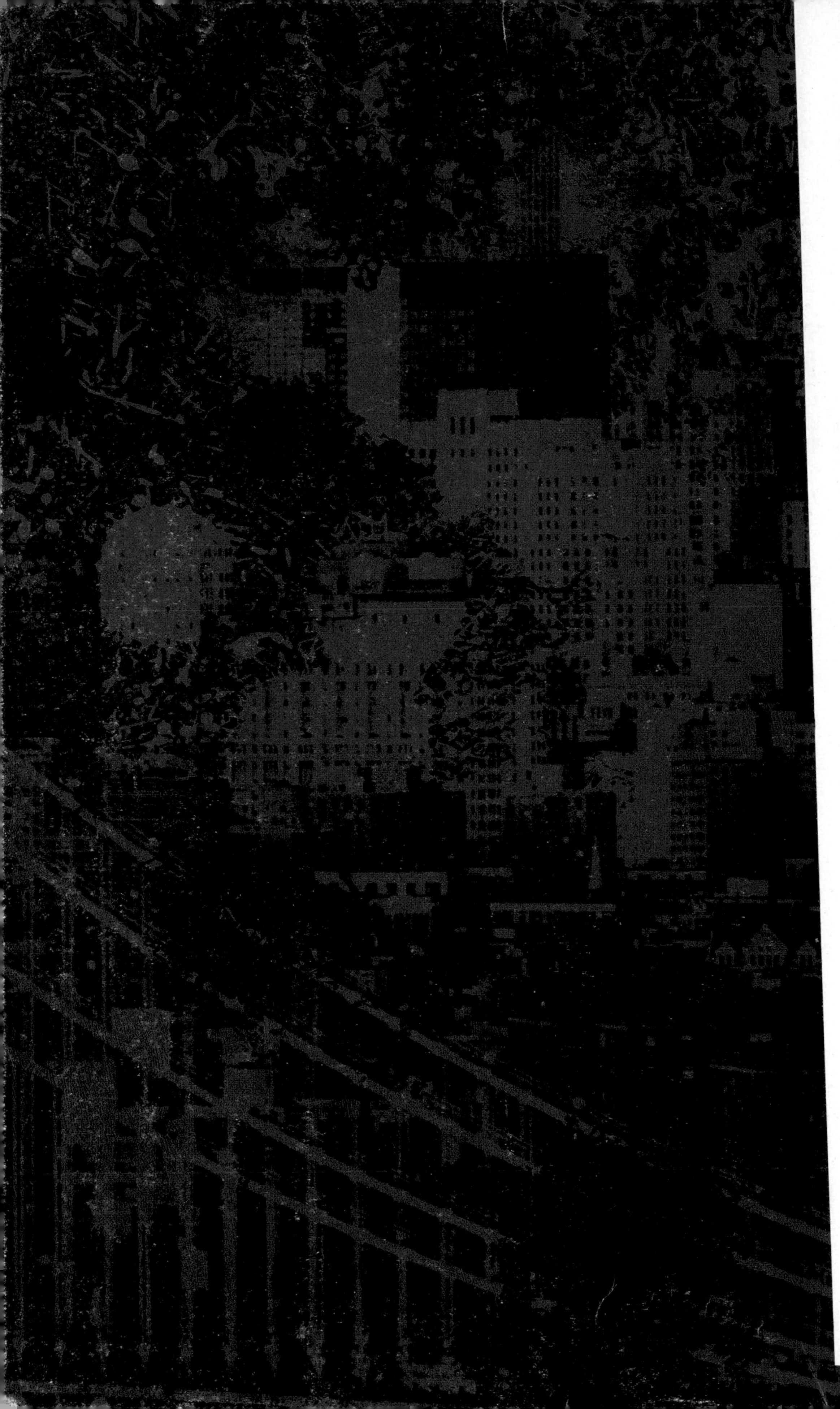